12-17-2008

"In a nuanced and creative inversion of traditional approaches to the treatment of anxiety, Eifert and Forsyth offer clients the possibility of relinquishing their struggles with anxiety, by "treating" the struggle as the problem and letting fear play out to an increasingly disinterested audience of one. Acceptance, commitment, and mindfulness are essential to this process, and this book clearly lays the type of experiential learning foundation that allows clients to embody these concepts and, through their actions, develop a new relationship with their fears. This book will certainly become a vital clinical resource for any therapist, student or educator in the field of anxiety disorders."

> —Zindel V. Segal, Ph.D., the Morgan Firestone Chair in Psychotherapy and professor of psychiatry and psychology at the University of Toronto and author of *Mindfulness-Based Cognitive Therapy for Depression*

"Eifert and Forsyth present the complexities and nuances of acceptance and commitment therapy for anxiety disorders in a fascinating and conceptually illuminating style and in a manner that is amply detailed to guide clinical practice. The principles that underlie acceptance and commitment therapy—to relinquish attempts to control internal states and instead focus upon valued life directions and goals—are brought to life with excellent case examples throughout their step-by-step guide for treating anxiety disorders. This book will be an invaluable resource for theoreticians and clinicians, novice and experienced alike."

> —Michelle G. Craske, Ph.D., director of the Anxiety Disorders Behavioral Research Program at the University of California, Los Angeles and author of *Origins of Phobias and Anxiety Disorders*

"Eifert and Forsyth have done something revolutionary! They have taken the treatment of anxiety disorders far beyond the disease model that CBT has been stuck in by brilliantly examining the core psychological processes that make fear and anxiety disordered and explaining in clear language what all anxiety disorders have in common. Their conceptualization of fear and anxiety demonstrates the cutting edge of clinical research and development within CBT and its development into the so-called third wave behavior therapies. The book contains innovative and user-friendly session-by-session guidelines on how to apply ACT for all the major anxiety disorders. This therapist guide should be on every clinical psychology program's reading list. It is truly an eye opener and a huge step forward in how we view and treat the suffering associated with anxiety disorders."

> —JoAnne Dahl, Ph.D., professor of clinical psychology at the University of Uppsala, Sweden, and author of *Living Beyond Pain* and *Pain: A Vital Friend*

"Behavior therapy is undergoing extraordinary change. Mindfulness, acceptance, and values-oriented interventions are increasingly being included in interventions for a wide variety of problems in living. Eifert and Forsyth's new anxiety text is a stunning example of the potential for this new wave of behavior therapies to remain connected to their scientific roots while exploring emerging treatment issues and technologies. This book is a must for the bookshelves of both clinicians and treatment developers."

> —Kelly G. Wilson, Ph.D., assistant professor of psychology at the University of Mississippi and coauthor of *Acceptance and Commitment Therapy*

"This book provides concrete treatment guidelines that are firmly grounded in a new and intriguing approach to emotion regulation: Acceptance and Commitment Therapy. The authors are well known for their rigorous scientific studies and theoretical contributions to the field of anxiety disorders and behavior analysis. This book further demonstrates that they are highly skilled clinicians and masterful educators who are able to translate complex theories into simple and clearly formulated treatment techniques. The book is a reflection of the current paradigm shift from the studies of behaviors and cognitions to the study of and emotion regulation and, therefore, is a must-read for both the present and next generation of anxiety researchers."

> —Stefan G. Hofmann, Ph.D., associate professor of psychology at the Center for Stress and Anxiety-Related Disorders at Boston University, and Editor of *Cognitive and Behavioral Practice*.

"*Acceptance and Commitment Therapy for Anxiety Disorders* provides a detailed, step-by-step account of how therapists can use ACT to help people who are suffering from these problems. Its comprehensiveness and session-by-session guides will help people who are novices to this approach understand and apply the fundamentals of ACT. Experienced ACT practitioners will also find this an extremely valuable resource, as Eifert and Forsyth have deftly tailored core ACT techniques to target the primary issues of people with anxiety-related problems. In addition, this book provides a considerable amount of new and innovative, out-of-session exercises and materials clients can use to strengthen their commitment to move through their anxiety and lead a vital life that they will value. In all, it's a one-stop-shop ACT guide for treating anxiety disorders."

> —Frank Bond, BA, P.G.Dip., M.Sc., Ph.D., C.Psychol., ICTLHE, senior lecturer in the Department of Psychology at Goldsmiths College, University of London

"This is an extremely useful book for professionals as well as educated clients. Focusing on the broad area of anxiety disorders, it does a superb job demonstrating how acceptance and commitment therapy can be applied to specific disorders. Avoiding the artificial constraints of DSM-IV or ICD-10 classifications of mental disorders, it emphasizes the functional similarities of the anxiety disorders and their common treatment strategies while at the same time taking into account some of their unique aspects."

—Rainer F. Sonntag, MD, psychiatrist and psychotherapist in private practice in Olpe, Germany

"Eifert and Forsyth are interpreters rather than the creators of acceptance and commitment therapy (ACT). So when they explain its value for the treatment of anxiety, they ground their commitment to this approach in their own extensive clinical and research experience in anxiety disorders, not in uncritical acceptance. Because they really understand the psychology of anxiety, they have produced an authoritative, beautifully written, usable manual for clinicians. Calling it a manual, however, belies its theoretical sophistication and its ability to inspire rather than stipulate. These properties make it particularly useful in diverse cultural and global contexts, where it can easily be molded to the real lives of real clients."

—Ian M. Evans, Ph.D., professor and head of the School of Psychology at Massey University in Palmerston North, New Zealand, fellow of the American Psychological Association and the Royal Society of New Zealand, and author of *Nonaversive Behavioral Interventions*

Acceptance & Commitment Therapy *for* Anxiety Disorders

A Practitioner's Treatment Guide to Using Mindfulness, Acceptance, and Values-Based Behavior Change Strategies

GEORG H. EIFERT, PH.D.
JOHN P. FORSYTH, PH.D.

New Harbinger Publications, Inc.

Publisher's Note

This publication is designed to provide accurate and authoritative information in regard to the subject matter covered. It is sold with the understanding that the publisher is not engaged in rendering psychological, financial, legal, or other professional services. If expert assistance or counseling is needed, the services of a competent professional should be sought.

Library of Congress Cataloging-in-Publication Data

Eifert, Georg H., 1952-
  Acceptance and commitment therapy for anxiety disorders : a practitioner's treatment guide to using mindfulness, acceptance, and values-based behavior change strategies / Georg H. Eifert, John P. Forsyth ; foreword by Steven C. Hayes.
     p. cm.
  Includes bibliographical references and index.
  ISBN 1-57224-427-5
  1. Anxiety. 2. Stress (Psychology) 3. Cognitive therapy. 4. Behavior therapy. 5. Behavioral assessment. I. Forsyth, John P. II. Title.
  RC531.E36 2005
  616.85'2206—dc22
                              2005010587

07 06 05

10 9 8 7 6 5 4 3 2 1

First printing

Contents

PART III
ACT TREATMENT OF ANXIETY

Acknowledgments
and Preface

Acceptance and Commitment Therapy (ACT) is a new and rapidly evolving third-wave behavior therapy. Numerous journal articles and book chapters have appeared outlining the nature of the treatment, its philosophical roots, its conception of human suffering and behavior change, and, of course, its empirical base in basic and applied clinical science. Ideas are also shared with colleagues every day through open exchanges on the Acceptance and Commitment Therapy electronic Listserv, typically years before they ever get published and copyrighted. We are particularly grateful to Steven Hayes, who has generously made his work and ideas available to us from the very start of this project—including giving us a copy of an unpublished ACT treatment manual for agoraphobia that he and his colleagues developed back in 1990. We are also grateful to Kelly Wilson and Joanne Dahl for sharing with us their work on values, which included assessment tools, illustrations, and therapist-client dialogues.

We thank Hank Robb for allowing us to include his version of the famous serenity prayer and Peter Thorne, a British clinical psychologist, for letting us use his "Bad News Radio" metaphor in this book—and thanks also to Steven Hayes for letting us reprint his rewording of part of that metaphor. All this generous sharing of ideas and materials by our ACT colleagues has occurred in the spirit of spreading what is good, which unfortunately is not the norm in the competitive world of science. We also acknowledge with gratitude Joanna Arch for her thoughtful comments on earlier drafts of the mindfulness sections of this book, and Michelle Craske and her graduate students at UCLA for their critical comments and suggestions for improving the treatment chapters as we prepared to launch our clinical trial comparing ACT with cognitive behavioral therapy for anxiety disorders.

We also thank the following professionals and organizations who kindly gave us permission to reproduce their work: John Blackledge, Frank Bond, Joseph Ciarrochi, David Mercer, the Association for Behavioral and Cognitive Therapy (ABCT), and the American Psychological Association.

During the writing of this book we often said to each other, "This is the best and most fun thing we have ever done in our professional lives." The reason is that many aspects of our previous work have propelled us exactly to the place we have arrived at with this book. In this sense, writing this book was a destination, but, as is often the case, it is also a starting point on a new and exciting path in our personal and professional lives. About ten years ago, neither of us would have thought of writing this sort of book. We were trained in the behavioral tradition. Our roots are in behavior therapy and basic and applied behavior analysis. We were conducting clinical experiments with the goal of trying to understand the nature of fear conditioning in the anxiety disorders. We were writing about language and cognition from a behavioral perspective. We knew much about the cognitive revolution. This revolution was, in the early 1990s, hard to ignore. Yet, we found cognitive theory and techniques cumbersome and difficult to use in our own lives and with our clients. Cognitive techniques addressing problematic psychological content seemed to prolong our own struggle and that of our clients.

The same was true of traditional behavior therapy techniques for anxiety disorders. All seemed to emphasize undoing client suffering by removing problematic psychological and emotional content almost like a mechanic might swap out a faulty spark plug to fix a car engine. While this movement was underway, overwhelming evidence was mounting that the ultimate vehicle for clinical improvement is behavioral change and activation. A growing undercurrent suggested also that clients may want more from psychotherapy than symptom alleviation. They come to therapy because their lives are not working. Mainstream behavior therapy and cognitive behavioral therapy were paying little attention to this larger problem. This made sense given that these mainstream therapies were largely cast within a symptom- and syndrome-focused change agenda.

We felt a new stage of development dawning upon our field when we saw Steve Hayes demonstrating the "empty chair" technique (borrowed from gestalt therapy) to a group of partly bewildered and partly bemused behavior analysts in a talk at a national conference of behavior analysts in the midnineties. Around that time, the notion of balancing acceptance and change was promoted by a number of well-respected clinical scientists in a book edited by Hayes, Jacobson, Follette, and Dougher (1994). We were intrigued by the fact that this approach had grown out of behavioral science just as the first-wave behavior therapies had. This basic science foundation was (and still is) different from the second-wave *cognitive* behavioral therapies, developed as they were from clinical practice rather than advances in behavioral theory and research. We had always hoped that behavior therapy would eventually find a way to address human language and cognition in a more direct, fundamental, and functional way. It has done so with ACT and other third-generation behavior therapies that emphasize nontraditional concepts such as the self, acceptance, mindfulness, and value-guided behavior change using behavioral concepts and principles. A growing number of behavioral and other therapists are ready to explore the therapeutic potential of this new approach. Helping you do that was one of our main reasons for writing this book.

We sincerely hope you will benefit from reading this book as much as we have benefited from working on it. We particularly hope it will be useful to you. It has profoundly and deeply changed how we view the emotional pain and suffering of the people we encounter (our clients, colleagues, family, and friends) and how we approach our own and their pain and suffering in ways that keep us all moving in directions we value.

Finally, we would like to thank our wives and children for giving us extra time, space, and support to complete this book. They saw the value in this work and showed a willingness to make personal sacrifices to see that it would come to fruition. We truly hope it was worth it, and we'll commit ourselves to making it up to them!

—Georg H. Eifert, Ph.D.　　John P. Forsyth, Ph.D.
　　Chapman University　　University at Albany, SUNY
　　Orange, California　　Albany, New York
　　　　　　March 2005

Foreword

Taking a New Direction in the Behavioral and Cognitive Approach to Anxiety

Empirical clinical psychology as we know it in the modern era is only about fifty years old. Before the advent of the first generation of behavior therapy, clinical psychology documented its impact in relatively uncontrolled studies. Interventions were divided up into schools of thought: analytic, existential, and so on. The clinical issues these broad traditions addressed were deep, but the theories were not scientifically precise, the technologies were poorly specified, and the empirical support was weak to the point of nonexistence.

Early behavior therapy brought two key ideas to the table: the importance of the link between basic psychology and applied psychology, and the importance of well-crafted experimental tests of the impact of specific treatment technologies. The basic principles considered most important at the time were those drawn from learning theory, and traditional behavior therapy and applied behavior analysis proved to be spectacularly successful in applying these principles for the betterment of clinical problems and in testing them in well-designed studies. There were several downsides to this earliest manifestation of modern empirical clinical thinking, however. In its fervor for precision, traditional behavior therapy ignored too many of the interesting and important clinical questions being addressed by other traditions in favor of very direct targeting of specific problem behaviors. This increased the distance between schools of thought, raising even higher barriers between various camps. Just as bad, the set of behavioral principles utilized was too small to address language and cognition adequately. Philosophy of science matters were often left somewhat ambiguous, and when they were discussed, perhaps too much emphasis was put on the more mechanistic aspects of behavioral psychology, which limited the degree to which more functional analytic and pragmatic aspects of the behavioral tradition could be applied.

One of these problems was soon addressed, but at the cost of an important part of the behavioral tradition. As traditional learning theory collapsed, behavior therapy embraced the modification of cognition as a central goal of treatment and cognitive behavioral therapy (CBT) was created. Unable to link new treatment technologies in the cognitive domain to specific basic principles, however, a set of more clinical or even commonsense theories of that domain were used in CBT. Broadening and deepening the targets of clinical interventions to cognition solved one of the weaknesses of early behavior therapy, but at a large cost: a defining characteristic of behavior therapy (its link to basic psychology) was weakened or even abandoned. Other clinical traditions followed suit as they entered the empirical clinical camp, and empirical clinical psychology came to mean little more than the collection of controlled outcome data.

The other strengths and weaknesses of the behavior therapy movement remained. On the one hand, systematic experimental tests of well-specified technologies persisted and even increased in traditional cognitive behavioral therapy, and CBT took over the lion's share of attention in empirical clinical psychology. On the other hand, many clinical questions were still largely ignored, divisions between clinical traditions were still great, targets of change were still almost exclusively first order (even though the range of targets was now broader with the inclusion of cognitive targets for change), and the domination of mechanistic approaches was still obvious or even increased to the degree that information processing accounts were discussed.

The book you have in your hands is part of something new. Acceptance and Commitment Therapy (ACT—which should be said as the single word "act," not as its initials A-C-T; Hayes, Strosahl, & Wilson, 1999; Hayes & Strosahl, 2004) is a "third-generation" behavioral and cognitive therapy. Like most of these approaches (see Hayes, 2004b, and Hayes, Follette, & Linehan, 2004, for more thorough discussion), ACT is a contextualistic approach that embraces elements of both traditional behavior therapy and traditional CBT, but adds new elements that carry this tradition in a new direction.

ACT has maintained its commitment to empirical tests of well-specified procedures (Hayes, Masuda, Bissett, Luoma, & Guerrero, 2004). As of the end of 2004 there were controlled studies for ACT in psychosis (Bach & Hayes, 2002; Gaudiano & Herbert, in press); anxiety and stress (Bond & Bunce, 2000; Zettle, 2003; Twohig, Hayes, & Masuda, in press); depression (Folke & Parling, 2004; Zettle & Hayes, 1986; Zettle & Raines, 1989); smoking (Gifford et al., 2004); pain (Dahl, Wilson, & Nilsson, 2004; McCracken, Vowles, & Eccleston, in press); management of diabetes (Gregg, 2004);

heroin addiction (Hayes, Wilson, et al., 2004); and stigmatizing attitudes of therapists toward their clients (Hayes, Bissett, et al., 2004), among others. Many more studies are currently underway. ACT research is still fairly young, but its commitment to empirical development is obvious and the early results are promising.

The commitment to treatment specification is also clear. This very volume demonstrates that commitment, as do other recent manuals and books in the area. Someone who wants to test or apply ACT can acquire the skills through a variety of means, and do so without hierarchy, excessive payments, centralization, certification, and other proprietary restrictions.

ACT also brings several new things to behavioral and cognitive approaches. ACT is based on a well-specified philosophy of science: functional contextualism (Biglan & Hayes, 1996; Hayes, 1993; Hayes, Hayes, Reese, & Sarbin, 1993). Not only does this allow an exploration of the utility of more contextual forms of behavioral thinking, it also allows a good deal of clarity about the assumptions underlying ACT, so that it is relatively easy to detect and eliminate inconsistencies between assumptions, principles, and procedures. ACT puts aside the linear, mechanistic qualities of much of the behavioral and cognitive therapies and in so doing creates a more dynamic, interactive, holistic approach that still retains the precision of traditional methods.

ACT is the only behavioral and cognitive therapy I know of that has its own active basic research program into the nature of human language and cognition. ACT is based on Relational Frame Theory (RFT; Hayes, Barnes-Holmes, & Roche, 2001), which is the first new, comprehensive, behavioral approach to human language and cognition since Skinner's attempt in the late 1950s. There are already over seventy studies on RFT and the data are almost uniformly positive (Hayes et al., 2001, reviews much of this work). This development has allowed the close linkage between basic studies of behavioral processes and clinical application to finally be applied to both behavioral and cognitive domains within behavior therapy.

The relative clarity about treatment processes has had two other important effects. First, it has been possible to test ACT processes of change. It is important that there are already several mediational studies that have shown that ACT works through its specified processes (see Hayes, Luoma, Bond, & Masuda, in press, for a review of these studies). Second, it has been possible to test ACT components such as acceptance (e.g., Gutiérrez, Luciano, Rodríguez, & Fink, 2004; Hayes, Bissett, et al., 1999) and defusion (e.g., see Masuda, Hayes, Sackett, & Twohig, 2004). Several of these studies (e.g., Eifert & Heffner, 2003; Levitt, Brown, Orsillo, & Barlow, 2004) have been done in the anxiety area. So far, all of the published tests of ACT components have been positive. As a result, ACT is not merely a package; it is a model, an approach, and a set of associated technologies, with data spanning the range from basic process, to experimental psychopathology, to inductive studies of treatment components, to studies of processes of change, to outcome research.

ACT is helping to break down artificial barriers between clinical traditions, not by vapid eclecticism, but by taking the issues addressed by other traditions seriously. ACT is behavior therapy, but it is using behavioral principles as a foundation and not a fence.

Issues of meaning, purpose, emotion, self, spirituality, values, experience, commitment, and so on are central to ACT, and based on systematic theoretical and empirical development. ACT is not afraid to examine questions such as "Why is it hard to be human?" or "What does it take to create a meaningful life?" It does not call these questions vague or dismiss them out of hand. ACT embraces the experiential, spiritual, and paradoxical elements of other clinical traditions, and puts them through the dual filters of empirical tests and specification of theoretical processes. This provides a better balance of breadth and focus.

Finally, ACT challenges the empirical clinical traditions to take second-order change seriously. As comports with both the philosophical assumptions and the theoretical principles that underlie it, the ACT clinician can truly embrace the old maxim that it is function, not form, that is important. As such, ACT greatly broadens the targets for change and the possible methods that can be used to produce change. For example, ACT is not as much concerned with whether a given thought or emotion occurred; instead, it is concerned with how to change the pathological functions those thoughts and emotions might have.

The present volume is written by researchers and clinicians who have been in the forefront of recognizing the revolutionary implications of this shift in direction, even while emphasizing the evolutionary continuity between ACT and the hard-won knowledge of first- and second-generation behavioral and cognitive therapy. In this well-crafted book you will be guided by skilled hands to bring both the best of existing procedures for anxiety (e.g., exposure-based methods) and the new clinical context established by ACT to bear on the problems faced by your anxiety patients. Eifert and Forsyth are sensitive to the philosophical and theoretical subtleties of this work on the one hand, and to the need for practical clinical guidance on the other. I particularly like the way they have worked to reduce unnecessary jargon and to find ways of speaking (e.g., FEEL exercises) that have a better chance of maintaining the connections between ACT methods and ACT principles and assumptions. If you know nothing of ACT, this book will help you get up to speed quickly and effectively. The approach is accessible to clinicians from a wide variety of backgrounds and can be combined with other elements once you understand the core processes and purposes of ACT interventions.

This book is about anxiety, but the theory underlying ACT suggests that struggles with anxiety are just an example of a more general set of human problems. Thus, what you learn in this volume should apply, with some modification, to several other clinical problems and to those comorbid problems faced by your patients

This book opens a door into a clinical approach that is both familiar and strange; both evolutionary and revolutionary; both broader and yet more focused than what has gone before. It will become clear very quickly that, yes, this is behavior therapy, but it is also behavior therapy pointed in a new direction. The possibilities are exciting; this book will help other clinicians and researchers discover if the possibilities are real.

—Steven C. Hayes
University of Nevada

PART I

UNDERSTANDING ANXIETY DISORDERS

CHAPTER I

What Is ACT?

The purpose of life is not to be happy—but to matter, to be productive, to be useful, to have it make some difference that you have lived at all.

—Leo Rosten

WHERE WE HAVE BEEN

Over the last forty years, behavior therapy has led the field in the development of empirically derived and time-limited psychological interventions to assist those suffering from anxiety- and fear-related problems. Most of these interventions now exist in the form of manuals and have been remarkably successful. Yet, all is not well. Despite some impressive short-term gains, we are still far from producing overwhelming success rates in terms of long-term recovery and prevention of relapse. Indeed, many time-limited cognitive behavioral interventions for anxiety-related disorders appear to produce equally time-limited treatment gains (Foa & Kozak, 1997a). And, despite numerous theoretical and conceptual advances in understanding the etiology and maintenance of anxiety-related disorders, we still lack agreement on the critical variables that may be involved, and do not yet agree on how best to approach the problem (Rapee, 1996).

Cognitive Behavioral Views of Anxiety Disorders

The result has been a growing literature of conflicting and unrelated findings, numerous disagreements and controversies, and a proliferation of disorder-specific mini theories and models that implicate so many different variables and processes that it is difficult to make any meaningful sense out of them (e.g., Barlow, 2002; Beck & Emery, 1985; Lang, 1993). This state of affairs is somewhat frustrating given that the anxiety disorders represent one of the more homogeneous diagnostic categories. Finally, despite refinements in our current diagnostic system (*Diagnostic and Statistical Manual of Mental Disorders-IV-TR*; American Psychiatric Association, 2000)—a system that has become ever more atheoretical, symptom-based, and categorical in nature—our field is still undecided about how best to classify and assess the problems in living that are grouped under the anxiety disorders, with diagnostic reliability often taking precedence over validity (Brown & Barlow, 2002). What *is* certain is that anxiety and fear-related problems are ubiquitous in human affairs. They often represent the main concerns of clients seeking outpatient psychotherapy and help from primary care physicians. What is more uncertain is whether cognitive behavioral therapies are addressing the real problem of anxiety and fear in the most useful fashion possible.

Most texts on the anxiety disorders describe etiological, theoretical, and treatment differences for each anxiety disorder consistent with the *DSM-IV-TR*—a system that classifies disorders and anxiety subtypes based on symptoms defined topographically and structurally rather than functionally or dimensionally. Using the *DSM* system as a bedrock for conceptual and treatment development is problematic for a number of reasons, but two stand out. First, the *DSM* tells us little about processes involved in how individuals come to have the symptoms they do. Second, the *DSM* does not address how those symptoms and associated problems in living can be effectively influenced in therapy. Despite such concerns, the *DSM* is widely used as a road map for thinking about psychopathology and has greatly influenced how we all think about anxiety disorders. For instance, it has become customary, if not mandatory, for behavior therapists to approach the anxiety disorders as discrete diagnostic entities, with each having its own separate etiologies and assessment and treatment strategies. As a result, the bigger picture is lost. Readers of standard chapters, texts, and treatment manuals on the anxiety disorders can easily be left with the false impression that the anxiety disorders are more different from one another than they really are.

Clearly, there is considerable overlap across the anxiety disorders. Such overlap, in turn, suggests that common behavioral processes are involved in the development, maintenance, and treatment of anxiety disorders. Perhaps if we were to come to grips with the common processes involved in how anxiety-related problems develop and are maintained, we might be in a better position to produce more impactful and meaningful behavior changes with our treatments and alleviate a wider range of human suffering. This is the more general aim of this book.

Cognitive Behavioral Therapies for Anxiety

For better or for worse, cognitive behavioral therapies (CBT) have become the treatments of choice for the anxiety disorders. Such treatments focus heavily on symptom alleviation as a therapeutic goal, are matched to specific *DSM*-defined anxiety disorders, and are set within a mastery and control framework. Such treatments imply several things.

First, they suggest that the "symptoms" are the problem. This perspective, by the way, is similar to how clients tend to view their problems (at least early on in therapy). In this sense, CBT therapists and clients appear to be in agreement that symptoms of anxiety cause impairment and suffering. If this were the whole story, then an obvious treatment strategy would be to target the symptoms. Yet there is usually a more important life to be lived behind the symptoms. It is this aspect of living that is of deep concern to clients, as it is to most human beings. In the past, traditional CBT has not paid sufficient attention to this and, as a consequence, may have missed important aspects of a person's life situation. It is for this reason that acceptance-based approaches put living front and center on the therapeutic stage—as we show in this book.

Second, we must provide a more process-oriented answer to the question: What are the so-called symptoms of anxiety a sign of? If we refer to the problem responses that our clients seek treatment for as symptoms of anxiety, then we must explain what the disorder is. Calling the disorder "anxiety" sounds reasonable, but is not a viable solution. A problem response (symptom) cannot define a disorder and be a symptom of the disorder at the same time (Williams, 2004). The alternative we suggest in this book is to go after the processes that turn normal anxiety into the often life-shattering problems we refer to as anxiety disorders and then target those processes during treatment.

Third, the strategy of matching treatments to different anxiety disorders suggests that the anxiety disorders are truly distinct, and thus warrant different approaches for each. This issue alone is interesting and certainly deserves more comment than space would allow for here. Most therapists, however, are quick to point out the high degree of functional and symptom overlap across the presumably different anxiety disorders. Similar treatment technologies work for different anxiety disorders (e.g., exposure, cognitive restructuring, relaxation). This is a further indication that the disorders are more similar than they have been made out to be. It is interesting that this perspective has actually been gaining ground in CBT, too. For instance, David Barlow has recently proposed a unified treatment protocol and modular approach directed at the core features of all anxiety and related emotional disorders with the goal of condensing the existing various versions of CBT to *one* strategic approach that targets those core features (Barlow, Allen, & Choate, 2004).

Finally, virtually all cognitive behavioral treatments are cast within a mastery and symptom control framework. The chief therapeutic goal of such interventions is to teach clients more effective ways to gain control over their anxiety, fear, and related symptoms. Again, this is precisely what clients have come to expect from therapy, and a posture that most clients are all too familiar with by the time they enter therapy. That is, clients have tried this or that to master and control their anxiety and fear, often without much success. Now, they expect therapists to provide them with new, "better," gold-plated strategies to do essentially more of the same, hoping that such strategies will be more workable than those they have tried in the past. As we will suggest, this mastery and control agenda is unnecessary and may even be counterproductive. Thoughts and emotions need not be managed to live a valued and meaningful life. Human experience tells us as much. Management and control of our internal private world is not a necessary prerequisite for living a meaningful life.

If this all sounds like a slam against cognitive behavioral therapies, it is not. Rather, our intent is to suggest ways that we can improve upon existing CBT interventions while retaining those components of CBT that have clearly proven effective, such as exposure exercises and strategies to counteract avoidance behavior. Helping clients to improve their life situations, however, may require that we rethink the mastery and control change agenda within standard cognitive behavioral therapies for anxiety disorders.

Before proceeding, we would like to challenge you to put aside for a moment some of the following commonly held assumptions about anxiety: (a) anxiety is bad; (b) anxiety is the cause of human suffering and life problems; and (c) our task as therapists is to help clients "get rid of," "control," "replace," or "eliminate" disturbing feelings or irrational thoughts, memories, and urges associated with anxiety and fear. In place of these assumptions, we offer a different view of anxiety and fear and their treatment and, hence, of psychological health.

WHERE WE ARE GOING

The treatment approach described in this book is based on *Acceptance and Commitment Therapy* (Hayes, Strosahl, & Wilson, 1999). Acceptance and Commitment Therapy (ACT) is a relatively new third-wave behavior therapy. It goes after various forms of experiential and emotional avoidance that keep people stuck and suffering. The basic goal of ACT is to help the client become better at living a full, rich, and meaningful life, rather than becoming better at feeling good (i.e., being symptom free) in an attempt to have such a life.

Acceptance and Commitment Therapy

Acceptance and Commitment Therapy is a unique behavior therapy approach that aims to address human concerns about anxiety and fear in a mindful, compassionate way, while encouraging people to pursue what really matters to them. In a nutshell, ACT is about helping clients to do three things: accept themselves and others with compassion, choose valued directions for their lives, and commit to action that leads them in those directions. ACT teaches clients that it is okay to have whatever unwanted thoughts and feelings their minds and bodies come up with. Rather than struggling with these thoughts and feeling, clients learn new ways of relating to them as experiences to be had.

ACT has two major goals: (1) fostering acceptance of unwanted thoughts and feelings whose occurrence or disappearance clients cannot control, and (2) commitment and action toward living a life that they value. This is why ACT is about acceptance *and* it is about change at the same time. Applied to anxiety disorders, clients learn to accept and live with their unwanted thoughts, worries, bodily sensations, and other feelings *and* take charge and move their lives in directions that they value.

ACT is not just short for Acceptance and Commitment Therapy. The ACT acronym also nicely captures the three core steps or themes of this approach—*Accept* thoughts and feelings, *Choose* directions, and *Take* action:

1. **A**ccept Thoughts and Feelings: Accept and embrace thoughts and feelings, particularly the unwanted ones (anxiety, pain, guilt, inadequacy). The idea is for clients to accept what they already have anyway and end their struggle with unwanted thoughts and feelings by not attempting to eliminate or change them, by not acting upon them, and by ultimately letting them go. Through various mindfulness exercises clients learn to live with their critical, evaluative mind.

2. **C**hoose Directions: This step is about helping clients to choose directions for their lives by identifying and focusing on what "really matters" and what they value in life ("What do you want your life to stand for?"). It is about helping clients to discover what is truly important to them and then making an important choice. It is about choosing to go forward in directions that are uniquely theirs *and* accepting what is inside them, what comes with them, and what accompanies them along the way.

3. **T**ake Action: This step is about committed action and involves taking steps toward realizing valued life goals. It is about making a commitment to action and changing what can be changed. The therapist encourages clients to behave in ways that move them forward in the direction of their chosen values. In this stage of ACT, clients learn that there is a difference between them as a person, the thoughts and feelings they have about themselves, and what they do with their lives. We will describe this process in detail as it is fundamental to ACT work, regardless of the clinical presenting problem.

The philosophy of ACT is somewhat similar to the serenity creed that many people love: *Accept with serenity what you cannot change, have the courage to change what you can, and develop the wisdom to know the difference.* Most people find that it is much easier to agree with the serenity creed than to do what it says. The reason is that often people simply do not know what they can change and what they cannot change. As a result, they do not know how to apply this profound statement in their daily lives and become frustrated with it. ACT teaches people to put the serenity creed into action.

ACT accepts the ubiquity of human suffering and does not seek to reduce pain or to produce a particular positive feeling. It is not about producing quick fixes or using culturally sanctioned feel-good formulas and methods to reduce suffering. ACT seeks instead to reduce suffering by increasing people's vitality and ability to do what they want to do with their lives. This is what the ACT approach is all about: Accept and have what there is to be had (anxiety, anger, joy, memories, the whole package) while also staying committed to doing what needs to be done to live a fulfilled, rich life guided by chosen values. People can choose to do things they enjoy and value regardless of what it is that they think or feel. Anxiety need not stand in the way of doing. If anxious clients start to move down this path, they are likely to feel more anxiety at first. Eventually they will probably feel more enjoyment and less pain and anxiety. If that happens, it is considered a welcome by-product of therapy—it is not an explicit goal of ACT.

An ACT Approach to Anxiety Disorders

CBT approaches to anxiety disorders have rightly focused on helping clients confront rather than avoid situations and stimuli that have been associated with anxiety. More recently, however, clinical researchers have begun to focus on a more general type of avoidance called *experiential avoidance*. Experiential avoidance refers to an individual's attempts and efforts to avoid, suppress, or otherwise alter the form of negatively evaluated private events such as bodily sensations, emotions, thoughts, worries, and memories (Hayes, Wilson, Gifford, Follette, & Strosahl, 1996). According to this view, when persons with agoraphobia avoid public places, they are not avoiding the places per se. What they are really avoiding is experiencing their thoughts and emotions associated with panic in such places (Forsyth, 2000; Friman, Hayes, & Wilson, 1998). Similarly, when people with obsessive-compulsive disorder avoid touching a doorknob that might have germs on it, they are not doing so to avoid being contaminated. What they are doing is avoiding the negative affect associated with touching the doorknob. In other words, in all these cases of phobic avoidance, people are avoiding their own psychological and emotional experiences.

This type of avoidance is at the core of all anxiety disorders. For instance, individuals with specific phobias do not really avoid snakes, elevators, or airplanes per se. They avoid experiencing paniclike responses in the presence of these stimuli (Forsyth & Eifert, 1996). Likewise, combat veterans with post-traumatic stress disorder do not avoid the sound of helicopters simply because they are afraid of them. They avoid the intense negative affect that is associated with that sound and its potential to remind them of past traumas that they wish not to think about. We therefore agree with the notion that the core issue in anxiety disorders is a fear of fear (Chambless & Graceley, 1989) or, more generally, a fear of negative affect. This is certainly part of the problem, but not the complete story. In fact, we would add to and rephrase fear-of-fear notions to read: The core issue in anxiety disorders is a fear of fear *and doing everything possible to avoid experiencing the fear*. The primary function of such experiential avoidance is to control or minimize the impact of aversive experiences. In fact, this avoidance tendency (not wanting to have the fear) is what drives fear of fear. Without avoidance, there would be no reason to fear the experience of fear.

Rigid and inflexible patterns of emotional and experiential avoidance are common to all anxiety disorders and function to make anxiety and fear problematic for anxious clients. Within ACT, such avoidance is viewed as a core toxic process driving "disordered" experiences of anxiety and fear. This is why experiential avoidance is one of the most important explicit treatment targets. ACT is not about helping clients to control or manage their anxiety, only to leave them stuck with lingering fears and concerns, such as "When is anxiety going to come back?" This prolongs the client's struggle and effectively sets up a relapse trap for them. Instead, ACT attempts to teach clients to approach fear and anxiety more fundamentally, more deeply, and in a different way. Specifically, an ACT approach to anxiety disorders is designed to teach clients the following:

1. Rigid and inflexible attempts to control, reduce, and avoid experiencing anxiety are the problem, not a solution.

2. Acceptance (as opposed to struggle) is a viable alternative agenda when faced with anxiety responses and the circumstances that occasion such responses.

3. Practice mindful acceptance and willingness when experiencing aversive bodily sensations, thoughts, and feelings during anxiety and other emotional states, regardless of whether they occur spontaneously or are elicited during exposure exercises. The goal here is not to help clients to feel *good* (i.e., be anxiety free), but to become good at *feeling* a full range of private experiences (i.e., thoughts, memories, emotions, bodily sensations) for what they are.

4. Client concern about overcoming anxiety has resulted in a restricted life and a great deal of suffering. Thus, clients are encouraged to take a hard look at their lives. In the process, they are encouraged to identify their own values while committing to put those values into freely chosen action. This will invariably result in what CBT manuals usually refer to as *naturalistic exposure exercises*. Yet, unlike typical CBT approaches, the primary goal is not to extinguish and reduce anxiety. The goal is to help clients live a valued life. ACT-style exposure, therefore, is always done in the service of client values and life goals, not as a means to

reduce or get a handle on symptoms. Though symptom alleviation may come about via the exercises contained in part 3 of this book, it is not an explicit focus nor a requirement for living life as a complete, fully functioning, capable human being.

Building upon these and other core ACT concepts, this book provides an alternative *mastery of experiencing* context for the exposure-type interventions that lie at the core of virtually all cognitive behavioral interventions for persons suffering from anxiety disorders. The ultimate therapeutic prize within ACT is to help the client live a full, rich, and meaningful life. Any exercise that facilitates movement in such directions is considered worthwhile.

HOW TO USE THIS BOOK

This book explores and describes ways to integrate the most successful components of traditional cognitive behavioral therapy within an Acceptance and Commitment Therapy framework. It is not meant to replace texts and manuals focusing on conventional CBT interventions. Most CBT texts provide comprehensive accounts of the current conceptual and research-based knowledge on the causes and assessment of anxiety disorders (Barlow, 2001, 2002; Craske & Barlow, 2000). These books also give clinicians detailed session-by-session instructions on how to conduct CBT for the various anxiety disorders. We summarize CBT approaches and review their efficacy in chapters 2 and 3 in enough detail so that you know where we are coming from and where we are going.

A word of caution, however, on how *not* to use this book. Please do not move to the treatment guidelines in part 3 without first reading part 2. There are several reasons we recommend against doing so that will become clearer to you as you read on. An increasing number of conference presentations, journal articles, professional books, and self-help books have focused on acceptance and mindfulness notions. Such topics, in turn, are becoming ever more popular in clinical science and practice. The tide is shifting. Many researchers and clinicians are curious about what this shift may offer them and the clients with whom they work. Though the basic ideas are certainly old, they are new in the field of psychology. Yet, the rapid dissemination of such notions has raced ahead of the practical, how-to translation. The underlying theory, rationale, and practical technology have not been disseminated in an easily understood and useable form. Acceptance- and mindfulness-based approaches remain somewhat shrouded in mystery for this very reason. This is unfortunate and a problem we hope to begin to remedy with this book. This book is, at its core, about describing and applying acceptance- and mindfulness-based notions to understanding and treating anxiety disorders. It represents our best effort to translate the underlying framework and technology. Our intention is to make ACT accessible and understandable so that it can be used by therapists and others who may benefit from it. We describe relevant concepts, principles, and techniques in an easy-to-understand language so that therapists may make use of this information in their daily practice with clients who present with anxiety disorders.

Part 3 of the book describes the application of ACT principles and techniques to the treatment of the major anxiety disorders. In this section you will find session-by-session guidelines on how to conduct acceptance-based behavior therapy. You will see that we present a unified approach to the treatment of anxiety problems, emphasizing emotional acceptance, experiential mindfulness, and actions that are consistent with what clients value and wish their lives to stand for. Most of the treatment guidelines are applicable to all anxiety disorders. Where appropriate and necessary, we also describe some disorder-specific considerations and procedural variations. We also provide detailed practical guidelines so that you may integrate ACT principles and techniques with the most successful and effective aspects of cognitive behavioral interventions for anxiety disorders (e.g., exposure and behavioral activation). The material is outlined in sufficient detail so that you may put what you read into therapeutic action and readily use it in your clinical work. As already mentioned, however, we do *not* want you to go immediately to part 3 of the book, read it, and then apply the interventions in a cookbook-type fashion with your clients. The results could be disastrous for them and disappointing for you. Understanding the rationale for the interventions is critical.

Rather than a technology, ACT truly is an *approach* to understanding and treating anxiety. It is not a set of techniques, metaphors, and exercises, although there are many. You should individualize and tweak techniques based on the specific circumstances and responses of each patient, an understanding of the core processes involved in maintaining your client's behavior, and what it is you want to change at the process level. We encourage you to use exercises and metaphors in a flexible and creative fashion. You should tailor and match the specific techniques to the unique circumstances of the client and the client's responses in the therapeutic interaction. So, do not feel compelled to use the exercises in exactly the same way, or in the exact same order, as we suggest. These are simply meant to be starting points. We expect that you will alter and adapt them to your clients' specific needs. You will probably also create new ones along the way. This is all fine and desirable as long as you target the critical processes that underlie disordered anxiety. It is for this reason that we consider it essential to read and learn about these processes in part 2 first before moving to the treatment guidelines in part 3 and attempting to apply any of the techniques we describe.

You will see that this book focuses on the functional overlap and similarities amongst the major anxiety disorders in terms of both etiology and treatment principles and techniques. This may be welcome news for you. It is a view that is quite different from the typical professional book about anxiety disorders. Such books, as you know, tend to emphasize unique aspects of each particular anxiety disorder. This we believe, does not jibe with clinical reality nor emerging evidence suggesting that we may have been artificially splitting up the anxiety disorders for too long. These and related issues are clearly laid out in part 2 of this book. For instance, chapter 4 describes a major commonality of all anxiety and related disorders: the toxic effect of experiential avoidance and efforts to control unwanted private experiences that most individuals with anxiety disorders engage in regardless of their particular DSM diagnosis. Rigid inflexible patterns of avoidance are common to all anxiety disorders. Such tendencies function to exacerbate and perpetuate client problems, regardless of the specific diagnosis or name we give them. We therefore encourage you to understand anxiety disorders as disorders of experiential avoidance. It is this experiential avoidance that becomes the explicit treatment target within the ACT approach we describe for you in part 3 of this book. Unless you have a good understanding of these processes and principles, including how they may play out in your own life, you will not be able to do ACT.

CHAPTER 2

Overview of Anxiety Disorders

When you change the way you look at things, the things you look at change.

—Wayne Dyer

In this book we focus on the features and processes that all anxiety disorders share rather than on the differences between them. Nonetheless, at the beginning of this book it may be useful to review the features that have come to define the most common anxiety disorders, including the latest data on the prevalence and demographics of such problems. We also present some commonalities and differences between disorders in terms of both symptom presentation and the core processes underlying disordered anxiety.

ANXIETY AND EFFORTS TO CONTROL IT ARE UBIQUITOUS

Despite some nuances, anxiety disorders are ubiquitous and can be found in all ethnic groups, countries, and cultures. In fact, anxiety disorders are among the most prevalent psychological disorders, affecting up to 25 percent of the general population at some point in their lifetime (Kessler et al., 1994). The core processes that contribute to such disorders—avoidance, escape, and other control tendencies to manage unpleasant emotions—are particularly common in Westernized countries. For instance, most of us learned early on to avoid touching a red-hot stove because it hurts. Some of us learned this the hard way, and others by listening to our parents or caregivers warn us about the consequences. We also learn how to manage physical pain when it comes and are socialized to use physical and psychological pain and suffering as reasonable reasons for our behavior and that of others. For instance, it is acceptable to miss a day at work or school for feeling ill, but it is not acceptable to miss a day of work or school for feeling full of life.

Through multiple examples such as this, we also learn to apply the very same control strategies to our thoughts, memories, and emotions—particularly to those that are unpleasant or painful. Anxiety and fear become much like the hot stove, and our behavior with respect to them must be managed somehow. Yet, the sensible strategy of dealing with potential sources of real pain and harm rarely works in the same way when applied to our thoughts and emotions. We can't turn them on or off in the same way we can move our hand on or off the hot stove. Our thoughts and feelings are with us wherever we go. We cannot escape or avoid them. They are part of us.

ANXIETY DISORDERS ARE EXPENSIVE

Barlow (2002) summarized the human costs of anxiety disorders as follows:

> In our society, individuals spend millions of dollars yearly to rid themselves of anxiety. The costs of visits to primary care physicians, and the utilization of health care services in general by individuals with anxiety disorders, are double what they are for those without anxiety disorders, even if the latter are physically ill. (p. 1)

People with panic disorder are indeed more likely to seek help for their problem than those with any other psychiatric diagnoses (including schizophrenia). Moreover, compared to people with other emotional problems, individuals with anxiety disorders are the highest users of emergency room services (Eifert, Zvolensky, & Lejuez, 2000; Eifert & Zvolensky, 2004). In addition, most anxiety disorders tend not to go away by themselves if left untreated. Instead, they tend to stay the same or get worse over time until people reach their fifties, with an increasing negative impact on quality of life for affected individuals and their families.

With high prevalence and chronicity, it is no surprise that anxiety disorders are associated with enormous personal and social costs as well as substantial economic costs. In fact, as Barlow (2002) aptly noted, "the actual expenses dwarf even the most pessimistic estimates … In recent years, anxiety disorders accounted for 31 percent of total costs of mental health care, compared to 22 percent for mood disorders and 20 percent for schizophrenia" (p. 26). Counting both the direct costs of services and lost productivity, the total annual costs of anxiety disorders in the United States are estimated at approximately $45 billion, with only 30 percent of that amount stemming from psychological and psychiatric treatment. In fact, over 50 percent of the costs come from excess (mostly unnecessary) utilization of primary health-care services. A number of studies have reported that the cost savings of effectively treating anxiety disorders far outweigh treatment costs. Not treating an anxiety disorder is ultimately more expensive than providing appropriate treatment (for a more detailed discussion, see Barlow, 2002).

NATURE AND FUNCTION OF FEAR AND ANXIETY

The nature and function of fear and anxiety teach us much about the core processes involved in "abnormal" or disordered anxiety. When we seek to understand the predicament of individuals with anxiety disorders, it is particularly important to consider the strong and mostly adaptive urge to escape from situations that elicit fear.

Fear—The Present-Oriented Basic Emotion

Fear is a present-oriented state that occurs in response to real or imagined danger or threat. Some of these threats are present in the here and now (e.g., a situation that is dangerous or distressing), others are in response to what is going on inside the client (e.g., a disturbing physical sensation, a thought, or a memory of the past), and some are a combination of these. Fear is typically characterized by an abrupt and acute surge of the sympathetic branch of the autonomic nervous system, accompanied by intense physiological changes (e.g., increased perspiration, rapid heartbeat, breathlessness, increased blood pressure) and a powerful action tendency to fight or flee from signs of threat or danger. Fear is also associated with greater vigilance and a narrowing of attention so that the individual's attention stays focused on the event that elicits the fear (Barlow, 2002). Under most circumstances, fear is perfectly adaptive because it serves an important function: it motivates and mobilizes the individual to take defensive action. Both the physiological and psychological changes that are associated with fear are designed to maximize the behavioral effectiveness of the individual to avert the threatening event.

Anxiety and Worry—The Future-Oriented Emotions

Anxiety, by contrast, is a future-oriented mood state that is accompanied by anxious apprehension, worry, increased muscle tension, restricted peripheral autonomic arousal, and marked increases in EEG beta activity reflecting intense cognitive processing in the frontal lobes (Borkovec, Alcaine, & Behar, 2004; Craske, 1999). Several studies have shown that people who are chronic anxious worriers show less physiological responsivity than people with phobic disorders (Roemer & Orsillo, 2002). Indeed, autonomic physiological changes associated with anxiety are much less pronounced and dramatic compared with fear. This may be due, in part, to the future-oriented and largely verbal-symbolic nature of anxiety. That is, people are typically anxious about something that may happen in the future, whereas people experiencing fear are afraid of what is happening right now. As an example, anxiety would be a more typical response to the thought of the possibility of living through an earthquake and its aftermath, whereas fear would be the more typical response when the earth is actually shaking. Behaviors that are most closely associated with anxiety are largely verbal or cognitive (e.g., worrying and making plans), whereas behaviors most closely associated with fear involve overt behavioral actions such as escaping, fighting, or freezing.

The Function of Normal Fear and Anxiety

Fear is an alarm response that makes us take some type of protective action when our safety or health appears to be threatened. These types of actions are in some cases reflexive and occur on an unconditioned (unlearned) basis, as when we close our eyes and turn our heads sideways in response to an object that flies toward us. In other cases, these actions occur on a learned (conditioned) basis, often with the help of language. Thus, when we take evasive action and jump to our left because someone shouts "danger on your right," we are doing so, in part, because of language learning. Even anxiety and worry about some future event that could threaten our livelihood can be useful and adaptive. For example, a bout of worrying can help us put together an action plan so as to more effectively respond to potential threats to our health, employment, safety, or the welfare of our family. In some instances, such plans need to be quite elaborate so that we can respond effectively when we are faced with an actual threat. A good example of such plans would be a family coming up with a plan in the event of a house fire.

Avoidance Makes Anxiety Problematic or "Disordered"

Thus, experiencing fear and anxiety is in many instances healthy and adaptive. Both emotions serve a purpose, namely, to keep us out of trouble and alive. This, by the way, is also an important fact to convey to clients in the beginning of a treatment program. Physical sensations, thoughts, and actions that accompany fear and anxiety are not abnormal or disordered per se. This is true even when fear and anxiety occur with great intensity. It is true even when fear and anxiety occur on a learned basis in response to a trauma. Consider, for instance, a client who has been bitten by a pit bull and subsequently experiences a strong fear response when encountering the same or similar dogs. Here, the tendency would be to describe the client's problems as a specific phobia—animal type. Yet, avoiding such dogs is not disordered or abnormal—it is a sensible response that is designed to avert another attack or injury and protect the client's physical health. Likewise, it is normal and adaptive for a woman who has been sexually assaulted to experience a fear response when encountering her assailant at a later time. If she were to encounter the man again, such fear could lead to a swift escape or other defensive responses to protect herself. Also, thinking about that man and worrying what might happen if she met him again can be adaptive and useful for her safety. It might help her devise an action plan of what she needs to do to protect herself and how she can best avoid being victimized in future. These learned alarm responses are normal and quite adaptive.

On the other hand, too much fear or anxiety can impede one's ability to take productive and effective action. Even animals don't do well under extreme fear. They freeze, shake uncontrollably, try to escape, or struggle to get away from the source of fear. Humans are the same as other animals in this respect. For example, false alarms, such as panic attacks, seem to occur for no good reason—out of the blue—in inappropriate or inconvenient situations (e.g., while getting ready to give a speech). They are quite often disruptive and challenging. Over time, some individuals seem to learn how to be with and experience such attacks, whereas others do not. This variation in responses is a critical point.

In many cases false alarms are not clinical problems that warrant clinical attention. What might help us understand how fear and anxiety can become disordered is to examine the much larger number of people in the general population who have panic attacks and no panic disorder. Epidemiological studies consistently place the prevalence of panic disorder in the general population at around 3 to 5 percent (Salkovskis, 1998). Several studies (for details, see Barlow, 2002) have shown that about 35 percent of presumably normal young adults had one or more panic attacks in a given year. The difference between such "normal panickers" and people with panic disorder is not primarily the intensity or frequency of panic attacks. Instead, it seems that people in these two groups react differently to their experience of panic attacks.

Most people who experience an occasional panic attack learn to wait it out and hang in there until it subsides. They do not attempt to escape from their fear. Rather, "nonclinical" panickers pick up from where they were before the attack and continue to live their lives without spending too much time worrying about future panic attacks—and, most importantly, without doing things to avoid the experience of panic and the places where they had panic attacks. We believe that this posture of acceptance and nonavoidance is one of the key preventive mechanisms that protects many of these nonclinical panickers from developing panic disorder or social phobia. It is only when people desperately and rigidly try to avoid the experience of panic attacks, and devote increasingly larger portions of their life energy and space to that task, that they are at high risk of developing actual panic *disorder*.

Both the *DSM* and anxiety researchers (e.g., Craske, 1999) have long emphasized that what turns nonclinical panic into clinical panic is fear of, and worry about, future attacks and associated behavioral changes (e.g., restriction of activities, avoidance behavior) to reduce the likelihood of having another attack. Nonhuman animals do some of this preparatory planning too. For instance, when an animal that is always shocked following a tone hears that tone again, the animal will interrupt its behavior and move its head and attention toward the tone. We could say that this animal is con-cerned with a real threat (i.e., the possibility of being shocked again) in the immediate future. Humans, by contrast, can go much farther in terms of both time frame and what might happen to them. This is possible, in part, because humans, unlike other animals, have the ability to think, imagine, and speak. These otherwise functional abilities also make it possible for humans to get caught up in a struggle with their own emotions in an effort not to have them. This struggle, in turn, can feed on itself in a self-perpetuating cycle, paradoxically creating more of the very emotions that are undesirable. More importantly, the struggle itself takes effort. Such effort directed at struggling to mini-mize or prevent anxiety and fear is energy and time no longer available to pursue other valued life activities. More fundamentally, this struggle for control is really a battle with one's own experiences. It is a battle that, somewhat paradoxically, cannot be won. We provide a detailed discussion of this struggle in chapter 4 because it is central to a deeper understanding of anxiety disorders and the ACT approach to treatment.

OVERVIEW OF ANXIETY DISORDERS

This section is designed to give the reader a brief overview of the central features of the major anxiety disorders as currently defined by the *DSM*.

Panic Attacks

Barlow (2002) noted that clinical manifestation of the basic emotion of fear is most evident in panic attacks. In addition to a strong autonomic surge that typically reaches its peak within ten minutes, and sometimes in as little as two minutes, individuals experiencing a panic attack report extreme fear and terror, thoughts of dying and losing control, and an overwhelming behavioral urge to escape and get away from wherever they are. Such fear responses are emergency or alarm reactions. They function to prepare humans and other mammals for action. Typically, such actions aim to ward off the potential impact of a threatening environmental stimulus or event. Thus, at its most basic level, the core of that response is a fight-or-flight action tendency. Classifying panic as an intense fear response and as an action tendency means that it is an *e-motional* alarm response: it serves to *elicit motion*. It is that strong urge to escape that leads people to avoid places where escape could be difficult (e.g., movie theaters, large shopping malls, formal social gatherings). If the action tendency is actually blocked, the intensity of fear increases.

Panic Disorder and Agoraphobia

Panic Disorder (PD) is characterized by recurrent panic attacks, fear of bodily sensations associated with autonomic arousal, and anxiety concerning the possibility of future panic attacks. Current diagnostic criteria for a diagnosis of PD require that an individual experiences recurrent and unexpected attacks. At least one of the attacks must be followed by at least one month of persistent worry about future attacks, worry about the consequences of the attacks, or a behavioral change because of the attacks (e.g., some type of avoidance). At the core, panic disorder is a fear of experiencing fear, where people are literally afraid of panic attacks and the potential consequences of such attacks. Agoraphobic avoidance occurs when people avoid places (e.g., malls, movie theaters, grocery stores) where they might have had a panic attack, and where escape may be difficult, in case they have another attack. Recall that agoraphobia is essentially a fear of having a panic attack in particular places, not a fear of those places as was previously thought. Accordingly, agoraphobia may best be viewed as a complication of panic disorder, where people attempt to avoid future panic attacks by staying in "safe" areas and avoiding stimuli and places that have previously been associated with panic. Nearly all persons who develop agoraphobia do so after first experiencing panic attacks; in fact, only 1 percent of people with agoraphobia do not experience panic attacks.

The onset of PD is typically in the mid to late twenties. Stressful life events frequently precede the onset of the disorder. Yet, absolute frequency of negative life events does not reliably differentiate persons with PD from persons with or without other anxiety disorders. Persons with PD do, however, report experiencing negative life events as more distressing compared to other people. Persons with PD also report a high degree of concern about their health status, particularly in regard to changes associated with bodily states. Without professional intervention, the course of PD is often chronic, with an increase in the number and intensity of attacks occurring during periods of stress. PD is twice as common in women as in men. This gender difference is consistently found in studies around the world and is largely due to sociocultural factors that moderate the experience and expression of emotion differently in males and females (Craske, 2003). For example, it is more socially acceptable for women to respond to fear by engaging in agoraphobic avoidance behavior, whereas men may attempt to endure fear and anxiety with the help of alcohol and other substances ("self-medication").

Specific Phobias

A specific phobia is a marked, persistent, and excessive or unreasonable fear of a specific object or situation. Exposure to the feared object usually produces an immediate and intense fear reaction (i.e., a panic attack). This alarm response is accompanied by a strong urge to flee from the object or situation and may be accompanied by significant impairment and distress about the fear. Persons suffering from specific phobias often act to avoid future encounters with the feared object as much as they can and will make great efforts to do so. Nonetheless, they typically recognize that their fear is excessive or unreasonable. This knowledge, however, has no impact on the urge to escape and avoid feared objects or the ability to control physiological and subjective responses that follow.

Specific phobias, along with other anxiety disorders, are typically defined as involving changes in three loosely connected "response systems" (Eifert & Wilson, 1991): motor behavior (e.g., avoidance or escape); elevated physiological activity (e.g., increased heart rate, perspiration, respiration, and muscle tension); and verbal-cognitive activity such as reports of distress and apprehension that precede, accompany, or follow the occurrence of anxiety.

Some specific phobias are situational (e.g., closed spaces, heights, or airplanes), whereas others focus on the natural environment (e.g., heights, storms, lightning, or water), animals (e.g., snakes, rats, or spiders), or bodily harm (e.g., diseases, injuries, or the sight of blood). Specific phobias are quite common in the general population, with large surveys showing a lifetime prevalence of 11 percent (Kessler et al., 1994). The most common phobias are (in descending order) fear of animals, heights, closed spaces, blood and injuries, storms and lightning, and flying.

In spite of this high prevalence, most people with specific phobias never seek treatment. Antony and Barlow (2002) report that in their anxiety clinics only 5 to 6 percent of patients present with a specific phobia as their major complaint. Yet, 26 percent of people presenting for other anxiety disorders also suffer from a specific phobia as a secondary problem. Most people with a specific phobia do not seek treatment for their fears, in part because they are quite adept at avoiding the objects of their fear and/or because contact with feared objects is not an issue in their daily lives (e.g., seeing a snake in midtown Manhattan). Such avoidance is possible because the fear-eliciting stimulus is clearly known and discernible. Yet even this "successful" avoidance occasionally comes at a high personal or social price. For instance, the family of one of Georg's clients in Australia could not take trips to a beautiful island just three miles offshore (a favorite weekend getaway destination for many people in the city) because she had a shark phobia and couldn't stand the thought of sharks swimming underneath the ferryboat during the crossing.

A number of specific fears may serve an evolutionary function. Researchers have observed that the most prevalent fears tend to involve stimuli that are associated with harm and have thus threatened survival (e.g., snakes, spiders, thunderstorms, heights). Over time, we have become "biologically prepared" to react in a hypervigilant, fearful manner to such stimuli to secure our survival (Seligman, 1971). Many studies, including several in our own lab (e.g., Forsyth & Eifert, 1998b), have demonstrated that fears of evolutionarily prepared objects are indeed more easily acquired than fears of other equally dangerous objects of more recent origin (e.g., electrical outlets, guns).

Social Phobia

Social phobia is characterized by an excessive and persistent fear and avoidance of situations that involve social interaction and evaluation by others. Persons with such problems tend to be particularly concerned about being negatively evaluated by others, show heightened personal awareness of autonomic activity in social situations, and experience real or perceived social inadequacy. They also worry that others might detect their social discomfort. These fears are often experienced as unreasonable and as causes of life distress.

Not surprisingly, people with social phobia typically avoid and escape from social situations as much as they can. Such situations include, but are not limited to, public speaking, interpersonal communication with persons of the opposite sex, group meetings, telephone-based communication, social gatherings, and at times quasi-social activities such as using public restrooms or public transportation. More than 90 percent of all persons diagnosed with social phobia fear and avoid more than one social activity. Researchers often differentiate a fear of specific or discrete social situations (e.g., public speaking) from generalized social phobia. The latter of these is characterized by fears and avoidance of most social situations. The generalized type also is associated with a greater degree of psychological suffering compared to specific social phobia (see Hofmann & Barlow, 2002, for a full discussion).

The problems experienced by individuals with social phobia typically go well beyond a fear of the actual social situation. Recall that individuals with agoraphobia, panic disorder, and specific phobias are not primarily afraid of public places, situations associated with panic attacks, or specific objects per se. They are afraid of experiencing unwanted psychological and emotional events in those contexts. The same is true of individuals with social phobia, where the fear is often focused on having a panic attack, somehow failing in front of others, or being humiliated or embarrassed while in a social situation. Thus, as with the other anxiety disorders, the core issue for individuals with social phobia appears to revolve around avoiding the experience of negative affect.

We know that the prevalence of social phobias is much more common than previously thought, with recent data (for a summary, see Hofmann & Barlow, 2002) showing a lifetime prevalence of 13.3 percent. This makes social phobia the most common anxiety disorder and the third-most-common psychological disorder after major depression (17 percent) and alcohol dependence (14 percent). Studies consistently show that about 70 percent of individuals with social phobias are female (Juster & Heimberg, 1998) and that social phobia tends to develop gradually over time. Few persons report a traumatic experience precipitating the disorder. In fact, many socially anxious persons report that they "have always had the problem." This is supported by other epidemiological data showing that the median age of onset occurs on or about puberty (i.e., twelve years of age), with more than 90 percent of individuals developing the disorder prior to age twenty-five (Juster & Heimberg, 1998).

Post-Traumatic Stress Disorder

The major clinical features of Post-Traumatic Stress Disorder (PTSD) fall into three broad clusters: reexperiencing of the traumatic event, avoidance of trauma-related stimuli, and chronically elevated bodily arousal. Great concerns regarding threats to personal safety (e.g., death) are central to the disorder.

The first cluster is also the most personally distressing feature of PTSD and involves reexperiencing aspects of the traumatic events by means of flashbacks, nightmares, intrusive thoughts, and emotional distress in response to internal or external cues that serve as reminders of the trauma (Jaycox & Foa, 1998). Trauma-related stimuli often trigger a reexperience of the trauma, heightened somatic activity, and behavioral manifestations of extreme terror, such as immobility. During flashbacks and nightmares, people with PTSD can relive traumatic experiences vividly and in a way that seems very realistic to them.

The second cluster involves avoidance behavior. For instance, persons with PTSD typically go to great lengths to avoid thinking about the traumatic event or any cues or situations that may serve as reminders of the event. The central function of such avoidance is to prevent reexperiencing the negative affect and psychological pain associated with the trauma. As with other anxiety disorders, avoidance behavior can vary from highly limited and circumscribed to highly generalized and extensive. As avoidance becomes extensive, it tends to restrict life functioning to such a degree that PTSD sufferers no longer engage in routine activities. For instance, some PTSD rape victims decrease contact only with certain types of males (e.g., males of the same race as the perpetrator), whereas other victims cease contact with all males. Another common form of emotional avoidance in PTSD is numbing, which refers to detachment from others and restricted range of affect. For instance, some rape victims with PTSD report a decreased level of enjoyment in sexual activity compared to other females despite achieving an equivalent number of orgasms. Many others simply report an inability to experience pleasure in life and an inability to trust and become close to others.

Lastly, the third PTSD cluster consists of experiences associated with elevated bodily arousal or the alarm response. Clinical features associated with arousal include sleep disturbances, elevated startle responses, irritability, anger outbursts, and hyper-vigilance. For instance, some rape victims constantly scan their environment for stimuli that are associated with the perpetrator and traumatic event. It is quite common for this elevated bodily arousal to spiral up into a full-blown panic attack.

PTSD is the only psychological problem with a clear etiological marker, namely one or more traumatic events. Although problem responses may manifest in a relatively short time after the trauma (e.g., within three to six months), they also can arise years after a traumatic event. Jaycox and Foa (1998) rightly called the prevalence of trau-matic experiences and clinical PTSD alarming. Approximately 39 percent of the U.S. population will experience at least one traumatic event in their lifetime. Yet, of those people, only 24 percent will go on to develop PTSD, accounting for a 9 percent lifetime prevalence of PTSD in the general population. These numbers are certainly high, par-ticularly when considering that up to 15 percent of the population suffers from subclinical PTSD. Nonetheless, we know from such studies that about two-thirds of trauma victims do not develop PTSD. Again, we must ask, why do most people emerge from traumatic experiences psychologically relatively unscathed? Why do some people only experience acute problems following trauma that dissipate on their own after a few months? And, why, in other cases, do problem responses persist and develop into the disorder we call PTSD? As we discuss in chapters 3 and 4, this is probably not a question of differences in traumatic conditioning, luck, or fate. Examining the core dimension of rigid avoidance of negative affect may hold the key to answering these and other crucial questions.

Generalized Anxiety Disorder

The clinical features of generalized anxiety disorder (GAD) are excessive worry about a number of events and activities occurring more days than not for at least six months, causing clinically significant distress or impaired functioning; unsuccessful attempts to stop or control worrying and to reduce anxiety by means of worrying; and a number of central nervous system problems such as muscle tension, restlessness, fatigue, difficulty concentrating, irritability, and sleep disturbance.

Approximately 5 percent of the general population will suffer from GAD at some point in their lives. Of these, about 60 percent of all cases are female. The onset of GAD is typically insidious, often beginning at an earlier age compared with other anxiety dis-orders. However, we should add that GAD onset late in life is common, too (Roemer & Orsillo, 2002). Worry and anxiety-related responses are likely to be particularly intense during periods of life stress and tend to decrease during periods of low stress. As with social phobia, the onset of GAD is not typically associated with negative life events. Rather, individuals commonly report that they are "stressed" and frequently over-whelmed by everyday life experiences ("daily hassles"). These observations further sup-port the view that it is the frequent experiencing of negative uncontrollable life events in general, rather than a specific traumatic experience, that determines individual susceptibility to GAD. As a result, persons with GAD learn that they can do little to predict and control such events and end up worrying about them and avoiding them as much as possible.

Obsessive-Compulsive Disorder

Obsessions are recurring persistent thoughts, impulses, or images that are associated with significant anxiety and are experienced as intrusive, unreasonable, and distressing. Compulsions, by contrast, are repeated behaviors (e.g., checking, hand washing) and mental acts (e.g., counting, praying) that people engage in rigidly and excessively to relieve anxiety provoked by the obsessions (Steketee & Frost, 1998). The goal of ritualistic thoughts or actions is to suppress, neutralize, or otherwise control disturbing obsessional content. The behavioral or mental acts serve to restore safety, reduce anxiety, and prevent the dreaded event from happening. Obsessions and compulsive rituals cause marked distress and interfere with daily routines and social functioning more significantly than any of the other major anxiety disorders. In fact, when individuals are hospitalized because of anxiety, it is typically because they suffer from obsessive-compulsive disorder (OCD) (Steketee & Barlow, 2002). Hospitalization often represents the culmination of the downward vicious cycle of compulsions and obsessive rituals. Both tend to put so many constraints on people's lives, while consuming so much time every day, that some individuals literally run out of time to do what they really need to do. Hospitalization in such cases is typically a last resort to break this cycle.

Unlike cognitions associated with GAD, the intrusive thoughts and worries experienced by persons with OCD are not simply excessive worries about real, everyday life problems. Instead, OCD is characterized by unrealistic, unreasonable, and often bizarre concerns. Most human beings have had such intrusive and bizarre concerns at some point. Yet, intrusive thoughts and images tend to elicit more anxiety and are more difficult to dismiss in OCD sufferers compared with other people (Steketee & Frost, 1998). Such thoughts, in turn, also often culminate in a paniclike reaction and are typically avoided and resisted. This is why Steketee and Barlow (2002) describe the response of individuals with OCD as another type of phobic reaction. This reaction is similar to that seen in panic disorder, except that the phobic objects in OCD are cognitions, not bodily sensations.

Most people with OCD realize that their rituals are excessive and unreasonable. Yet they continue to engage in behaviors that are designed to control or reduce unwanted thoughts. It is certainly possible that OCD sufferers engage in such control behavior because obsessive intrusions provoke more anxiety in them than in other people. Yet, it is also possible that the very tendency to neutralize and control intrusions inadvertently contributes to elevated anxiety. There is indeed mounting empirical support for the negative and backfiring effects of attempts to suppress or control unwanted thoughts and images (Hayes et al., 1996; Wegner, 1994). We will have more to say about this line of research in subsequent chapters.

Although the age of onset for OCD is typically mid to late adolescence, problems can start in children as young as five to six years of age. In childhood and adolescence, there are more males than females suffering from OCD (sex ratio 2:1), but by adulthood the gender distribution is approximately equal. OCD rarely begins after age fifty (Steketee & Barlow, 2002). If untreated, the prognosis of OCD is poor.

ANXIETY DISORDERS HAVE MUCH IN COMMON

In the past, researchers and therapists have focused on the differences between anxiety disorders. At the phenomenological level such differences are obvious, particularly if one focuses on events that elicit fear and anxiety across the anxiety disorders. In specific phobias, for instance, we have focused on a specific object, event, or situation. In social phobia, we have focused on social situations. In panic disorder, we have focused on discrete episodes of intense fear elicited by bodily sensations. In PTSD, we have focused on past traumatic events and associated memories. We also differentiate cued or expected fear responses, where we know the fear-eliciting stimuli (e.g., in specific and social phobias and PTSD), from uncued or unexpected types of fear responses that appear to occur out of the blue (e.g., in panic disorder), where we often have no clear understanding of the eliciting stimuli. We have also focused on differences in the duration and intensity of responses. For instance, fear and the associated physical changes in panic disorder are intense but relatively short-lived, whereas anxiety and physiological responses in GAD are less intense and occur over much longer periods of time.

Phenomenological Overlap

Despite these differences amongst the various anxiety disorders, there are some striking commonalities that have been studied extensively. For instance, although panic attacks most frequently occur in persons with PD, they also can and do occur in persons with all other anxiety disorders. For instance, at least 50 percent of people with social phobia and at least 30 percent of people with GAD and OCD experience occasional or frequent panic attacks.

Additionally, we have known for some time that there is little difference between a panic attack that occurs within the context of panic disorder and cued (situationally bound) panic attacks that occur in the presence of specific stimuli (e.g., in specific and social phobias, PTSD; cf. Craske, 1991). Most importantly, the tendency to avoid and escape from fear and anxiety is characteristic of just about every individual diagnosed with an anxiety-related disorder. The specific types of escape and avoidance behavior may differ at a phenomenological level. Yet, the basic function of those behaviors is the same: they serve to make the fear and anxiety go away and get the person out of the situation where they experience fear and anxiety. There is also much overlap between anxiety disorders and major mood disorders such as major depression and dysthymia. Barlow and colleagues (2004) report that 55 percent of patients with a principal anxiety or mood disorder had at least one other additional anxiety or depressive disorder at the time of assessment. This rate increased to 76 percent when additional lifetime diagnoses were considered.

Panic attacks are indeed common occurrences in persons with major emotional disorders. For instance, as many as 25 to 50 percent of persons suffering from major depression, and 35 to 60 percent of those with somatization disorder or hypochondriasis, experience panic attacks (Salkovskis, 1998). Brown and Barlow (2002) discuss several large-scale studies that all show that major depression is by far the most common additional lifetime diagnosis in patients with a principal anxiety disorder. A surprising finding was that the overwhelming majority of patients with mood disorders also presented with a current or past anxiety disorder. In fact, only 5 percent of 670 patients who had lifetime major depression or dysthymia did not have a current or past anxiety disorder. In the majority of cases of coexisting anxiety and depression, anxiety disorders preceded rather than followed the onset of mood disorders.

We therefore agree with Barlow and colleagues (2004) that there is a remarkable degree of functional overlap across the anxiety disorders. We also agree that all the emerging evidence points to the overriding importance of common factors in the genesis and presentation of emotional disorders. The observable overlapping features of the various anxiety disorders, as well as the large co-occurrence of anxiety and mood disorders, point to a more basic fundamental overlap at the process level:

> Deepening understanding of the nature of emotional disorders reveals that commonalities in etiology and latent structure among these disorders supercede differences [p. 205] … There is wide agreement that the *DSM-IV* represents the zenith of a splitting approach to nosology, with the obtained advantage of high rates of diagnostic reliability. But there is growing suspicion that this achievement has come at the expense of diagnostic validity, and that the current system … may be erroneously distinguishing categories that are minor variations of broader underlying syndromes. (Barlow et al., 2004, p. 211)

Common Core Pathological Processes

We believe that a better understanding of the common core processes by which normal anxiety and other emotions become disordered is essential to a successful approach to treating people with anxiety and other emotional disorders. There is increasing empirical support for the notion that the powerful and self-defeating impact of avoiding negative affect is the core pathological process that fuels all anxiety disorders. In our view, the way people with GAD use worry to avoid and reduce the stress associated with anxiety can teach us a lot about the core problem behavior that is at the heart of all anxiety disorders: rigid and excessive attempts to avoid experiencing anxiety.

GAD—The Prototypical Anxiety Disorder?

GAD used to be a catchall diagnosis for persons who presented with an anxiety problem that did not neatly fit into one or more of the other, more specific anxiety categories. In recent years, the shift in GAD diagnostic criteria from specific motor and autonomic symptoms to the core processes of worry and anxious apprehension has led to the notion that GAD may in fact be *the* "basic" anxiety disorder. Indeed, Barlow (2002) views anxious apprehension as a core process that can serve as a platform for the genesis and maintenance of all anxiety disorders. He defines anxious apprehension as a future-oriented mood state in which an individual becomes ready for, or prepares to cope with, upcoming negative events. This state is associated with heightened negative affect, chronic overarousal, a sense of unpredictability and uncontrollability, and an attentional focus on threat-related stimuli. Barlow points out that the process of anxious apprehension is present in all anxiety disorders, but the specific content of that apprehension varies from disorder to disorder.

Our much improved understanding of GAD gives us important clues as to what can make anxiety disordered and what behaviors we need to address in treatment. Worry functions as a cognitive avoidance response to threatening material. Borkovec and associates (2004), for instance, have gathered convincing empirical evidence that the function of worry is to avoid imagery and physiological arousal associated with anxiety and negative affect. When people worry, they are mostly talking to themselves. That is, worry involves more abstract verbal thinking than imagery (Borkovec & Newman, 1998). Hence, worry allows people to approach emotional topics from an abstract conceptual perspective and thereby avoid aversive images and intense negative emotions in the short run. In the long run, however, this strategy is ineffective. In fact, individuals tend to experience even more intense anxiety over the long haul, which is usually followed by efforts to reduce anxiety by engaging in more worrying (Mennin, Heimberg, Turk, & Fresco, 2002).

> [People with GAD] are thinking so hard about upcoming problems that they do not have the attentional capacity left for the important process of creating images of the potential threat, images that would elicit more negative affect and autonomic activity. In other words, they avoid all the negative affect associated with the threat … [As a result] they may avoid much of the unpleasantness associated with the negative affect and imagery, but they are never able to work through their problems and arrive at solutions. Therefore they become chronic worriers, with accompanying autonomic inflexibility and quite severe muscle tension. Thus, intense worrying for an individual with GAD may serve the same maladaptive purpose as avoidance does for

people with phobias. It prevents the person from facing the feared situation, and so adaptation and real problem-solving can never occur. (Barlow & Durand, 2004, p. 130)

It has proven difficult to explain why worry helps GAD sufferers avoid distressing emotional experiences and why these experiences are so aversive that such individuals feel they need to avoid them in the first place. Still, Mennin and colleagues (2002) have provided an explanation that we believe is quite compelling. These authors found that individuals with GAD have emotional reactions that occur more easily, quickly, and intensely than for most other people. At the same time, they also appear to have a poorer understanding of emotions, respond to their emotions in a negative way, and use maladaptive strategies to control and constrain their emotional experience to decrease this aversive state. Thus, GAD tends to be associated with indiscriminate avoidance of negative affect that is, in some sense, on autopilot.

Avoiding Fear and Anxiety at All Costs

There is increasing evidence that the key problem of most people with anxiety disorders is not their intense fear or pervasive anxiety. The problem is that such persons tend to be overwhelmed by the action tendency to avoid experiencing fear and anxiety. They quite literally live a life focused on trying not to have anxiety and fear, unwanted thoughts, past memories, worries, and the like. Such a life lived in the service of anxiety and fear can take several forms, such as avoiding people, places, activities, and situations that might lead to anxious and fearful feelings, using substances to minimize the occurrence of such feelings, and escaping from situations during unpleasant emotional states. A life lived in the service of not having anxiety and fear, particularly when rigidly and inflexibly applied, is quite limiting and likely has come to define how clients are living their lives by the time they enter therapy. It is when this strategy of avoidance and escape is applied rigidly and inflexibly to anxiety and fear, including the circumstances that occasion such responses, that we begin to talk about the shift from normal anxiety and fear to disordered experiences of anxiety and fear. Most of this activity is verbally constructed and evaluative, and hence the reason why ACT considers language at the heart of this experiential avoidance problem. Indeed, from an ACT perspective, anxiety and fear become problematic when persons:

- are unwilling to have anxiety and fear;

- routinely act to avoid, suppress, and escape from such emotions, associated thoughts, physical sensations, and the circumstances that may occasion them; and

- devote enormous effort and time to this struggle with anxiety and fear at the expense of other valued and important life activities and goals.

As we show in part 3, ACT aims to break up this cycle by undermining this natural tendency to avoid and escape and increasing flexibility and willingness to experience anxiety and fear for what it is. At the same time, ACT helps clients focus attention on important and valued life domains that are being sidelined during this struggle.

CHAPTER 3

Cognitive Behavioral Views and Treatments of Anxiety Disorders

*Clinical experience has shown that, ironically, it is often the
patient's very attempt to solve the problem that, in fact, maintains it.
The attempted solution becomes the true problem.*

–Giorgio Nardone & Paul Watzlawick

Behavioral and cognitive behavioral treatments are the treatments of choice for anxiety disorders. In fact, they represent the best psychosocial interventions that we have to offer persons suffering from anxiety disorders. Yet, cognitive behavioral therapies are still far from being curative. A significant number of anxiety sufferers fail to respond to cognitive behavioral therapies. More people than we'd like to admit never even start treatment when they hear what it involves (Becker & Zayfert, 2001). Many others drop out before completing treatment, and of those who complete treatment, many ultimately relapse and require additional treatment. It is simply not the case that we have reached the efficacy ceiling with regard to cognitive behavioral therapies for anxiety disorders (Barlow et al., 2004; Foa & Emmelkamp, 1983; Foa & Kozak, 1997a). Far from it. We can and should do better. In fact, we must do better. Meeting this challenge will require rethinking some of the basic assumptions guiding our views of anxiety-related problems and their treatment. In particular, we need to reexamine what makes anxiety and fear disordered. The aim of this chapter is to provide some background for this reexamination and a new perspective.

COGNITIVE BEHAVIORAL VIEWS

Early behavior therapy owes much of its success to its account of the etiology and maintenance of anxiety disorders. This account was based on the simple notion that anxiety disorders are learned or acquired via a process of conditioning and are maintained via escape and avoidance behavior (Mower, 1960). The logical consequence of this account was that successful treatment needs to involve helping clients to confront feared stimuli and situations in a safe therapeutic environment so as to allow for new corrective emotional learning and extinction of excessive fear and anxiety (Wolpe, 1958). This view survived more or less intact until the 1970s, when criticisms mounted suggesting that anxiety disorders are not solely about conditioning. There is more to the human experience than conditioning because of the human capacity for language and our propensity to engage in complex and infinite verbal-symbolic cognitive processes. A more cognitive view of disorders and their treatment ensued that focused on the role of memory, attention, catastrophic thinking patterns, irrational beliefs, unrealistic self-statements and appraisals, and the like. These notions were quickly integrated within behavior therapy and became known as cognitive behavioral therapy (Beck & Emery, 1985). Below we briefly trace some of these developments, and highlight where both the original conditioning and the cognitive behavioral accounts fall short.

Limitations of the Behavioral Account

Early behavior therapists tended to conceptualize the etiology of anxiety disorders in terms of straightforward Pavlovian or classical conditioning principles. Thus, when an otherwise benign stimulus occurs in close contingency with an anxiety-inducing event, it becomes highly likely that the stimulus will later elicit anxiety and fear without further trauma. In fact, a relation between otherwise neutral stimuli and a false alarm (i.e., a panic attack) may be enough to set this learning in motion (Barlow, 1988; Bouton, Mineka, & Barlow, 2001; Forsyth & Eifert, 1996; Wolpe & Rowan, 1988). For instance, several studies out of our lab group have shown that panic attacks can function as conditioning events in the etiology of anxiety disorders (Forsyth, Eifert, & Thompson, 1996; Forsyth, Daleiden, & Chorpita, 2000; Forsyth & Eifert, 1996, 1998a, 1998b). Importantly, this work suggests that conditioning involves, at least from an individual's perspective, relations between bodily and environmental cues and a highly unpleasant false alarm response (i.e., a panic attack; Barlow, 2002; Forsyth & Eifert, 1996; Wolpe & Rowan, 1988). It is the false alarm response, not necessarily the aversive stimulus capable of evoking it, that humans experience as traumatic. This view is at the core of contemporary thinking about the critical processes involved in fear learning, wherein panic attacks or paniclike responses function as critical conditioning events in the genesis of anxiety disorders (Bouton et al., 2001).

Nonetheless, numerous criticisms have been raised about the clinical relevance of a conditioning account of anxiety disorders. Our intent here is not to redress all of these criticisms (e.g., Marks, 1979; Menzies & Clarke, 1995; Rachman, 1977, 1991), as only one of them holds up in light of contemporary learning theory. The conditioning model of anxiety disorders has not fully explained how adaptive learning processes (i.e., conditioning) coupled with adaptive emotional responses (i.e., fear and anxiety) would send some individuals down the path to an anxiety disorder and not others. Indeed, critics and proponents of the conditioning model of anxiety disorders have largely ignored this critical issue. Yet, coming to terms with it has profound implications for understanding anxiety-related suffering (see Forsyth, Eifert, & Barrios, in press, for a detailed account). Here, we will briefly summarize a few key points.

First, consider classical fear conditioning. There is nothing disordered about this form of learning. In fact, it is ubiquitous and highly adaptive. Classical conditioning occurs in forms ranging from subtle to obvious across all mammalian species, and even has been found to occur in single-cell organisms (e.g., paramecia; see Hennessey, Rucker, & McDiarmid, 1979). The main function of this form of learning is to tinge stimuli with emotional significance or meaning, and thus direct behavior as a consequence (Staats & Eifert, 1990). At times fear learning can be quite dramatic, as with the trauma of 9/11, natural disasters, accidents, assault, or war. Yet, even in these and other more extreme examples, the learning is perfectly adaptive. It makes sense to learn to fear stimuli that have been associated with aversive consequences. As indicated in chapter 2, it also makes sense to avoid people and situations that have been associated with aversive and harmful consequences. In fact, the consequences of *not* doing so could be quite disastrous.

Second, the alarm response, whether conditioned or unconditioned, is no less adaptive. When fear is evoked in nonhuman animals, they engage in a number of behaviors that we describe as behaving fearfully. They freeze, shake, struggle to escape, cry out, and even urinate and defecate. Numerous neurobiological responses underlie such actions, involving in particular the amygdala and hippocampus and the sympathetic branch of the autonomic nervous system (LeDoux, 1996, 2000; Selden, Everitt, Jarrard, & Robbins, 1991). When such responses are evoked, the typical acute consequence is disruption and narrowing of ongoing behavior. Such disruptions make organisms ready to take immediate action to prepare for, and subsequently to escape from or avoid, potential sources of threat. Following such experiences, most mammals, including humans, will actively avoid exposing themselves to stimuli that predict such responses, in part because it makes adaptive sense to do so.

Classical fear conditioning has survived as a model of anxiety disorders largely because of Watson and Rayner's (1920) dramatic demonstration of phobic fear acquisition in Little Albert. The correspondence between the behavior of Albert and the phobias and other anxiety problems was so dramatic that behavior therapists never stopped to ask whether it would have made sense for Little Albert to have responded any differently than he did under the circumstances. We are suggesting that the emotion of fear and the classical conditioning of fear are not disordered processes, but rather normal and mostly adaptive dimensions of everyday human experience. The real challenge is to explain why classical fear learning would result in an anxiety *disorder*.

This issue, as we will suggest, requires consideration of what humans do to manage the experience and expression of emotions. This is a key point of difference between nonhuman animals and humans. There is no indication that nonverbal mammals suffer about their own suffering. Nonhuman primates will also learn to avoid the source and context of aversive stimulation, but as best we can tell, they do not act deliberately and purposefully to regulate their emotional experience. Humans, by contrast, can and do suffer about their own emotional pain and histories by responding to conditioned responses with evaluative verbal behavior and thinking, and by engaging in efforts to suppress, avoid, or escape from their emotional pain and related thoughts. Thus, humans can become fearful or fear, depressed about anxiety, worried about the future, tormented about the past, and struggle to avoid and escape from unpleasant thoughts, images, sensations, feelings, behavioral tendencies, and the circumstances that have evoked them or those that *may* evoke them in the future. The capacity of language, coupled with powerful social contingencies regarding the experience and expression of emotion, make all this possible.

Emotional Regulation Can Transform Normal Fear Into a Clinical Problem

When a fear learning process is juxtaposed with emotional regulation processes, something new may emerge that is far from functional. Emotion regulation simply refers to actions that are designed to influence "which emotions we have, when we have them, and how we experience and express them" (Gross, 2002, p. 282). Putting on a smile at a social gathering, despite feeling and thinking negatively about the situation, is one example of emotion regulation in action. Though emotion regulation is itself not a dysfunctional process, it can become dysfunctional when the emotions one is attempting to regulate cannot and need not be regulated, and when the very act of emotion regulation gets in the way of meaningful life activities.

Figure 1 illustrates the typical points where emotional experience tends to be regulated. In a somewhat simplified fashion, this model suggests that humans may regulate the antecedents and consequences of emotions. Antecedents, in the case of anxiety disorders, may include situations where anxiety and fear are likely to occur, bodily and environmental cues that tend to evoke such reactions, whether emotionally relevant

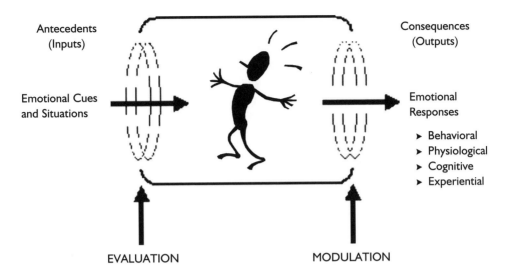

Antecedents
(Inputs)

Consequences
(Outputs)

Emotional Cues
and Situations

Emotional
Responses

➤ Behavioral
➤ Physiological
➤ Cognitive
➤ Experiential

EVALUATION   MODULATION

Figure 1. A consensual model of emotion regulation. Adapted from "Antecedent and response-focused emotion regulation" by J. J. Gross, 1998, *Journal of Personality and Social Psychology, 74,* p. 226. Copyright (1998) by the American Psychological Association. Reprinted with permission of the publisher.

information is attended to, and how such information is appraised (e.g., "This is bad," or "I can't get through this"). Strategies used to regulate emotions on the front end are important precisely because how one responds to emotional inputs, and particularly the verbal evaluation of those inputs (i.e., "This is dangerous [awful, harmful, etc.]"), affects the emotional consequences that may follow. Thus, escalation of the emotional sequence can be attenuated or avoided altogether depending on how one manages the antecedents of emotional experience. Once the emotion occurs, regulation efforts tend to focus on the intensity, duration, and general quality of the emotional experience and its consequences. Such response-focused regulation strategies may involve taking a break, relaxation, deep breathing, or doing something pleasant. There is nothing particularly disordered or problematic about such strategies, particularly when applied in a context-sensitive and flexible manner.

Emotional Dysregulation in Anxiety Disorders

The problems come about when persons make rigid and inflexible efforts to down-regulate the cognitive, physiological, or behavioral components of negative emotions such as anxiety and fear. Such strategies are often subtle and idiosyncratic in persons suffering from anxiety disorders, and usually take the form of suppression, control, avoidance, or escape (Barlow, 2002; Barlow et al., 2004). People suffering from anxiety disorders do not experience fear and anxiety as adaptive, normal emotional events. Rather, they are bad emotional events that need to be managed and controlled at all costs.

These emotion down-regulation efforts provide the context in which persons suffering from anxiety disorders experience anxiety, fear, and the circumstances that give rise to them. That is, down-regulation efforts function as important predispositions that make the otherwise adaptive emotions of anxiety and fear disordered. As we describe in chapter 4, emerging data on several fronts suggest that emotion regulation efforts only work to a point, and these efforts are particularly unworkable when the emotions are highly aversive. In fact, attempts to escape from and/or avoid unpleasant emotions typically backfire, resulting in an increase of the very emotion that is undesired, as demonstrated by the effects of attempts to control emotions after initial panic attacks (Craske, Miller, Rotunda, & Barlow, 1990).

The Role of Avoidance and Escape Behavior

Within the traditional behavioral account, avoidance and escape behavior are thought to represent the two main antecedent and response-focused emotion regulation strategies that emerge as a natural consequence of fear learning. Yet, this account begs the question as to why the powerful action tendency to avoid and/or escape fear-evoking stimuli would yield an anxiety disorder in some individuals and not others. When persons encounter a stimulus that was previously associated with danger, harm, or pain, they will indeed experience a powerful behavioral urge to escape and will often act to stay away from that situation as much as they can. In chapter 2 we used the example of a woman who was sexually assaulted and subsequently experiences a strong fear response when thinking of her assailant or the previous assault. If she were to encounter the man again, such fear would lead to an immediate escape or other defensive responses to protect herself. As we indicated, there is nothing disordered about such learned alarm responses and related avoidance and escape behaviors. They are normal and adaptive.

In our view, the main reason why fear learning becomes disordered is related to individual differences in the application of emotion regulation strategies when such strategies are unworkable and/or uncalled for by the situation. Going back to the sexual assault example, if this woman were to apply escape and avoidance behavior in a rigid and inflexible way, to avoid not only her assailant but all men (including those who have never harmed her, such as her husband), then she might well be on her way to developing an anxiety disorder. It is unworkable for this woman to avoid feelings of apprehension the first time she is about to have sex in a safe environment (e.g., with her husband) after she was sexually assaulted. It is unworkable because feeling anxious and apprehensive in this sexually charged situation is a natural consequence of the previous highly aversive experience with her assailant—even though the contexts could not be more different. It is simply impossible for her to shut down or avoid apprehension, anxiety, and perhaps even some aversion. Avoiding those feelings (and her husband) is also uncalled for in the sense that the situation does not require her to escape in order to be safe because her husband poses no danger to her safety. Nonetheless, the urge to escape is there and quite real. The woman must choose whether to give in to that urge or to stay *and* be anxious *and* be sexually intimate with her husband because that is more important to her than not being fearful. The choice she makes will be closely related to her values as well as to her history of handling aversive experiences. Thought and emotional regulation can get in the way of such choices.

A less complex example might help clarify the important distinction between flexible (healthy) and inflexible, rigid (possibly disordered) responses. When a child falls off her horse and hurts herself while learning to ride, she will be apprehensive about getting back into the saddle. After all, horse riding has just been associated with pain. So experiencing some fear at the sight of the horse is quite natural. Yet we all know that this child needs to get back into the saddle pretty soon, or else she will never learn to ride the horse. She will also miss the chance to experience that horse riding, for the most part and when done with caution, is not harmful and can be quite useful and enjoyable. Now consider the child who falls off the horse and does not get back onto the horse. In fact, she starts to avoid all horses as well as anything that is horse related (e.g., barns, the countryside, movies featuring horses). She may even come to avoid situations unrelated to riding where taking a fall is a possibility. This child will neither learn to ride a horse safely nor lose her apprehension about horses, and she may also very well be on her way to developing a horse phobia and broader problems related to a fear of falling.

Although we know woefully little about this process, it is likely that people learn such rigid avoidance strategies early on in life, with observational learning probably playing a major role (Hayes et al., 1996). People also learn not only to avoid the fear-related objects and events, but to avoid feeling fear and other aversive emotions themselves. In any case, persons who have learned to avoid unpleasant thoughts and feelings, and who do so rigidly and inflexibly, are likely to respond to fear learning experiences quite differently than persons who are not so predisposed. In this context, fear and anxiety, and the cues and contexts associated with them, must be managed even at significant personal cost. This quite literally traps people—it keeps them stuck—and creates the context that may help explain the shift from normal fear and anxiety to disordered fear and anxiety, and why fear learning may contribute to the development of full-fledged anxiety disorders.

COGNITIVE BEHAVIORAL THERAPIES AND THE MASTERY AND CONTROL AGENDA

Mainstream cognitive behavioral therapies for anxiety disorders tend to conceptualize anxious thoughts and feelings as problems that warrant clinical attention (e.g., Barlow, 2002; Beck & Emery, 1985). Accordingly, the therapeutic solution is to help clients to alleviate their symptoms as a means to attain psychological health (e.g., Barlow, 2002). Often this is achieved, or at least initiated, by getting clients to confront feared objects or aversive bodily events in a safe therapeutic context, which is believed to facilitate corrective emotional learning and fear reduction.

A variety of techniques can facilitate this process, including direct exteroceptive or interoceptive in vivo exposure, imaginal exposure, response prevention, flooding, systematic desensitization, worry exposure, decatastrophizing, cognitive restructuring, guided imagery, breathing retraining, and progressive muscle relaxation. Such techniques, in turn, have a more general objective; namely, to get clients to experience unpleasant thoughts and feelings that they have otherwise avoided and to learn how to reduce or control them in the future. Many of these and other related techniques have been shown to be quite efficacious, at least in the short term, in producing symptom reduction and relief for most clients most of the time. Many empirically-derived treatments for anxiety disorders include such techniques as components of comprehensive treatment manuals developed for many of the *DSM-IV-TR* anxiety disorders: panic disorder (e.g., *Mastery of Your Anxiety and Panic*, Craske & Barlow, 2000), specific phobias (e.g., *Mastery of Your Specific Phobia*, Craske, Antony, & Barlow, 1997), obsessive-compulsive disorder (*Mastery of Obsessive-Compulsive Disorder*, Foa & Kozak, 1997b), and generalized anxiety disorder (*Mastery of Your Anxiety and Worry*, Zinbarg, Craske, & Barlow, 1993), to name a few.

The word "mastery" as contained in the titles of such manuals is not accidental and reflects the underlying philosophy and approach of such treatments. For in most cases, the aim of the techniques outlined in manualized treatments is to assist clients in becoming better at controlling (i.e., mastering) their thoughts and emotional experiences (i.e., the symptoms) by giving clients more and "better" thought and emotion regulation strategies, and by replacing "dysfunctional" thoughts with more "functional" ones. Mastery and control-based techniques are simply another way of saying "you must regulate your anxiety, because such regulation is important for psychological health." This more general approach is what many anxious clients have come to expect from psychotherapy. That is, they want to learn better and more effective ways of regulating unwanted anxious thoughts and feelings. Virtually all cognitive behavioral therapies play into this system and teach clients that (a) their thoughts and feelings are the cause of their suffering and life problems; (b) in order to live a happy and successful life they need to become better at mastering (i.e., controlling or reducing) unwanted thoughts and feelings; (c) therapy is going to give them new techniques to accomplish better control of their private experiences; and (d) if and when they become better at controlling their anxious thoughts and feelings, they will then become better at living a happy and productive life.

As we describe throughout this book, we suggest a different strategy, which is to directly address the struggle to control and avoid unwanted thoughts and feelings. This means addressing the agenda of emotion regulation itself. Thus far, people have desperately tried to relax *away* fear and anxiety by pushing their unwanted thoughts and feelings away. Instead, we want to help people relax *with* their anxiety by being and moving with it.

Suppose instead that it is what clients do to regulate anxiety and fear, not anxiety and fear per se, that is the problem. Suppose also that anxious thoughts and feelings are not "symptomatic" of anything, but rather normal facets of human experience.

Attempts, therefore, to teach clients to become better suppressors or avoiders of their unwanted thoughts and fearful or anxious feelings is unlikely to work as a lasting solution, for this is what many persons with anxiety-related problems are already doing by the time they enter therapy. We must ask ourselves in all honesty, if that was a workable and functional solution, then why have they come into therapy?

Targeting unwanted thoughts or feelings in therapy can, at best, result in only short-term gains. The reason is that this approach implies that such private events are the problem and need to be dealt with. Such strategies also imply that psychological health occurs only at one end of the emotional spectrum (i.e., positive thoughts and feelings), and that negative emotional experiences are problematic and the cause of life problems. Thus, when anxious thoughts and feelings occur again (and they will occur again), they should be controlled or else more problems will result. Yet, we do not live in a world where people only experience good thoughts and feelings (Hayes, 1994). Indeed, what makes us human is our capacity to experience a wide range of emotional experience, willingly and without defense, and to adapt and behave effectively despite what we may think or feel. Those who do so willingly and without defense, and adapt and behave effectively despite what they may think or feel, are very healthy indeed.

In fact, at a very basic level, what differentiates psychological health from disordered suffering is not the absence of trauma, pain, and negative private events. The difference is whether people are willing to experience the totality of their psychological and emotional world and still do what matters most to them. *Willing* here is not about brute force of will. It means being open and experiencing and accepting what is for what it is. It is about finding a way to live a meaningful and productive life. It means being willing to live such a life *and* taking the totality of personal pains and joys along for the ride. This perspective is quite different from unwillingness, where lives can quite literally be about living to avoid or manage psychological and emotional pain. This is not a way most persons would want to live. Yet, this is what the lives of many anxious clients have become and why we now think that anxiety itself is not disordered. It is what people do to regulate anxiety that makes it disordered. This view, by the way, is now making its way into mainstream cognitive behavioral interventions, resulting in a rethinking of the mastery and control symptom-focused change agenda (Barlow et al., 2004).

NEW-WAVE BEHAVIOR THERAPIES FOR ANXIETY

Most behavioral and cognitive behavioral therapies for anxiety are predicated on the notion that changing anxious thoughts and feelings would naturally foster a more vital life. Newer-generation behavior therapies, by contrast, tend to focus on domains of human experience that go well beyond symptom alleviation and control as therapeutic goals. Instead, they emphasize topics traditionally reserved for less empirical wings of psychology, such as acceptance, mindfulness, values, spirituality, meaning and purpose, relationships, and quality of life, to name a few (Hayes, Follette, et al., 2004). Examples of approaches that are part of this movement include Dialetical Behavior Therapy (Linehan, 1993), Functional Analytic Psychotherapy (Kohlenberg & Tsai, 1991), Integrative Behavioral Couples Therapy (Jacobson, Christensen, Prince, Cordova, & Eldridge, 2000), Mindfulness-Based Cognitive Therapy (Segal, Williams, & Teasdale, 2002), and of course Acceptance and Commitment Therapy (Hayes, Strosahl, & Wilson, 1999). At the core, these approaches challenge the symptom- and syndrome-focused change agenda that has come to characterize much of mainstream cognitive behavioral therapy. In so doing, they offer a unique and expanded view of human suffering and what it means to foster psychological health and wellness. We will have much more to say about this throughout this book. How an ACT approach differs from, and at times complements, mainstream cognitive behavioral approaches for anxiety problems is described below.

Emotion Regulation Gets People into Trouble

Emotion theorists generally regard emotion regulation as an adaptive process that can go awry under some conditions (Gross, 2002). For instance, one could argue that persons suffering from anxiety disorders lack the appropriate emotion regulation skills, or tend to apply emotion regulation techniques (e.g., avoidance, escape, suppression, inhibition) that are counterproductive. From this perspective, it would make sense to teach clients more effective anxiety regulation strategies, or to correct instances where counterproductive strategies are being applied (e.g., distraction, avoidance, escape). In some sense most cognitive behavioral interventions are designed to correct for deficient and inappropriate anxiety regulation strategies. Most often, the correction simply involves substituting one emotion regulation strategy for another (e.g., tension with relaxation, catastrophic thinking with more realistic thoughts). This, as will be seen, is not what an ACT approach is about.

From an ACT perspective, the very act of emotion regulation can get people into trouble. Emotion regulation becomes troubling (psychologically and experientially) when it is unworkable or when there is no need for it (i.e., when the situational context does not require it). Such strategies, in turn, are often driven by the view that "I ought to be thinking and feeling something differently than I am." This tends to get people into trouble because it makes successful emotion regulation a prerequisite for effective action. For instance, anxious clients are quite often guided by the view that "To do X will require that I think or feel something differently than I am thinking or feeling right now." With anxiety disorders, this form of regulation usually centers on anxious thoughts and feelings that are unwanted or undesired, including the situations that might occasion them. In the process, many anxious clients spend their whole lives focused on the regulation of anxiety and fear, instead of doing what is most important to them. It is for this very reason that persons suffering from anxiety disorders have been described as suffering from an *experience phobia*. This is an important predisposition that anxiety sufferers apply to anxiety and fear, and quite often other unpleasant psychological and emotional content as well.

ACT tries to undermine the need for excessive and rigidly inflexible emotion regulation. It does so by fostering psychological and experiential flexibility, willingness, and openness to all human experience as it is, rather than how clients evaluate their experience (both the pleasant and unpleasant). When the full range of emotional experience is allowed in for what it is, the very notion that emotions need to be regulated becomes nonsensical under most circumstances. This acceptance posture, somewhat paradoxically, frees up clients to act and use their hands and feet to regulate how they live their lives—what they do—consistent with their values and goals. This is the kind of life regulation that ACT is after, even if living that way means bringing along anxious thoughts and feelings and other facets of clients' private world (e.g., their memories, behavioral histories, physical sensations) into situations where they make no sense and where it might be easier to act effectively if they weren't there.

Narrowband Versus Broadband Outcomes

Cognitive behavioral interventions typically focus on narrowband clinical outcomes, most often in the form of symptom reduction and alleviation. Clients typically want this too, guided by the view that "In order to live better, I must first think and feel better." Yet, to get there, clients typically must go through quite a bit of pain by confronting anxiety and fear-evoking cues and situations during in vivo or imaginal exposure exercises. Interestingly, this is the point at which some anxious clients drop out of therapy. In fact, two recent studies completed in our labs showed the positive effects of an acceptance context for preventing dropouts. The first study (Karekla, 2004; Karekla & Forsyth, 2004) showed significant differences in the pattern of attrition rates between CBT and ACT-enhanced CBT for persons suffering from panic disorder. Prior to the introduction of the rationales for interoceptive and exteroceptive exposure, none of the CBT clients and only three ACT clients dropped out of therapy prematurely. However, following the introduction of the exposure rationales, five persons discontinued therapy in the CBT group whereas only one person discontinued treatment in the ACT group.

The main difference between the exposure rationales was in how they were framed (i.e., mastery and control of panic versus mastery of experiencing panic) and for what purpose (i.e., controlling panic symptoms versus living more fully and consistently with what one values). The results of this study suggest that exposure conducted in the service of feeling better is somewhat limiting and not very inspiring. Clients appear to recognize this too. All the pain of therapy and for what? The hope of feeling less anxious? At some level, anxious persons also recognize that feeling less anxious does not mean that they will be anxiety free, or that somehow their lives will be better, richer, or more meaningful. In the second, related study with highly anxious females (Eifert & Heffner, 2003) who experienced paniclike responses in an acceptance or a control context, we found that 20 percent of control participants dropped out of the study, whereas none of the acceptance participants did. Here, too, by giving up their efforts to gain control, people felt they had actually gained control and strength.

While ACT allows room for symptom alleviation, it is not a main target or *the* therapeutic goal. Rather, the real focus is on what we call *broadband outcomes*. Such outcomes are about helping the client move in life directions that they truly care about. For instance, a client may value having deep and meaningful relationships with her children, but is letting her anxiety regulation efforts get in the way of that. Within ACT, the focus would be about removing barriers to having that kind of relationship with her children (e.g., unnecessary emotion regulation strategies). Anxiety reduction may occur as a consequence, but it is not an explicit target. As you will see, ACT is very much about fostering the development of fully functioning human beings who are able to live in a manner consistent with meaningful values and goals. Making and keeping value-guided commitments are very important parts of an ACT approach to anxiety disorders. Valued living dignifies the treatment and makes the hard work of therapy worthwhile.

Use of CBT Interventions in an ACT Context

There are several other ways in which CBT and ACT differ in their philosophy and approach to the alleviation of human suffering. Many of these differences will become apparent as you go through this book. In the process, you will see that we have not thrown the baby out with the bathwater. There are several useful CBT interventions for anxiety sufferers. It would be misguided to dismiss them given the strong evidence for their efficacy. This applies in particular to all CBT techniques (e.g., exposure, response prevention) that aim to help clients do the opposite of what clients think ought to be done about their anxiety. The reason is that these techniques let clients experience that escape and avoidance are uncalled for and do not serve any functional adaptive purpose. One could speculate that this process may underlie the extinction of fear over time, as approach behaviors begin to predominate over escape and avoidance behaviors. This is why exposure-like techniques are also part of an ACT approach.

Yet, you will see that the traditional CBT exposure interventions for anxiety have a different feel as used throughout this book. Virtually all of them are recast within an acceptance and mastery of experiencing framework. We talk very little about symptoms, because anxious thoughts and feelings are not symptoms of anything. They are what they are, namely facets of human experience that anxious clients happen to respond to much as they would when placing their hands on a hot stove. The approach we describe in detail is very much about altering how clients with anxiety respond to their emotional and psychological experiences, not the structure or content of those experiences. In so doing, we are trying to make room for those experiences, while freeing up psychological and behavioral space for clients to use to get on with the task of living their lives consistently in the direction of their chosen values.

Summary of Key Concepts

In this chapter, we began with an overview of first- and second-generation behavior therapies, represented early on with classical conditioning as a model of anxiety disorders, and later with the notion that anxiety-related suffering has to do with problematic cognitive and psychological content. Within a coherent theoretical and philosophical framework, ACT illuminates the ways that language entangles clients into futile attempts to wage war against their own inner lives. This war, as we have described, is fundamentally about the application of unworkable emotion regulation efforts in contexts where such regulation efforts are unnecessary. It is such emotion regulation efforts (i.e., control, suppression, avoidance, and escape) that make fear learning, anxiety, and related thoughts and physical sensations problematic or disordered. ACT, in turn, is very much about loosening the hold that emotion regulation has on the lives of anxiety sufferers. It shows how interventions based on metaphor, paradox, and experiential exercises can help clients make contact with thoughts, feelings, memories, and physical sensations that have been feared and avoided. As a consequence, clients learn to recontextualize and accept these private events, develop greater clarity about personal values, commit to needed behavior change, and embark on the journey to put those commitments into action.

PART II

HOW ACT REFRAMES THE ANXIETY DIMENSION

CHAPTER 4

Controlling Anxiety Is the Problem, Not a Solution

Two mice fell into a bucket of cream. Immediately, each began to struggle frantically in an effort to get out. Around and around they went, but without success. Growing tired, one mouse had had enough. Believing that the situation was hopeless, she ceased to struggle and eventually drowned. The other mouse, determined to get out of the bucket, kept swimming and swimming against all odds. This mouse would not give in to her fate. So, on and on she went, though deep down inside she had every reason to believe that she was wasting her time. What happened next came as a complete shock to the little mouse. With each stroke, the cream began to stiffen, and shortly thereafter turned into butter. The mouse then climbed on top of the butter and out of the bucket to safety.

It may seem that this simple story only has two messages. The first message is that continued struggle is generally the way out of life's hardships. The second message is that giving up always leads to death. Here is a third one: Struggle can keep us safe and alive when we are responding to *real* danger and threat. Yet the crucial question to ask is: Can anxiety ever turn into sweet butter so long as one desperately struggles to get out or away from it? None of us would choose to be thrown into a situation like the two little mice found themselves in. Yet, most of us can probably see a bit of ourselves in how the two mice responded to it. Animals prefer controllable aversive events and will act to maintain a sense of control, and to regain it if it's lost, in the wake of uncontrollable aversive events.

Humans do this too. Under most circumstances, this is a highly adaptive and workable strategy. For instance, if we can act to reduce the possibility of real pain and suffering, then it makes sense to do so. There is comfort in knowing this and responding accordingly. Our direct and indirect experiences with the world tell us as much, and a voluminous psychological literature supports the benefits of a control posture in the promotion of psychological health and physical well-being (Barlow, 2002; Chorpita & Barlow, 1998; Zvolensky, Lejuez, & Eifert, 2000). Life may not always be fair, but we can and should do something about it to make things right.

Managing and overcoming life's daily challenges often requires hard work, effort, and persistence. Success and happiness never come easy, and never come at all for those who wait, give in, or do nothing. We have all heard variations of this credo from a very young age and are in some sense guided by it. Though there is no guarantee that these coping strategies will produce desired outcomes, they are valued and useful precisely because they tend to produce desired outcomes more often than not.

Persons suffering from anxiety disorders are all too familiar with the mantra of struggle and control. By the time they enter therapy, most have tried numerous strategies in the struggle to manage and control their anxiety, unwanted thoughts, worries, and physical sensations. Unfortunately, the success of the strategies has typically only been limited. Like the mice in the opening story, individuals are stuck in a bucket with their anxious thoughts and feelings and are desperately swimming around trying to find a way out. They may even feel powerless, hopeless, and alone. It does not occur to them that the bucket may be their friend, not their enemy.

The goal of this chapter is to describe anxiety-control efforts and why they are largely unworkable as a means to cope with anxiety. We will also indicate that control efforts are related to another "toxic" process, which has to do with not accepting our reality and an unwillingness to experience what we have, when what we have is aversive to us. At first, some of these ideas may sound a bit odd to you. In your clinical work, you have been very much involved in your client's struggle with anxiety, actively trying to help them cope. At a more basic level, you may also wonder how control can work so well as a strategy to handle the demands and strains of the world, and yet be so ineffective when applied to unwanted anxiety-related thoughts and feelings inside the skin. Anxiety is an aversive emotional state that brings with it suffering, right? Should it not be controlled? Is it not your task to help your client be more successful in their control endeavors? As you will see, control efforts have a more insidious side as a solution to anxiety, and can make the anxiety and the client's life worse, not better. Anxiety never turns into sweet butter if one is unwilling to have the experience of anxiety.

EXAMPLES OF CONTROL EFFORTS

Control means quite literally to order, limit, instruct, or rule something or someone's actions or behavior. Control is, by definition, purposeful and effortful. It requires an investment of time, energy, and resources and deliberate action directed toward some outcome or goal. For example, if you no longer like some of your clothes, you can simply take those tops, pants, or shoes and throw them away or pass them on to someone who may actually like them. Likewise, if you are in a job that you do not like, you can simply quit that job, go to a different employer, and work there. If you are fed up with the color of the walls in your bedroom, then you can paint the walls red, green, blue, or whatever color your heart desires. The common element of these examples is that they all involve situations where control is possible because they involve objects and events in the external world (the world outside our skin). We can literally use our hands and feet to manipulate and physically change those objects and events. These kinds of actions can work well in the external world and often have a positive impact on our lives.

When Does Control Work?

One of the main psychological purposes of control is to manage our world, our behavior within it, and at times the behavior of others. This strategy works so successfully in most spheres of life that it only makes sense to apply it deliberately to manage emotional and physical pain, and in some instances, this strategy leads to desirable outcomes. For instance, control may be directed to prevent or manage external sources of pain while maximizing contact with pleasant activities and outcomes. Thus, we tend to avoid situations that may result in physical injury or death, and we act to escape from them when and if they occur.

For example, if we see a previously hidden car approaching us as we cross the road, we run for safety. If another person or an animal threatens to attack us, we take evasive, defensive, or offensive action to the best of our abilities. As we indicated in previous chapters, this type of fear-related behavior is adaptive and works to our advantage. Controlling or reducing our fear by responding to an identifiable cause in the external world is a workable solution. There is nothing dysfunctional about this form of control.

Now let us consider the case where control behavior is directed to prevent or minimize internal sources of physical and emotional pain (e.g., illness, unpleasant thoughts, feelings). This latter form of control is also quite common, may work, and again can be quite functional. For instance, you may take an aspirin for a headache, see a doctor for an illness or injury, take time to relax so as to feel more energized, and exercise regularly and watch what you eat and drink so as to promote health and feel better about yourself.

When Does Control Not Work?

Problems arise when either of these control strategies is taken to the extreme—when control efforts become overly intense and rigid and when they are applied in situations where they do not work. An example would be the young woman who becomes so fearful of gaining weight that she restricts her eating and exercises for three hours every day to control her weight and how she feels about herself. In the case of anxiety disorders, problems arise when control efforts are applied in circumstances where they simply do not work, either because they do not produce the outcome desired by the client (anxiety reduction), or because the partial relief they offer restricts the person's life.

Take the case of Susan. Susan had a full-blown panic attack in her car while making a right-hand turn. To control subsequent panic attacks, she would avoid making right-hand turns while driving. Although this tended to reduce Susan's anxiety somewhat, she paid a high price for her relative comfort. Even short trips to work or to run errands became convoluted, difficult excursions requiring a map, careful planning beforehand, and constant vigilance. Spontaneous drives on unfamiliar routes were out of the question. It seemed that controlling anxiety—maximizing feeling good while minimizing pain and emotional suffering—had become the focus and purpose of Susan's life. Yet, this strategy left her neither panic free nor feeling good. Far from it. Susan's life was lived in the service of controlling panic, and it became more restricted as a consequence. A related example is the man with a history of panic attacks who quits his job and stays at home for fear of having more panic attacks if he leaves the house. In these and other examples, control efforts are typically life constricting, not life expanding.

As in Susan's case, control efforts often end up becoming a way of life for persons suffering from anxiety disorders. Anxiety is, in many respects, an unpleasant emotional state. So it is understandable when people simply say, "Anxiety is bad" or "I don't like anxiety." Most people without anxiety disorders do not like experiencing anxiety. Yet, not liking anxiety does not make it a problem. If this were true, then many of us would likely suffer from anxiety disorders.

Instead, anxiety becomes problematic when an individual experiences anxiety in the absence of real threat or danger and acts "as if" anxiety is a cause of suffering and misery. Statements like "I cannot do ABC or go to XYZ because I have anxiety" imply that "If I did not have anxiety, I would be able to do ABC or go to XYZ." From this posture, anxiety needs to be managed and controlled like other external sources of pain and misery in order for a person to be happy and healthy and to have a good quality of life. Yet, there is good reason to believe that control over anxiety is not particularly workable as a solution and may actually be part of the problem. Although your clients can probably sense that control is not working as a solution to their anxiety, they may not yet see how it has become problematic.

WHY ANXIETY CONTROL IS PROBLEMATIC

Control efforts are intimately fused with our evaluations of the world. We make an effort to have more of what we like. What we dislike, we often try to avoid or escape from. This strategy works to the extent that the good and unpleasant in life are, in fact, within our control.

Emotional Control Is Often Illusory

One of the greatest illusions about control is that we have it most of the time. Yet, many life experiences, both pleasant and unpleasant, happen outside our control. A simple example is the weather. A bitter cold wind blowing at our face can cause some discomfort. A natural reaction in this case might be to turn our backs to the wind. This act may provide some relief, but it will not stop the wind or the cold. Cursing the cold wind will likely not do much good either. We would like to think that the situation is different when it comes to controlling our own emotional reactions and thoughts, and the behavior of others. Yet, control in such circumstances is typically, at best, only partial.

Consider a somewhat humorous example of John's younger brother Kevin. As a child, Kevin loved having spaghetti and meatballs for dinner. It was his favorite meal and he would request it often. This all changed shortly following Kevin's fifth birthday. During the summer of that year, Kevin had been playing outside in the dirt with some friends. One of the kids found a worm and then tossed it in the air. The worm happened to land on Kevin's shirt collar and then slipped inside his shirt and down his back. Kevin screamed and cried to have the worm removed. A few days following this event, Kevin once again sat down to a spaghetti dinner with his family. Remember, this was his favorite meal! Before they started eating, one of Kevin's older brothers jokingly said, "Hey, the spaghetti noodles look like worms." From that point on, Kevin would not eat spaghetti or noodles in any form. He had made an arbitrary association (spaghetti = worms = disgust/aversion). This association, in turn, was established by a sequence of events that occurred outside of Kevin's control. This example illustrates the subtle forms of conditioning that we all experience on a daily basis as well as the great illusion of control, namely that we should always act to have and maintain control when it comes to unpleasant thoughts and feelings. One of the main psychological challenges for all of us, and particularly persons with anxiety disorders, is to learn that this need not be so and is indeed a myth.

We Cannot Turn Emotions On and Off

Human emotions are a good example of events that cannot be readily controlled, either by turning them on or by turning them off. Emotions have no on/off switch.

Emotions happen to us as a consequence of our interactions with the world. They are not something we deliberately do apart from that world. To illustrate, try making yourself extremely happy. Go ahead and try it now. If you were successful, then you likely induced the state as a response to something else (e.g., a memory of a pleasant past experience or by thinking about something you like or an event you are looking forward to). Yet, this is not what we were asking of you. We want you to feel exuberant for the sake of it, not as a response to something that may help make you feel that way. Now, try to do the same by making yourself feel really anxious or afraid. We want you to try really hard. Again, the point is that controlling our emotions is extremely difficult. This is actually a useful exercise to do with clients, and we will come back to it later.

Persons suffering from anxiety disorders often come to therapy believing anxiety should be controlled in the same way that many other aspects of human experience can be controlled. Implicit in this is the notion that anxiety is bad. And, like other bad things in life, one should act to not have it, or to diminish the probability of having it, because we simply must not and cannot have it. Ellis (2004) has written extensively about this human tendency that we all share to some degree and how it can get us into trouble (Ellis & Robb, 1994). So we should not fault persons suffering from anxiety disorders for doing what appears to come naturally for many, if not all of us. Westernized notions of personal happiness and success are intimately bound up with feeling good, not bad. Thus, being able to control unpleasant thoughts and feelings would seem like a sensible strategy in order to be happy and successful. This assumption, as we described in an earlier chapter, is at the core of many empirically supported psychosocial interventions for anxiety disorders. It is also part of the "dark side" of emotional control.

The Dark Side of Emotional Control

Our reference to the dark side of emotional control is based on an increasing amount of solid research evidence. Several independent lines of research suggest that attempts to suppress and control unwanted thoughts and feelings can result in more (not fewer) unwanted thoughts and emotions (Clark, Ball, & Pape, 1991; Gold & Wegner, 1995; Lavy & Van den Hout, 1990; Wegner, Schneider, Carter, & White, 1987; Wegner, Schneider, Knutson, & McMahon, 1991; see also Purdon, 1999, for a recent review). This is possible because the human body is a closed system with a series of built-in feedback loops. Within this system, therefore, trying not to have anxious thoughts and feelings will contain aspects of the unwanted event and other events to which it might be related. Thus, reacting to our own reactions can actually amplify those reactions in a vicious self-perpetuating cycle.

For example, a person suffering from obsessive-compulsive disorder may try not to think about shouting out profanities during a church service. Yet, trying not to think about yelling profanities is itself a thought about profanities. Here the very act of suppressing the thought may bring about the very unwanted thought and emotional experience exactly when it is most unwanted, such as during a church service. Kevin tried this too. He tried to suppress the thought of worms so that he could eat spaghetti. Yet, it only made things worse. This is quite like the activity of trying not to think about a pink elephant. It is hard to do because not thinking about a pink elephant is itself a thought of a pink elephant.

Controlling Emotional Experience Versus Behavior

We do not wish to imply that all emotional regulation is problematic. In fact, in many cases it is the failure of emotional regulation that is a problem. It is important, however, that we clearly distinguish between regulating the experience of emotions and regulating the actions that are associated with that experience. For instance, anger and rage are examples where emotional regulation is highly desirable because uninhibited outbursts of verbal and other anger and rage-related behavior can be very destructive. Even in such cases, however, the initial experience of anger feelings cannot be controlled. The emotional experience of anger, just like fear, may show up in a fraction of a second. What can be controlled is how individuals respond to their felt anger. For example, individuals can learn to choose whether they respond with attack, avoidance, or compassionate understanding when anger shows up. The first step in this process is to notice anger and accept its presence. The next step involves making a choice about how one responds to it.

The point here is that emotional *experience* can be inhibited and controlled only to a point. Attempts to do so often do not work and may actually make matters worse. Gross and Levenson (1997), for example, found that attempts to suppress either a positive or a negative emotion do not provide relief from the psychological experience of that emotion. In fact, just the opposite occurs. The emotion becomes stronger and more salient. We are much better at controlling what we do with our hands and feet in response to unwanted emotional experiences than we are at controlling the emotional experiences themselves. Paradoxically, the first step toward healthy emotional regulation is letting go of our attempts to control unwanted emotional experience and accepting what we have for what it is; that is, to acknowledge the presence of fear, anxiety, worry, sadness, and anger. This stance puts us in a much better position to exert control where we do have it—how we respond to our ecmotions.

The Effects of Control Versus Acceptance

In our own research lab, we have seen firsthand the problem of trying to control uncontrollable emotional experiences (Eifert & Heffner, 2003). In this study, we compared the effects of creating an acceptance versus a control treatment context on avoidance behavior and reported fear in women scoring high in anxiety sensitivity. All women were asked to breathe carbon dioxide–enriched air for two ten-minute periods. This challenge procedure reliably produces involuntary and largely uncontrollable physiological sensations that are similar to those experienced by people during panic attacks. Thus, participants really had no control over their reactions to the challenge. Through the use of an interactive metaphor, we taught women in the acceptance context not to fight their symptoms and to accept them instead. Women in the control context were taught a special breathing skill and were encouraged to use the breathing skill to control their paniclike symptoms.

Nearly half of the participants instructed to conquer their fear worried that they would lose control. Interestingly, quite a few of them (20 percent) actually did lose control—they dropped out of the study altogether. In contrast, acceptance-context participants were less avoidant behaviorally. They also reported less intense fear and fewer catastrophic thoughts during the panicogenic carbon dioxide (CO_2) inhalations. In short, participants who accepted the annoying (but harmless) panic sensations without trying to fight them did not worry about losing control. None of them dropped out of the study. Paradoxically, by giving up their efforts to gain control, they actually had more control!

Our results were replicated in a study examining the effects of accepting versus suppressing the effects of a panicogenic CO_2 challenge in clients with panic disorder (Levitt, et al., 2004). Clients in that study were simply instructed to either accept or suppress their responses to the CO_2 challenge. This study found an almost identical pattern of results as we did. The acceptance group was significantly less anxious and less avoidant than the suppression or no-instruction control groups. Yet, the groups did not differ in terms of self-reported panic symptoms or physiological responses. It is important to reiterate that people in these studies, just like people with panic attacks in natural life, had no choice about having or not having the physical sensations. People cannot learn or choose *not* to have the sensations. What they can learn and control is what to do when they have them. That is, people can accept and be with their psychological and emotional experiences, or they can fight them.

There are also multiple clinical studies suggesting that client attempts to control anxiety may have paradoxical negative effects (Ascher, 1989). For example, Wegner (1994) found that attempts to control anxiety in the face of ongoing stress exacerbate physiological arousal. Increased tension during relaxation training was also reported in a study by Heide and Borkovec (1983). Likewise, studies suggest that adding slow diaphragmatic breathing ("breathing retraining") might not increase the effectiveness of interoceptive exposure treatment for panic disorder (Craske, Rowe, Lewin, & Noriega-Dimitri, 1997). In fact, breathing retraining even led to poorer outcomes compared to treatment without such training (Schmidt et al., 2000).

In a more general way, active coping efforts that attempt to minimize the experience of anxiety may, paradoxically and unintentionally, maintain pathological anxiety and increase the anxiogenic effects of interoceptive stimulation (Craske, Street, & Barlow, 1989). For instance, Spira, Zvolensky, Eifert, and Feldner (2004) found that avoidant coping strategies such as denial, mental disengagement, and substance abuse predicted more frequent and intense CO_2-induced physical and cognitive panic symptoms than acceptance-based coping strategies. These findings are consistent with earlier studies showing that attempts to avoid aversive private events are largely ineffective and may be counterproductive (Cioffi & Holloway, 1993; Pennebaker & Beall, 1986).

Collectively, these studies suggest that hiding, actively suppressing, escaping from, or avoiding negative thoughts and emotions are all unlikely to help one feel better in the long term. In fact, purposefully trying to control feeling anxious may, in turn, increase the very anxiety one wants to control (Gross & Levenson, 1997), while also increasing the probability that unwanted emotional responses will recur again, often in more severe form, in the future (Cox, Swinson, Norton, & Kuch, 1991; Hayes, 2004a; Hayes et al., 1996). Worse yet, anxiety suppression and control efforts also act to decrease positive emotional experiences (Gross, 2002). The result is more anxiety, not less, which will likely be followed by more effort to control the anxiety, in a self-perpetuating cycle.

EXPERIENTIAL AVOIDANCE AND CONTROL

The lack of control over life stress, whether real or imagined, is thought to function as a core diathesis and risk factor for anxiety disorders (Barlow, 2002). If one starts from this perspective, then it makes perfect sense to teach clients new ways to manage and control anxiety and the circumstances that give rise to this feeling. In one form or another, most contemporary cognitive behavioral treatments for anxiety disorders attempt to do just that. In effect, such treatments are playing into the struggle and control agenda that is familiar to all of us, and particularly to individuals who have been suffering from anxiety disorders.

Nonacceptance and Rigid Control Efforts Make Anxiety Disordered

Let us suppose that control itself is not the issue and that control is merely one of several manifestations of a more basic and toxic underlying diathesis (i.e., a predisposition or vulnerability). We will describe that diathesis in a moment, but for now consider a person who is fully willing to experience a full range of human emotions, even intense anxiety and fear, without acting to control them. Those feelings and associated thoughts are welcomed and experienced just as they are, and are acknowledged as such. This person neither acts to reduce, avoid, or escape from them, nor does she let them get in the way of important and meaningful life activities. At first glance, one might think such a person is the exception, not the rule.

Yet even in Westernized societies where the culture of feel-goodism is the rule, there are many people who do not let anxiety rule their lives—recall the data presented in chapter 2 on the number of people with panic attacks who never develop panic disorder or the majority of people who experience trauma but never develop PTSD. There is nothing disordered about people feeling anxiety and the accompanying physical sensations. There is nothing harmful or disordered about anxious or "negative" thoughts.

They are what they are, thoughts and feelings, nothing more or less; they do not harm or kill; they are, in a very real sense, what makes us fully human.

Now consider anxiety in the context of someone who does not accept it and is unwilling to have it. Anxiety in this context is not just a feeling, it is a bad, even dangerous, feeling and necessitates a response. Now, anxiety is no longer just anxiety. It is a problem that cannot be had and must go away. Thoughts are no longer thoughts, they are bad thoughts. Anything associated with anxiety or the likelihood of experiencing anxiety is now a problem. Anxiety is now likely to be responded to with anxiety, and fear with fear. What follows are efforts to manage anxiety and the circumstances that give rise to it. As we have seen, such efforts are unlikely to be successful in the long term. Instead, these apparent "solutions" create a host of life problems.

Linehan (1993) succinctly defined suffering as pain plus nonacceptance. In other words, what turns adversity and emotional pain into suffering is the nonacceptance of such pain. Sadness after a loss is pain. Fear, humiliation, and shame after experiencing repeated sexual assaults is emotional pain. Life unfortunately serves up these events, and it is normal and appropriate when we respond to such events with sadness and fear and make efforts to remedy the situation. Pain turns into suffering when we do not accept our emotional reactions to painful events. When we do not accept our feelings of apprehension and instead struggle to get rid of them, the pain of normal anxiety may turn into the suffering associated with disordered anxiety. Such suffering occurs when we don't want to be hurt or fearful. Suffering manifests when we do not acknowledge and accept the reality of such experiences and instead act to avoid or escape from them. This leads us to become fearful about having fear and to experience sadness about being sad, and we start doing things to avoid our feelings.

Types of Control-Oriented Strategies

The following chart gives examples of control-oriented strategies that usually do not work in the long run. Such strategies are a natural consequence of unwillingness, and make little sense as a response to anxiety and fear in the context of willingness. They represent forms of experiential avoidance that may turn normal fear and anxiety into disordered fear and anxiety. We've included technical and nontechnical definitions for each strategy.

Strategy	Definitions	Examples
Avoidance	*Nontechnical* • Not doing things that cause you to experience uncomfortable anxious thoughts or feelings *Technical* • Any response that prevents or postpones the onset of, or contact with, an aversive event	*People, Places, Situations, Activities* • Avoiding situations or events where anxiety is likely to occur and escape may be difficult (e.g., social events, intimacy, crowds, standing in line, doctor's office, driving, flying, taking a train) • Being hypervigilant for signs of danger • Creating order, cleanliness, symmetry • Only spending time in "safe" places (e.g., home) where anxiety is less likely to be experienced • Exercising and physical exertion • Oversleeping and/or overeating • Taking medications (e.g., anxiolytics, antidepressants) • Excessive drinking, drug use *Thoughts and Emotions* • Distraction (e.g., thinking pleasant thoughts, developing a workaholic lifestyle) • Past experiences and memories
Escape	*Nontechnical* • Getting away from anything that is causing you to experience uncomfortable thoughts or feelings *Technical* • Any response that terminates an aversive event after it has begun	*People, Places, Situations, Activities* • Leaving any situation (e.g., mall, work) during a state of acute anxiety or panic • Excessive orderliness and rule following to feel better and to make things "right" • Using alcohol, drugs, medications to get away from emotional pain • Assuming the sick role *Thoughts and Emotions* • Using suppression to try to stop unwanted thoughts or emotions (e.g., "Don't think about traumatic event"; "Don't feel anxious") • Distraction • Daydreaming and/or detaching from the self and the world to get away from anxious thoughts and feelings

EXPERIENTIAL AVOIDANCE AND THE ANXIETY DISORDERS

Anxiety disorders are characterized by experiential avoidance, which is defined as a tendency to engage in behaviors to alter the frequency, duration, or form of unwanted private events (i.e., thoughts, feelings, physical sensations, and memories) and the situations that occasion them (Hayes, 1994; Hayes et al., 1996). Unlike acceptance, experiential avoidance reflects a cutting off from human experience (both good and bad) and a commitment to follow a change agenda where it is not workable; namely in the realm of thoughts and emotions (Hayes, 2004a; Hayes et al., 1994).

Examples of Experiential Avoidance in the Anxiety Disorders

The lives of those suffering from anxiety disorders are replete with examples of experiential avoidance or nonacceptance. This common element may take different forms, but its function is the same across disorders, namely to not have anxiety. Clients with post-traumatic stress disorder, for example, often avoid or escape from physical sensations, reminders of the trauma, memories, and the effects of those events (i.e., flashbacks, dissociation, numbing, increased arousal, tension, disrupted interpersonal and occupational functioning), in an attempt not to have or experience them. Similarly, persons with specific phobias often "rationally" acknowledge that they should not be afraid and yet still avoid any verbal, physical, or other reminders of the phobic stimulus because they "must not" experience the fear that would be elicited by such stimuli.

Persons with panic disorder likewise respond to their own intense and benign symptoms of arousal (e.g., heart sensations, sweatiness) by fighting and resisting them as if they were threatening or dangerous and must not be had under any circumstances. Such individuals are quite literally fearful of experiencing their own fear. As a consequence, they often do everything they can to not experience fear by engaging in agoraphobic avoidance or by using anxiolytics and other drugs. Persons suffering from social phobias and generalized anxiety disorder also are unwilling to experience what are otherwise normal physical and emotional reactions. Concerns about social evaluation and failure or worries about everyday life problems, even when they are intense and exaggerated, are normal. They are normal so long as we allow them to be there *and* continue to do what needs to be done in our lives. Problems arise when we do not accept negative affect associated with those concerns and worries as they are, and instead act to avoid them. The same is true of persons struggling with obsessive-compulsive disorder, where the issue shifts to unwanted thoughts and needless rituals. As indicated in chapter 2, most people with OCD realize that their rituals are excessive and unreasonable. Yet they continue to engage in behavior that is designed to control or reduce their unwanted thoughts because they want to reduce the negative affect associated with them.

Thus, all the anxiety disorders have at least one fundamental thread in common; namely, persons do not like how they think and feel. As a result, they engage in behaviors to reduce, control, or avoid their anxious thoughts and feelings. The paradox, however, is that persons can never truly escape from or avoid their bodies or their psychological experiences. For instance, a man who panics in a mall and escapes outside takes his unwanted thoughts and emotional experiences outside with him. A woman with PTSD who experiences flashbacks seeing a man in the street who faintly resembles her abuser, and then turns around and runs to her car, takes her unwanted images and emotional experiences into the car with her.

Costs Associated with Experiential Avoidance

Experiential avoidance is a potentially self-destructive process that is associated with significant costs, the least functional and most significant of which is the taking of one's own life. Suicide is the deliberate and purposeful act of terminating one's life to escape pain and suffering. There is no good evidence that nonhuman species commit suicide (Hayes, Strosahl, & Wilson, 1999) nor any evidence that relief from pain follows suicide. Most major religions teach as much. Suicide will be met with eternal suffering in the afterlife, not bliss. There is no perspective taking, no relief, even for those who do not hold any religious beliefs. You are alive, and then you are dead.

There is ample evidence that humans, unlike nonhuman animals, will take their own lives to end pain and suffering, with suicide ranking as the eleventh leading cause of death in the United States (Centers for Disease Control, 2002). Though suicide rates in the anxiety disorders have been inconsistent across studies, a recent meta-analysis suggests that the risk may be greater than previously thought (Khan, Leventhal, Khan, & Brown, 2002). In fact, the rate appears to be over ten times greater in patients with anxiety disorders, regardless of the type of anxiety disorder, than age-adjusted rates found in the general population, which are .01 percent (= 1 in every 10,000 persons; Centers for Disease Control, 2002). These data point to the need to evaluate suicide risk in anxiety disorder patients. That risk, from an ACT perspective, increases as a person more rigidly and pervasively engages in experiential avoidance behavior.

Most anxious persons will not resort to suicide to end their struggle with anxiety and fear. Instead, they will live in the world and not fully participate in it. Avoidance and escape behavior gives the impression to an outsider that persons with anxiety disorders wish they were not fully part of the world. Yet this is typically not the case. Clients with anxiety disorders do want to go out and live a full, meaningful life. It is just that they are not willing to take their anxiety along with them on this path.

To illustrate, we saw a woman in our clinic who had been struggling unsuccessfully to control her worry and physical tension. Initially she viewed her worry, physical tension, and nervousness as the main problem in her life and the reason why she could not be happy and do the things she previously enjoyed doing. She was, however, an avid baker. Over the course of therapy, the therapist used the client's baking activities to undermine her struggle to control and avoid by directly challenging this agenda in session.

Therapist: You said that you love to bake and that you are quite good at it.

Client: Oh yes, I'm quite a good baker.

Therapist: You also said that your worry and tension have been getting in the way of several meaningful activities in your life.

Client: Yes … It has been brutal … I wish I could get rid of it and move on with my life.

Therapist: From the sounds of it, I bet that your worry and anxiety must keep you from baking too. Also, I'd bet, given what you've said, that if I made you really anxious and worried you couldn't bake a thing.

Client: Like hell! Nothing can keep me from baking when I want to.

Therapist: I see … So you can bake *and think what you think and feel what you feel.* Yet, somehow you can't do other things *because of* how you think and feel. Is that true?

Client: Well … uh … not really.

From this point on in therapy, our client began to see her former solutions to her problems as problems in themselves, and eventually committed herself to doing the things she wanted to do *and* taking whatever thoughts and feelings she had along with her. A variety of experiential exercises, such as in vivo and imaginal exposure, were included to facilitate this process. Such exercises were used to help our client more fully experience her thoughts and feelings for what they are. In so doing, such exercises also likely had the indirect effect of changing the aversive functions of such events and, more importantly perhaps, her responses to them. As she told us during a six-month follow-up visit, "I used to cross bridges before I got to them. Now I don't cross those bridges until there is a real bridge to cross. Then, I just deal with it and move on."

The life problems that persons with anxiety disorders experience are, in one form or another, a direct consequence of the tendency for humans to suppress and avoid suffering. As indicated in the previous chapter, evaluative thinking and destructive language conventions largely fuel this tendency. Perhaps, humans do have an innate tendency to believe that we absolutely must not have discomfort, as Albert Ellis (2004) so vehemently states. In any case, avoidant-style coping is associated with a range of negative outcomes, including weakened immune system functioning, illness, and impairment in interpersonal, social, and occupational domains, overall poorer quality of life (Gross, 2002; Hayes et al., 1996; Pennebaker & Beale, 1986), and even greater mortality risk (Denollet et al., 1996). Impairments in social, interpersonal, and occupational functioning are manifestations of this struggle and control agenda and often the main reasons why persons with anxiety problems seek professional help. For example, a socially anxious person may avoid social interactions as a means to decrease anxiety. Typically, this strategy will result in temporary relief from anxiety, but it also comes with a more delayed cost of long-term social isolation (Leary, 1986). Experiential avoidance is a life-constricting type of behavior precisely because humans cannot avoid their psychological experience of the world. Our emotions and thoughts do not force us to behave in certain ways, they only make it more likely that we will do so (Gross, 2002). It is what we do with them that counts!

Unwillingness to Struggle

Below is a very simple metaphor that illustrates the negative consequences that follow from being cut off from the experience of pain and struggle. Your clients may see a bit of themselves in this story, particularly in how they may rely on others to help them control their experience of anxiety and fear. Here, however, the issue is not about fighting back, but rather about allowing struggle to occur as a normal process underlying health and wellness.

■ The Moth Metaphor

A man found a cocoon of an emperor moth. He took it home so that he could watch the moth come out of the cocoon.

On the day a small opening appeared, he sat and watched the moth for several hours as the moth struggled to force its body through that little hole. Then it seemed to stop making any progress. It appeared as if it had gotten as far as it could and it could go no farther. It just seemed to be stuck.

Then the man, in his kindness, decided to help the moth. So he took a pair of scissors and snipped off the remaining bit of the cocoon. The moth then emerged easily, but it had a swollen body and small shriveled wings. The man continued to watch the moth because he expected that, at any moment, the wings would enlarge and expand to be able to support the body, which would contract in time. Neither happened! In fact, the little moth spent the rest of its life crawling around with a swollen body and shriveled wings. It never was able to fly.

What the man in his kindness and haste did not understand was that the restricting cocoon and the struggle required for the moth to get through the tiny opening was the way of forcing fluid from the body of the moth into its wings so that it would be ready for flight once it achieved its freedom from the cocoon. Freedom and flight would only come after the struggle. By depriving the moth of struggle, he deprived the moth of health.

Experiential Avoidance Differs from Our Typical View of Avoidance

Experiential avoidance is thought to function as a core psychological diathesis—a way of relating with oneself and the world—underlying the development and maintenance of several forms of psychopathology and human suffering more generally (Blackledge & Hayes, 2001; Hayes et al., 1996; Hayes & Wilson, 1994). It is a process related to how we go about influencing the emotions we have, when we have them, and how we experience and express them. As such, experiential avoidance is best described as one of several emotion regulation strategies (see Gross, 2002). As we describe below, experiential avoidance helps make the normal emotion of anxiety disordered and functions to maintain disordered experiences of anxiety and fear. That is, avoidance is both a risk factor for the development of anxiety disorders as well as a consequence of having anxiety disorders.

Avoidance as a Consequence of Anxiety Disorders

Most of us tend to think of avoidance as a response-focused emotion regulation strategy (Gross, 1998, 2002) that develops as a consequence of having an anxiety disorder. As such, avoidance serves to maintain anxiety-related problems by preventing opportunities for corrective emotional learning that would come about via direct experience (Dollard & Miller, 1950; Eysenck, 1987; Mower, 1939, 1960; Rachman, 1976; Solomon & Wynne, 1954). For instance, almost all persons suffering from anxiety disorders engage in activities designed to avoid, escape from, or limit the probability, intensity, and duration of experiencing anxiety and the contexts that occasion it (Barlow, 2002). As escape and avoidance behaviors tend to reduce anxiety (at least temporarily), they are thought to maintain and exacerbate anxiety-related problems via the process of negative reinforcement, thus setting up a vicious self-perpetuating cycle (Bouton et al., 2001). This is why exposure techniques are at the core of all cognitive behavioral therapies of anxiety disorders. Such techniques are designed to counteract covert and overt forms of avoidance and escape behavior by promoting approach behaviors in a structured way. The general goal is to provide a context for corrective emotional learning (Forsyth & Eifert, 1998a).

Avoidance as a Diathesis for Anxiety to Become Disordered

Within the traditional cognitive behavioral account, avoidance follows from anxiety disorders. As we indicated in chapter 3, negative reinforcement maintains this cycle, in part, because it reduces the probability of experiencing aversive feelings and seemingly provides relief from such feelings following escape from situations that evoke them. This account makes sense if one starts from the perspective that too much anxiety, fear, and the like are problematic and need to be reduced. Now consider the possibility that a tendency toward experiential avoidance may be learned and may itself be problematic. Consider also that this tendency may function as a psychological diathesis that binds with anxious thoughts and feelings to send human beings down the road to an anxiety disorder.

The question, then, is why do we avoid feelings and thoughts as if they are the enemy? The learning of such avoidance starts very early, is pervasive, and is fundamentally built into the very nature of human language and cognition. In Westernized societies, the typical and acceptable response to unpleasant thoughts and feelings is often to change or get rid of them (Blackledge & Hayes, 2001). Our culture (parents, schools, the media) teaches that some thoughts and feelings (happiness, pride) are good and that other thoughts and feelings (anxiety, sadness) are bad and should be eliminated or at least minimized. From the time we are little children, we are taught that we can and should control what we think and how we feel, particularly those negative thoughts and feelings. For instance, the little boy who cries on the playground is told, "Pull yourself together; don't be a baby." Just think of how many times you have heard parents or teachers saying things like, "Don't worry, there's no reason to be afraid," or "Stop crying, or I'll really give you something to cry about." The crying child now learns to be a mute child, and to hide emotional pain. What we are left with is a silent child who may be suffering inside. Through these and other experiences, children and adults quickly learn to regulate the experience and expression of their emotions in the eyes of others. Emotion regulation tendencies do not emerge in the absence of other people. The sky, the earth and the objects and animals that inhabit it have no stake in what humans think and feel at any moment—only humans do.

From an ACT perspective, social learning creates a context where forms of experiential avoidance and nonacceptance can thrive (Hayes, Strosahl, & Wilson, 1999). Here, the stakes are quite high. Emotional regulation is used as evidence of maturity, emotional stability, health and wellness, success, fulfillment, and happiness. We typically do not question what life might be like if unpleasant emotions and thoughts were treated simply as events to be experienced as part of being fully human, and not as "things" to be managed and controlled (cf. Blackledge & Hayes, 2001). We do not question the cultural mandate that equates failures of emotional regulation with suffering and misery. We leave unchallenged the generally accepted cultural view that connects "positive" thoughts and feelings with an ability to engage life to its fullest. In this cultural context, anxious thoughts and feelings become obstacles to living and the achievement of valued goals. They are reasonable justifications for inaction and are quite often fused with our sense of self-worth (e.g., "I'm not good enough," "Something is wrong with me," "I'm an anxious person," "I am broken"). Thus, the feelings and thoughts must be managed and controlled, even if that control comes at significant cost to the individual.

Emotional avoidance is a natural outcome of this process and represents a predisposition that people use to cope with anxious thoughts and feelings, some more so than others. As we describe in later chapters, this is the general system or diathesis that an ACT approach seeks to undermine. The strategies used to "not have" anxious thoughts and feelings are the problems. This, by the way, may include use of medications and psychosocial treatments for anxiety (including some of the skills taught in cognitive behavioral treatments) that aim to help clients reduce or eliminate unwanted anxiety and fear. Such treatments, from an ACT perspective, are part of a larger problem-solving control-oriented strategy that does not work as a long-term solution (Hayes et al., 1996). Remember, it is what we do with anxiety and fear that counts!

Anxiety Disorders Are Experiential Avoidance Disorders

From an ACT perspective, anxiety becomes disordered when persons:

- do not accept the reality that they will experience certain emotions, thoughts, memories, or physical sensations they do not like;

- are unwilling to be in contact with such emotions, thoughts, memories, physical sensations, and behaviors as they are;

- take deliberate steps to alter their form and frequency or the circumstances that occasion those experiences; and

- do so rigidly and inflexibly even at significant personal and interpersonal *cost* (cf. Forsyth, 2000; Forsyth & Eifert, 1996, 1998a; Friman et al., 1998; Hayes et al., 1996).

These four behavioral predispositions, and the verbal-cognitive processes that guide their regulation, are at the core of understanding the development and maintenance of anxiety disorders and figure prominently in the ACT approach to treatment. Anxiety becomes problematic when we do not accept its presence, when we are unwilling to have it, when actions are geared toward not having it, and when such actions disrupt or impede movement toward valued goals (Blackledge & Hayes, 2001; Wilson & Murrell, 2004). This sequence is illustrated somewhat humorously in figure 2. It nicely captures the ACT model of psychopathology and the essence of an ACT approach.

Figure 2. "Emotional avoidance detour" was illustrated and conceptualized by Joseph Ciarrochi and David Mercer, University of Wollongong, NSW, Australia. Reprinted with permission of the authors.

The road to the mountains depicts going in the direction of what is important in life for the client. You can actually show clients this picture when you talk about the effects and costs of experiential avoidance: "Imagine you are driving through life on a long winding road toward a mountain. Let's call this mountain your 'Value Mountain.' It represents everything you care about in your life and what you want to be about as a person. This is the place you want to go. Suddenly anxiety jumps out and blocks the road. You slow down, and try to avoid hitting anxiety. So, you quickly turn right, and find yourself on the 'emotional avoidance' detour. Note how experiential avoidance functions here. You are trapped in a loop, going round and round, and getting nowhere. You are sidetracked, stuck, and miserable as a consequence."

This loop is disruptive precisely because it neither works as a solution to anxiety (e.g., it doesn't make it more bearable, go away, or less likely to recur) nor is it a way most persons would choose to live. As we outline in later chapters, ACT attempts to undermine this struggle and change agenda by breaking the cycle of avoidance and control. All ACT strategies promote greater psychological flexibility, that is, a willingness to participate in life fully and a commitment to go in the direction of personal values. Note that controlling, getting rid of, and replacing anxious thoughts and feelings play no part within the ACT model of treatment. Clients can take them, along with other thoughts and feelings, on their ride through life.

Evidence Supporting Experiential Avoidance as a Toxic Diathesis

To show that emotional avoidance functions as a behavioral diathesis and risk factor for anxiety-related pathology, it is important to demonstrate that this predisposition functions to exacerbate aversive emotional responses in individuals with no known history of psychopathology. Consistent with this view, we have shown that greater predispositions toward emotional avoidance (as assessed using the Acceptance and Action Questionnaire; Hayes, Strosahl, et al., 2004), including the deliberate application of instructed emotion regulation strategies (i.e., emotion suppression), result in more acute emotional distress, but not greater autonomic reactivity (Feldner, Zvolensky, Eifert, & Spira, 2003). This study is important, for it is the first to show that emotional avoidance and emotion regulation strategies potentiate experimentally induced acute episodes of emotional distress (i.e., induced via panicogenic inhalations of 20 percent CO_2-enriched air). Most notably, such effects were shown in healthy individuals with no known psychopathology.

We have since replicated these findings and found that emotional avoidance, but not other psychological risk factors for panic (e.g., anxiety sensitivity), tends to covary with more severe panic response, even in healthy individuals (Karekla, Forsyth, & Kelly, 2004). After several trials of inhaling CO_2-enriched air, individuals high in experiential avoidance reported more panic symptoms, more severe cognitive symptoms, and more fear, panic, and uncontrollability than their less avoidant counterparts. Interestingly, as in all previous studies we conducted in our labs, the magnitude of autonomic responses did not discriminate between groups. Only one study that we know of has shown a relation between experiential avoidance and physiological reactivity to pleasant, unpleasant, and neutral film clips. In that study, persons with a greater predisposition toward experiential avoidance tended to experience their positive and negative emotions more intensely, but also showed greater heart rate suppression to unpleasant stimuli relative to their less avoidant counterparts (Sloan, 2004). These studies provide further strong evidence that experiential avoidance exacerbates aversive emotional responses and may constitute a risk factor for the development and maintenance of anxiety disorders.

Collectively, the work discussed above and other related studies (Hayes et al., 1996) suggests that a rigid repertoire of emotional avoidance may constitute an important psychological diathesis and risk factor for the development, maintenance, and potential exacerbation of anxiety-related problems. Simply put, "If you don't want it, you've got it." It is for this reason that experiential avoidance and control efforts must become a primary treatment target.

Summary of Key Concepts

This chapter began with a simple metaphor of two mice trapped in a life-or-death struggle. We end with the view that this struggle, when applied to unpleasant thoughts and feelings and the circumstances that might occasion them, is *the* toxic process that underlies a good deal of human suffering. Nonacceptance and the struggle with anxiety are, in a real sense, what makes anxiety disordered. Addressing this struggle head-on is what an ACT approach to treatment is about. In the process, clients learn how to experience their anxious thoughts and feelings in a new, less frightening way, as they are. The therapeutic prize here is to foster greater psychological flexibility and choice and a willingness to contact a full range of human experience as it is, always with an eye on helping clients move in valued life directions. As clients learn to give up the struggle and control change agenda, they are no longer owned by it or their unwanted experiences. They are free to live. This somewhat counterintuitive notion builds upon the model we outlined earlier, where *feeling* good is not a necessary requirement for *living* good.

CHAPTER 5

Balancing Acceptance and Change

Radical acceptance is the only way out of hell—it means letting go of fighting reality. Acceptance is the way to turn suffering that cannot be tolerated into pain that can be tolerated.

—Marsha Linehan

One of the most important themes of this chapter (and this entire book) is acceptance and helping clients learn to accept themselves with all their flaws, weaknesses, strengths, and talents—the whole package. Acceptance is willingness to participate in life in an active and open manner. Yet when clients hear the word "acceptance," they often think acceptance means giving in or even giving up and losing. Giving in or giving up is what we call *passive acceptance* or *resignation*. This is not what this chapter or ACT is about. We certainly don't want our clients to give up. We are not asking them to grin and bear their anxiety and do nothing.

This chapter is about active acceptance and balancing acceptance with meaningful life change. In fact, acceptance is what allows change and what really makes change possible. Acceptance breaks apart the fundamental struggle and control agenda that many anxious clients are consumed with. It removes the need to engage in a constant struggle with thoughts, emotions, and life circumstances first, so as to live with meaning and purpose later. Acceptance provides clients with the space and psychological flexibility to make life changes now that are consistent with what they truly care about. When clients begin to accept themselves the way they are right now, they begin a new life with new possibilities that did not exist before. Anxiety and fear are no longer obstacles to living. They are part of living and a natural consequence of a life lived well. The key to transforming anxiety-related suffering into meaningful life changes is to accept first that suffering and pain do exist, but they are not the same. Acceptance is the way to turn suffering that seemingly cannot be tolerated into pain that can be tolerated—or put differently, radical acceptance turns suffering into ordinary pain (Linehan, 1993).

ACCEPTANCE AS AN ALTERNATIVE AGENDA FOR BEING WITH ANXIETY

Acceptance involves a counterintuitive approach toward constructive living in which clients are encouraged to give up their struggle to change what cannot be changed for the sake of promoting change in domains of their life where change is possible (Heffner, Eifert, Parker, Hernandez, & Sperry, 2003; Heffner, Sperry, Eifert, & Detweiler, 2002). The basic idea is to let go of ineffective and unworkable change agendas to open the door for genuine, fundamental change to occur. When clients experience that they need not run from or struggle against their anxious thoughts and feelings, they become free to live. In fact, freedom is an emergent property of this process. It comes from being liberated from the grip of nonacceptance and the losing battle against oneself and one's own life experiences. You cannot fight against yourself and win.

Technical and Nontechnical Definitions of Acceptance

In a nontechnical sense, acceptance involves taking a nonevaluative posture toward living with oneself and the world, characterized by compassion, kindness, openness, present-centeredness, and willingness. More technically, acceptance "involves experiencing events fully and without defense … and making contact with the automatic or direct stimulus functions of events, without acting to reduce or manipulate those functions, and without acting on the basis solely of their derived verbal functions" (Hayes, 1994, p. 30). When applied to anxiety disorders, acceptance means letting go of the fight with fear and anxiety. Such an acceptance posture would translate into willingness to experience anxious thoughts, memories, sensations, and feelings as they are, without acting to avoid or escape from these experiences and the circumstances that may give rise to them, and without acting solely on the basis of what the mind may say about the meaning of these events (e.g., "I'm losing control," "I must be dying or going crazy," "I can't do such-and-such because I might feel anxious").

Acceptance is closely related to willingness and purposeful action because "willingness is accepting what is, together with responding to what is, in an effective and appropriate way. It is doing what works and just what is needed in the current situation or moment" (Linehan, 1993, p. 103). This relation between acceptance, willingness, and life goal–related behavior is also evident in the definition provided by Orsillo, Roemer, Lerner, and Tull (2004), who describe experiential acceptance as a willingness to experience internal events such as thoughts, feelings, memories, and physiological reactions, in order to participate in activities that are deemed important and meaningful. Please note that acceptance and willingness are not feelings. They are a stance toward life and are very much about behavior and action.

In the context of treatment, acceptance is highly experiential. At its core, acceptance is about approaching and making contact with thoughts, emotions, and life experiences fully and without defense. It is doing with feeling, not doing because of feeling. This means that acceptance must be experienced directly. The procedures and exercises outlined in later chapters (e.g., creative hopelessness, defusion, mindfulness, and exposure-like exercises) are designed to facilitate the development of acceptance as an experiential process.

Whether acceptance can simply be instructed is unclear at this time. Our sense is that acceptance is unlikely to develop via instructions alone and that it needs to be experienced. In fact, in one form or another, clients have already heard someone else tell them that they should stop doing what they have been doing and just accept their fear and anxiety. Many have told themselves the very same thing, without much success. The problem here is neither lack of motivation nor lack of desire or willpower. The problem is that changing our experience with the world requires that we allow ourselves to experience the world directly, unedited—as it is. Unless the change and control agenda is first challenged and undermined, clients will likely use acceptance as another new, snazzy tool to feel less anxiety, worry, fear, and other forms of psychological pain (Hayes & Pankey, 2003). The transformative power of acceptance comes about via directly experiencing life as it is: nothing more, nothing less.

We should add here that acceptance is an active, vibrant process that does not come easily or naturally for most of us. We tend to color our world with our own preconceived notions of what is or what should be. This is especially true for anxious clients, who seem tangled up in a web of doubt, what-ifs, and patterns of experiential avoidance and escape focused on events that exist mostly in the mind. Clients can, however, learn to be open to "what is" without contaminating this experience with their evaluations, justifications, and reasons for "what is" and "what ought to be." Acceptance is ultimately about choice: choosing to make contact with how one has lived up to this point, some of which might be painful, and then choosing to make the commitment to act differently and consistently with what one values. An acceptance posture on one day will not necessarily carry over to the next day. It is an ongoing process and a choice that needs to be made every day—again and again.

Acceptance is not about liking our experience (past or present), nor is it about approving of what happened or did not happen to us. It is also not about being right. It is about being proactive, not reactive, and acknowledging and experiencing what is, as it is. It is also about acknowledging, not condoning, what happened to us in the past. This move is courageous, empowering, open, honest, and compassionate. This move is also liberating. When we ask clients who have made the choice to accept, "How does acceptance feel to you?" they often say things like, "A burden has lifted" or "I feel free and ready to move on."

Acceptance Is Not Giving Up

There is an importance difference between the active form of acceptance we have been describing and a passive form of acceptance. To distinguish passive from active acceptance, let us go back to the serenity creed: Accept with serenity what you cannot change, have the courage to change what you can, and develop the wisdom to know the difference.

In this book, we define passive acceptance as failing to muster the courage to change what can be changed. Passive acceptance or resignation is akin to just giving up and failing to take action in areas of life that can be controlled. For instance, if your client is a student who decides not to go to class because she fears what others might think of her when she makes a class presentation, she lets her feelings (which she cannot control) guide her actions (which she can control). This type of passive acceptance and resignation is narrowing and limiting. It is not what we want clients with anxiety problems to do.

In contrast, active acceptance means letting go of the struggle with what cannot be controlled. As we mentioned in previous chapters, these are the thoughts and feelings anxious clients have about themselves, many of which they understandably do not like and would rather not have. Active acceptance means mindfully acknowledging thoughts and feelings without taking them as facts, approving or disapproving of them, or doing anything about them. By embracing an acceptance posture, clients are positioned to regain energy and time that might otherwise be wasted on attempting to change what cannot and need not be changed. Active acceptance liberates clients to take action toward what truly can be controlled and what really matters as part of living.

Hank Robb (personal communication, 2004) recently offered a spin on the serenity creed—the "Formula for Serenity in Action"—that nicely illustrates the nature of acceptance as an active process within an ACT approach. He has kindly allowed us to share it here:

> Let me seek acceptance of life as I find it, even though I may not approve of what I find, wisdom to see what would be good to change, willingness to act as well as willingness to follow through, and gratitude for the opportunity to live my life as best I can.

The reason why we refer to this type of acceptance as *active acceptance* is that clients must be willing to experience thoughts, situations, and emotions that they have strived to avoid. This move is about choice and shows that active acceptance is a challenging and courageous activity.

Initially, clients will find it difficult to be willing to have anxiety-related thoughts, images, or sensations deliberately and to do what is important to them anyway regardless. Yet, this is precisely what needs to be done to get on the path of living. In fact, active acceptance actually creates space and allows people to move their hands, feet, and mouth in directions that are important. Acceptance is easier than nonacceptance precisely because the avoidance, struggle, and control ropes that would normally tie up and bind a client with their anxiety are let go. There is no need to struggle, no need to fight. The battle and tug-of-war with one's thoughts and feelings need not be fought. In fact, with acceptance there is no fight left to fight. Acceptance ends the tug-of-war by letting go of the control ropes—a core metaphor we use in treatment (see chapter 8). Mindfulness exercises that encourage present-centeredness and nonevaluative experiential knowing of reality as it is can help facilitate the development of active acceptance. We describe mindfulness approaches briefly below and include such exercises in later treatment chapters.

ORIGINS OF ACCEPTANCE-BASED STRATEGIES

Acceptance-based ideas are not new within psychology, and yet it is only recently that they have made their way into cognitive behavioral therapies (Hayes et al., 1994; Hayes, Follette, et al., 2004). For instance, variations of therapist- and client-focused acceptance are at the core of humanistic (Rogers, 1961) and existential psychotherapies (Greenberg, 1994; Perls, 1973). Even Freud (1920) considered repression and avoidance of unwanted thoughts and emotions to be toxic psychological processes (Hayes & Pankey, 2003). We could go on and on with other examples of acceptance playing a key role in psychological theory and practice, including several religious traditions that predate psychology as a discipline. Such examples simply illustrate that most therapists believe that some form of acceptance is necessary for meaningful therapeutic change.

What is new about acceptance within mainstream psychology is its manualization, systematic conceptualization, operationalization, and inclusion in established, empirically supported psychotherapies (e.g., Acceptance and Commitment Therapy: Hayes, Strosahl, & Wilson, 1999; Hayes & Strosahl, 2004; Dialectical Behavior Therapy; Linehan, 1993, 1994; Integrative Behavioral Couples Therapy: Jacobson et al., 2000). Acceptance is viewed not as a therapeutic goal itself but rather as a means of empowering the achievement of valued life goals (Hayes & Pankey, 2003). It is a process, not merely an outcome, and shares an affinity with Eastern traditions emphasizing acceptance and mindfulness.

Eastern Philosophy and World Views

Mindfulness is fundamentally an acceptance-oriented psychological process derived largely from 2,500 years of Buddhist philosophy and meditation practice (Kabat-Zinn, 2005; Robins, 2002). Its origin can be traced back to as early as the first millennium B.C., to the foothills of the Himalayas, when Shakyamuni Buddha, the Buddha of this era and founder of Buddhism, attained enlightenment. Buddhism is intensely empirical and more closely aligned with experiencing life fully and openly than with any particular religious beliefs. Its focus is on the fluid aspects of reality as it unfolds, and it includes a microscopic examination of the very process of perception and experience. To reveal reality as it really is, its intention is to strip away that screen of evaluative distortions of reality that normally color how we see the world. This process undermines responding to evaluations rather than experiences, while promoting openness, flexibility, and contact with experience. Thus, it allows for contingencies to shape and guide behavior. This is precisely what ACT aims to do as part of the process of getting the client to move in life directions that are freely chosen and valued.

There are several strands of Buddhism, and two main forms of meditation stem from them: Vipassana (insight) and Samatha (concentration or tranquillity). Vipassana, the oldest form of Buddhist meditative practice, involves a clear awareness of exactly what is happening as it happens. Samatha is a state in which the mind is brought to rest, focused only on one item and not allowed to wander. Most systems of meditation emphasize the Samatha component, sometimes referred to as a *concentrative* approach. Here the meditator focuses the mind upon a single object, such as prayer, a certain type of box, a chant, a candle flame, a religious image, or some other thing, and excludes all other thoughts and perceptions from consciousness. The goal is a state of calm and peace. If achieved, however, such effects are temporary and only last as long as the meditator is meditating. Most systems of meditation focus on the achievement of peace and tranquillity as goals on the path to enlightenment. Not so with Vipassana meditation. Vipassana meditation is most closely aligned with mindfulness meditation. Mindfulness is about the act of purposefully paying attention to experiences as they are, and not how we say they are because of our conditioning histories. As such, mindfulness is to be used deliberately in daily life with eyes wide open, not simply during meditation sessions (Kabat-Zinn, 2005). It is this feature of practicing mindfulness in all life situations that makes mindfulness so relevant and useful for ACT.

Mindfulness as Process and Practice

Life is lived in the present, and living is ultimately about the fluid unfolding of a series of present moments. Yet, it is notoriously difficult for humans to remain psychologically present in the here and now. We frequently live in the past or the future, and we cloud our present experiences with evaluations of them, while failing to recognize that the evaluations are not the experiences. They are evaluations of the experience; the experience will be regardless of our evaluations of it. Yet our minds constantly fuse our experiences and our evaluations of those experiences, creating a language trap that is responsible for much human suffering. For instance, when the neighbor's dog starts barking loudly and uncontrollably before dawn, what do we do? We probably say something like, "Damn it … there goes that dog again," "I really can't sleep with this noise," "I'm not going to be alert today," "Why can't they shut him up," "Why don't they keep him inside," and so on. We may even think about calling the neighbors to request that they do something about their dog, and may consider calling the police. In the process, we fail to notice the experience of the dog barking—sounds that have a unique quality and beauty in their own right. It never occurs to us that we can simply experience the dog's barking as it is.

Several researchers (Bishop et al., 2004) have suggested an operational definition of mindfulness that contains two components. The first component involves the self-regulation of attention so that it is maintained on current experience, that is, observing and attending to the changing field of thought, feelings, and sensations from moment to moment. The second component involves adopting an orientation of curiosity, openness, and acceptance to one's experiences in the present moment. In this manner, a stance of acceptance is taken toward each moment of one's experiences. This involves a conscious decision to abandon one's agenda to have a different experience and an active process of allowing current thoughts, feelings, and sensations, no matter whether we like or dislike them.

In its most basic form, mindfulness is about making direct contact with our present experiences, with acceptance and without judgment (Kabat-Zinn, 1990; 2005). If you can imagine taking a neutral, scientist-like perspective while also observing your internal and external experiences from a nurturing, loving, compassionate perspective and with intention, then you can imagine what a mindfulness posture is like. Such observation without judgment and with compassion is actually an active response—just not in the way we usually think of being active (as in running, fighting, struggling, etc.). This stance is an antidote to the stimulus control exerted by literal language (Hayes & Shenk, 2004) and thereby facilitates acceptance and full contact with life experiences, both inside and outside the skin. At the core, mindfulness is very much about running into reality, not away from it!

This process of mindfulness is quite different from what most of us usually do. We usually do not take the time to see what is really there in front of us. Instead, life is viewed through a screen of thoughts and concepts. We all have a tendency to mistake those mental objects for reality, to focus on outcomes and not the process, and to get so caught up in dealing with an endless stream of evaluative thoughts that reality flows by unnoticed. Clients with anxiety-related problems spend an enormous amount of time engrossed in this activity, caught up in an endless pursuit of calm and peace and an ongoing flight from pain and unpleasantness. They expend lots of energy trying to make themselves feel better by burying fears, doubts, worry, and pain. Meanwhile, the world of real experience flows by untouched and untasted. Recall that an essential aspect of mindfulness is observing without evaluation or judgment and without holding onto, getting rid of, suppressing, or otherwise changing what we experience. The paradox is that real peace and joy come when we stop chasing them.

Though a deep sense of peace, calm, and relaxation may be a natural consequence of a mindfulness posture, this is not *the* goal of mindfulness from an ACT perspective. The transformative and therapeutic power of mindfulness practice derives directly from openness to all experience as it is. The goal of mindfulness is full awareness of experience—to become liberated from the blinders of our learning histories, evaluations, preconceptions, self-talk, and the like, and to wake up to life as it really is, not as our mind says it is. In this sense, mindfulness meditation has been described as the "Great Teacher." This teacher is one of several forms of acceptance behavior, and like any new behavior, it must be practiced regularly before it can be applied freely as part of daily living. Meditation practice creates a context in which experiential avoidance directly interferes with the process of meditation itself (Hayes & Shenk, 2004).

Incidentally, meditation practice is only one way to develop mindfulness skills. Other behavioral techniques foster mindfulness by teaching clients to distinguish experiences from evaluations of their experience; we introduce some of these cognitive defusion techniques (including mindful exposure) in the treatment chapters. The goal of all these practical exercises is to apply a mindful, accepting posture to all our experiences. Mindfulness that is only applied to meditation practice but not to daily living and anxiety-related situations is sterile and of limited value.

Mindfulness Is a Cognitive Defusion, Not an Anxiety Control Strategy

It is essential that our clients do not use mindfulness or any exercises as a control strategy to manage their anxiety. Our experience tells us, however, that clients are likely to do so. You can recognize it when clients come in saying, "Mindfulness doesn't work for me" but also when they enthusiastically say, "Mindfulness really works for me." In both cases, they may be trying to combat anxiety with mindfulness.

To address such behavior, therapists need to have a clear understanding of the function that mindfulness and other exercises serve in ACT. Instead of an evaluative avoidance stance, these exercises are designed to foster a nonevaluative approach toward the world of experience. For instance, mindful breathing is not designed to be a relaxation strategy to control or manage anxiety. It is a defusion strategy that aims to help the client make contact with experience as it is, without all the other evaluative baggage, including verbal rules and reasons, that usually come along with it. As with acceptance, mindfulness allows clients to notice the *process* of thinking, evaluating, feeling, remembering, and other forms of relational activity, and not simply the *products* of such activities (Hayes, 2002). Relaxation, peace, and a sense of calm may occur as by-products of mindfulness. Similarly, mindfulness might result in the experience of distressing thoughts, memories, and feelings. In both cases, the real aim of mindfulness is to help clients experience their experiences fully, including their evaluations, thoughts, and memories as they are, in a context where experiential avoidance is unnecessary and counterproductive.

In ACT, we consider mindfulness exercises a useful tool to help people experience their anxiety without trying to fix it. We do not consider mindfulness to be therapeutic in itself. We do not encourage it as a way of life to feel *better*. Mindfulness is not an escape hatch, emergency exit, or ejection seat (like the ones used by fighter pilots) to break away from aversive experiences. Instead, it is a way to become better at *feeling* on the path to *living* better. The prize here is a life, and as many casino signs read, "You need to be present to win." Mindfulness is designed to help clients wake up to their own experiences as fully functioning human beings. The danger here is that clients may start using mindfulness and other exercises to get relief from anxiety as a new way of avoiding, escaping, or fixing what they experience. This may work in the short run and reinforce old control patterns. As a consequence, clients may do more of the same in the future. At the same time, it would prevent a lasting change and be a step back to the old, unworkable control agenda.

LINKING ACCEPTANCE TECHNIQUES TO BEHAVIOR THEORY

Cognitive behavioral therapies are intensely empirical, experiential, practical, time limited, and present focused. Their popularity and effectiveness stem largely from these characteristics. Acceptance-based behavior therapies retain the core elements that have made behavior therapy so popular and add to them in several ways, chief among them being how psychopathology is conceptualized. We have already outlined many of the core elements that comprise an ACT approach to anxiety-related suffering. A few additional characteristics are worth mentioning here, particularly as it has become increasingly clear to us that ACT is quite different from mainstream cognitive behavioral therapies for anxiety disorders. For therapists to practice ACT, they really need to get their own head and heart around what acceptance is about.

We have said that ACT is an approach, not a set of techniques targeting symptoms. Its characteristics—focusing on experiential openness and values, and developing the human capacity to live on purpose and with meaning—follow directly from the view that a good deal of human suffering stems from actions that cut persons off from such uniquely human characteristics. One initial goal of therapy is to create a new context where such human qualities can thrive. Doing so requires therapists to rethink the symptom-focused change agenda that has come to characterize many mainstream cognitive behavioral therapies for the anxiety disorders.

The Language Trap

Recall that anxiety does not become disordered because of what people feel, or because anxiety and fear are too intense, or because such emotions often occur in situations that do not demand such a response. Rather, it is the language-based capacity for humans to evaluate, and respond relationally to their own evaluations, thoughts, and feelings with more evaluations, while acting not to have them, that sets up a trap for anxiety to become an anxiety disorder. Such tendencies do not come from nowhere. They are socialized and learned by about the age of two and are fundamentally built into human language and cognition:

> Humans have a hard time accepting the present moment with openness and curiosity … since the present moment may contain events that are … evaluated as undesirable. A primary benefit of language in an evolutionary sense is its contribution to problem solving, and typically the primary goal of problem solving is to produce desirable rather than undesirable events. Avoiding psychological pain is thus built into the normal function of language itself, even if that process causes harm. (Hayes & Shenk, 2004, p. 252)

As a therapist, you can think of the basic process that sets up this trap as a tendency to respond to one's own responses, or more technically behavior-behavior relations. These relations, in turn, are at any moment situated in and within a context. The context controls the nature of a relational response and the kinds of evaluative relational activity that might occur, including what clients ultimately do with their hands and feet as a consequence. As Hayes (2002) put it, "mindfulness and acceptance catch this bird in flight, and like an audience that learns how a magic trick is accomplished, they can profoundly change the effects of the language illusion" (p. 104). Consider, for instance, the case of Jerry.

Jerry suffered from panic attacks while driving. During such attacks, he would routinely focus on his evaluations of the physical sensations he experienced, saying to himself things like, "My God, I must be having a heart attack … I must be dying." Typically, Jerry would immediately pull over during such attacks, and eventually ride out the attack until he felt well enough (another evaluation) to drive home. Ultimately, Jerry sought out consultation from a cardiologist and underwent a routine exercise EKG. While undergoing this test, Jerry experienced a range of physical sensations, many of which were quite similar to those that normally would accompany his panic attacks while driving. However, in the "safe" context of the doctor's office, Jerry neither thought "I must be having a heart attack," nor did he stop the exercise or escape. This case illustrates a key point about how context controls our evaluative relational activities and overt behavior, and it can help you, as a therapist, conceptualize client problems and how to work with anxious clients from an ACT perspective.

The Fusion-of-Evaluative-Thinking-with-Reality Trap

First, the events felt during anxiety and other emotional responses are characterized by physical sensations that are well within the range of normal human experience. The responses "I am having a heart attack" and "I must be dying" are purely derived forms of evaluative activity. Note that the form or content of evaluative activity is not problematic in itself. To illustrate, go ahead and say to yourself "I am crazy," "I am worthless," "I can't breathe," "I might be dying," or "My heart is racing." These statements likely had little effect on you, showing that an evaluative thought or statement is just that: an evaluation, a series of words. Yet, evaluations have a tendency to become fused with our experience and can entail other relations. For example, "I must not stand up and speak because I will make a fool of myself in front of this crowd" is no longer just an evaluative thought. The thought takes on the function and is experienced as a representation of the actual event (e.g., social rejection) that then needs to be avoided. Also, the thought "I am a social failure" is likely related to other evaluations, such as "I am not happy," "I am sick," "People will think badly of me," or "I can't do X, Y, or Z." Many of us, in fact, are guided more by our evaluations of the world then by events in the world as they are. This is not to say that the fusion of evaluative thought with actual experience is necessarily and always a bad thing. The point is to help clients recognize the difference between what the mind says and how the world is, and to respond flexibly as the circumstances require while moving in the direction of valued goals.

The Avoidance Trap

Our second point has to do with the typical outcome of this fusion process and its treatment implications. The outcome for anxious clients is almost universally to engage in obvious and sometimes more subtle forms of experiential avoidance. Clients with anxiety disorders typically find themselves ensnarled in evaluative fusion activity (thoughts = feelings = reasons = justifications = action and inaction), and then do what appears to be the most sensible thing to do: avoid or run from the circumstances that contribute to the anxious thoughts, unpleasant memories, and associated feelings. What they are really doing, however, is responding to the evaluation—not the real contingencies of the situation—and they often do so in an inflexible and rigid manner. As a therapist, you could think of this as the product of a generalized insensitivity to contextual factors that would normally promote a more flexible and less evaluation-driven repertoire of responding. These actions, as we described earlier, function as the nails on the coffin door for human beings who want to have a life worth living.

IMPLICATIONS FOR TREATMENT

The acceptance and mindfulness posture of ACT can be thought of as a way to "defuse" or loosen and disentangle the fusion of events or experiences with the evaluations of such experiences. This is important because evaluative forms of cognitive activity that set up relations amongst feelings, thoughts, and experiences, and action tendencies (e.g., anxiety suppression, control, and avoidance) are typically unworkable as solutions. There are several obvious and not-so-obvious treatment implications that follow from an ACT approach. These implications are simply different, rather than better or worse, than those typical of mainstream cognitive behavioral therapies.

Reframing the Clinical Context

As a therapist and human being, take a moment to think about what you are ultimately trying to accomplish when working with other human beings who come to see you because they are suffering. You may have come up with several responses. Perhaps you focused on intermediate goals, achieving insight, and, more likely, symptom alleviation. You probably use a wide variety of techniques to get there. Ultimately, however, most therapists want to see their clients *living* better, not simply *feeling* better.

There are countless examples, some quite extraordinary, of human beings who experience emotional and psychological pain, hardship, and just about every possible disadvantage and, in spite of having every reason to feel bad and give up, they nonetheless choose to live life to its fullest. There are also many examples of individuals with many advantages and reasons to feel good who still suffer miserably. As a therapist, you have likely seen clients who represent both ends of this spectrum. Feeling good is a sensible and reasonable starting point if one starts from the posture that feeling better is a prerequisite for living better. This is also the same posture that many clients operate from and expect from therapy. Most mainstream cognitive behavioral therapies for anxiety disorders similarly focus on helping clients feel better in order to live better. Implicit in this move is the notion that one needs to manage the symptoms first so as to live a life later. The stakes are high if client and therapist buy into this change agenda. What if that anxiety management program does not work? They better get on top of the "anxiety problem" or else … there will be no life!

With ACT, the relation is reversed and the clinical context reframed to focus on the real prize—a life lived well, not living to feel well. Feeling better may happen as a by-product of living a full, rich, and meaningful life—or it may not happen. The clinical focus is first and foremost on helping clients get on the path of living consistently with their values and goals. This focus actually takes a lot of pressure off the shoulders of clients and therapists alike.

More Flexible Treatment Goals and Targets

The emphasis on living well redirects clinical attention away from symptom-focused eliminative techniques so often used in cognitive behavioral therapies for anxiety disorders. In fact, clients are often surprised to hear us say that an ACT approach to anxiety disorders is not simply about anxiety. The focus is much broader than that. ACT is about enriching a human life and undermining destructive forms of human activity that get in the way of living. For instance, learning to be fully present in the moment will likely enhance a client's quality of life, whether anxiety shows up or not. It also serves to broaden the range of events that might regulate behavior, while undermining narrow forms of verbally regulated behavior that get in the way of effective actions (Hayes & Shenk, 2004).

Similarly, loosening the experiential avoidance and change agenda is likely to help clients when confronted with various forms of human suffering, by enriching their experiences with the world and relationships with others in that world. Choosing to accept what cannot be changed and choosing to live a valued life with meaning and purpose are likewise broadband repertoire-expanding actions that are not specific to anxiety. In fact, anxiety-related problems could be thought of as one of several consequences of unwillingness, avoidance, and inaction. ACT intervention strategies, as we outline in later treatment chapters, are ultimately about fostering the development of whole, fully functioning human beings. Who ever said that behavior therapy cannot be "humanistic"? Acceptance-based behavior therapy is deeply experiential and humanistic. Therapists, therefore, need to think in terms of fostering psychological flexibility, growth, and meaningful life change when working with anxious clients from an ACT perspective. A variety of strategies may be used to accomplish such goals. This is why ACT, and behavior therapy more generally, is not limited to a specific set of techniques.

Recontextualizing Exposure

In vivo and imaginal exposure exercises are at the core of virtually all cognitive behavioral therapies for anxiety disorders, and for good reason. Exposure is designed to counteract the powerful action tendency to avoid or escape from anxiety and fear-provoking events. This is accomplished by arranging structured approach activities, usually in the form of a fear hierarchy. Corrective emotional learning comes about as clients make full contact with anxiety-provoking events, usually in increasing order of difficulty. Within standard cognitive behavioral therapies, repeated exposure takes advantage of extinction processes, and thus results in attenuation of anxiety and fear to previously avoided cues and situations. In fact, exposure is ultimately an eliminative technique and is conducted with the explicit goal of reducing anxiety. Implicit in this move is the assumption that anxiety needs to be reduced so that the client can feel and function better. Otherwise, exposure as traditionally practiced within cognitive behavioral therapy would not make much sense.

Within ACT, exposure is recontextualized in several ways. It is no longer an eliminative technique to be applied within a framework of mastering and controlling anxiety. To do so would be inconsistent with an ACT therapeutic stance, for it sends a message to the client that the anxiety is the problem and thus must be reduced or managed before a client can feel better. Rather, exposure within ACT is best thought of as one of several experiential exercises, with the goal being to *feel* better (i.e., become better at feeling), not to feel *better* (i.e., feel less anxiety). This mastery of experience framework for ACT exposure exercises is again about creating a fully functioning human being. The goal is not to help clients manage or get rid of anxiety and fear, but rather to help them develop willingness to experience thoughts and feelings for what they are. Thus, exposure exercises within ACT are framed in the service of fostering greater psychological flexibility, experiential willingness, and openness. They are about growth and are always done in the service of client values and goals. This is an important point, and it's why we refer to them in later treatment chapters as *Feeling Experiences Enriches Living* (FEEL) exercises. As you will see, FEEL exercises are included along with several other *Experiential Life Enhancement Exercises* in the treatment chapters.

As a therapist, you should always frame exposure in such a way that it is linked with a client's values and goals. The goal of exposure is to help move a client toward living consistently with their valued life goals. When in doubt, ask yourself, "What is this exposure exercise in the service of?" If a client's values and goals do not show up in the answer, then the purpose of the exercise will need to be clarified. Along the way, continue to be mindful that anxiety reduction is not a necessary prerequisite for meaningful behavior change. In fact, an acceptance-based approach allows for the possibility that anxiety levels may remain unchanged, so long as the client is showing greater willingness and is taking steps to use their hands and feet to live consistently with what matters to them. Again, it is likely that clients will experience some anxiety reduction or at least learn new ways of relating with their anxiety. Yet, even without anxiety reduction, therapy can still be a success, as long as the client is living a more meaningful and richer life. This posture is quite different from mainstream cognitive behavioral therapies, where anxiety reduction is seen as the main goal of exposure exercises.

> Mindfulness, acceptance, and defusion are not just a different way of treating … problems of depression or anxiety. They imply a redefinition of the problem, the solution, and how both should be measured. The problem is not the presence of particular thoughts, emotions, sensations, or urges: It is the constriction of a human life. The solution is not removal of difficult private events: It is living a valued life. (Hayes & Wilson, 2003, p. 165)

IMPLICATIONS FOR ASSESSMENT

We see assessment closely tied with case conceptualization and treatment as well as monitoring of outcome. Within ACT, the assessment and treatment relation is ongoing and recursive. It starts from the moment a client walks through the door and continues throughout treatment, and, when feasible, for some period of time after treatment. This is simply good clinical practice. Thus, we adopt this approach throughout the treatment chapters that follow.

We should add that ACT presents an enormous opportunity for therapists to make a difference, not only in their clients' lives but also within the clinical professional community. Although the empirical base of ACT is growing rapidly, it is still in its infancy (Hayes, Masuda, et al., 2004). Thus, therapists who collect assessment and outcome data using ACT with their clients, and who make an effort to disseminate their data via case conferences, workshops, and traditional publication outlets, truly stand to make an impact on the development of ACT in the years to come. This is no exaggeration. You, as an ACT therapist, can make a contribution to researchers and clinicians using, and attempting to further develop, acceptance-based treatments. What follows in this section is meant to help orient you to some broader assessment considerations. The issues we address are not meant to be inclusive. Rather, we provide an overview of some available assessment measures and their suitability in the context of an ACT approach to treatment.

Current Measures and Their Suitability Within ACT

There are numerous empirically supported assessment devices you may use with persons suffering from anxiety disorders. Most are designed to evaluate emotions, thoughts, and overt actions consistent with the tripartite model of fear and anxiety. As a therapist, you will likely not have the time or resources to include more expensive assessment technologies such as physiological monitoring. Thus, we limit this brief overview to the chief modalities for gathering information about your clients, beginning with the clinical interview.

Though the clinical interview is typically unstructured, there are good structured interviews available for anxiety-related problems. For instance, both the *Anxiety Disorders Interview Schedule for DSM-IV* (ADIS-IV; Brown, DiNardo, & Barlow, 1994) and the *Structured Clinical Interview for DSM-IV Axis I Disorders, Clinician Version* (SCID-CV; First, Spitzer, Gibbon, & Williams, 1996) are suitable if the goal is to conduct a thorough diagnostic assessment. Yet, we encourage you not to limit your assessment to diagnosis alone. This recommendation is based on several considerations.

First, psychiatric diagnoses are limited to symptoms and syndromes, whereas ACT is about behavior and processes that contribute to human suffering. Recall that symptoms are less important from an ACT perspective than getting the client unstuck from the pattern of avoiding and controlling those symptoms. Second, psychiatric diagnoses are widely known to have limited treatment utility. Simply because we build our treatments around diagnostic labels is not a good reason to use diagnosis as a guide for treatment. Many of the issues addressed from within an ACT approach are not disorder specific; ACT instead means to address variables and processes that underlie human suffering more generally. Third, and consistent with the aims of an ACT approach, diagnoses—however necessary for insurance purposes—create the false impression that disorders are more dissimilar than they truly are. This book in particular is about addressing the core processes that underlie disordered experiences of anxiety and fear. Though the particular issues will vary from client to client, the nature of the treatment is quite similar across each of the anxiety disorders. Remember, ACT is an approach, not simply a technology. It is about helping clients live fully and richly, rather than about alleviating disorders. Thus, psychiatric diagnoses have only limited utility from an ACT perspective.

You may also consider using one or more empirically supported paper-and-pencil self-report measures to assess common and more specific characteristics of anxiety-related suffering. The universe of options here is large, and we simply cannot describe each of the available measures. A good starting point is the *Practitioner's Guide to Empirically Based Measures of Anxiety* (Antony, Orsillo, & Roemer, 2001). This volume contains information on almost all of the measures that have demonstrated usefulness in assessing core features of anxiety and related disorders. Many of these measures are also quite useful in that they provide information about various forms of experiential avoidance. In fact, virtually all of the available self-report measures for anxiety, in one form or another, assess the psychological consequences of experiential avoidance.

Take, for example, the *Anxiety Sensitivity Index* (ASI; Peterson & Reiss, 1992; Reiss, Peterson, Gursky, & McNally, 1986), a sixteen-item questionnaire designed to assess fear of anxiety-related physical symptoms. Not surprisingly, fear of anxiety-related symptoms is characteristic of most persons with anxiety disorders and particularly persons suffering from panic disorder. From an ACT perspective, however, anxiety sensitivity is simply a manifestation of a toxic and more basic underlying process, namely experiential avoidance. Persons who are unwilling to have physical sensations and who consider them bad and something to be avoided tend to respond to their own responses, and the circumstances that occasion them, with apprehension and fear. In fact, in the context of experiential avoidance, fear of fear (i.e., elevated anxiety sensitivity) makes sense as a natural outcome. Now consider anxiety sensitivity in the context of willingness or acceptance. Here, anxiety sensitivity makes little sense, for now we are left with the experience of physical sensations as they are, willingness to have them for what they are, and consequently no need to do anything about them. They are just feelings, sensations, and related thoughts. As a consequence, we would expect to see a reduction in ASI scores following ACT treatment. Responses to many other anxiety-related measures can be conceptualized similarly and should show pre-post treatment changes as a result of a decrease in experiential avoidance. Thus, we encourage you to include them routinely in your work with clients.

Numerous other more traditional forms of assessment may prove useful in the context of an ACT approach, and these are only limited by the creativity and skill of the therapist. For example, direct observation of a client's behavior in session and outside of session can be enormously useful. In particular, many of the exercises outlined in later chapters are introduced and practiced in session. How clients respond to you as another human being can provide valuable information about how they may respond to other human beings in their daily lives. Similarly, be attuned to how your clients respond to the treatment exercises (both verbally and nonverbally). Watch for subtle and more obvious clues to patterns of rigidity, experiential avoidance, and struggle. Address such issues with compassion as they unfold, and be mindful of how you respond to your client and how your client is responding to you in the present moment. Such present-centeredness can help you develop a clear formulation of your client's difficulties, while also helping you more appropriately tailor treatment to your clients' unique circumstances.

ACT-Specific Process and Outcome Assessment

Assessment technology suitable for ACT is developing at a rapid clip. Some assessments exist in published format and others were developed or adapted specifically for the purpose of this treatment program. For instance, in the treatment sections of this book, we provide several measures that may be used to assess ACT-relevant clinical processes and outcomes. You will also find electronic versions of all these measures and worksheets on the CD that accompanies this book. This, we hope, will make it easy for you to incorporate these measures into your clinical practice. Although these measures can be used to document pre-post treatment effects, they are equally useful as ongoing measures to monitor changes in experiential avoidance and willingness, as well as difficulties clients may be experiencing between sessions.

Experiential Monitoring Forms

Living in Full Experience (LIFE)

Right from the beginning, we ask clients to monitor contexts where anxiety and fear show up, associated experiences (thoughts, physical sensations, and overt behaviors), their willingness to have those experiences, and how they respond to them in ways that get in the way of their values and goals. At the end of chapter 7 (and on the book CD) we provide a worksheet—Living in Full Experience (LIFE)—that can be used to track some of the above domains. The acronym LIFE is not accidental. It's a deliberate effort to frame this exercise in terms of what really counts: living.

Daily ACT Ratings

Throughout treatment, we also ask clients to complete the Daily ACT Ratings at the end of every day. You'll find this rating form at the end of chapter 7 and on the book CD. Clients make simple ratings on a scale from 0 (not at all) to 10 (extreme amount) for each of the following domains: (a) how upset and distressed over anxiety they were that day, (b) how much effort they put into making anxious feelings or thoughts go away that day, (c) to what degree they would consider that day to be part of a vital, workable way of living, and (d) how much they engaged in behaviors that are in accord with their values and life goals.

Assessing the Major Components and Processes of ACT

Let us now outline the main component processes of ACT and what therapists might want to assess specifically within each area.

Assessing Creative Hopelessness

The goal here is to assess your clients' efforts to manage and solve their anxiety-related difficulties and how well such efforts have worked for them. The assessment is not about the feeling of hopelessness, but rather the workability of former solutions. Such assessment is important and needs to be thorough. The focus here should be on what clients have done in the past to manage anxiety and how well such strategies have worked. You do not want to spend time in therapy doing more of what has not worked for your client. Additionally, it is useful to begin to relate such strategies with broader issues that pertain to client values and how they wish to live their life. For instance, you may ask how each of these solutions has gotten in the way of your client's ability to live a full, rich, and value-consistent life. What was given up in the service of not having anxious thoughts and feelings? Perhaps the most crucial question to ask with insistence and compassion is, "What have been the short-term versus long-term costs of these strategies; have they moved you closer to or further away from your values?" Such questions begin to plant the seeds for the values work to come.

Assessing Control and Avoidance Versus Acceptance and Willingness

The goal here is to identify avoidance and control efforts that the client has been using. Most of these, as we have discussed, can be described as experiential avoidance strategies, and many will center on unwanted thoughts and feelings, as well as the situations that occasion them. Such strategies function to distance human beings from contact with the world of experience as it is, and when rigidly and inflexibly applied to private events, they manifest as struggle, control, and avoidance, or value-inconsistent actions. Experiential avoidance may seem like a trait, but it's best thought of as a predisposition to relate with oneself and the world in particular ways. It is something that people do, not something they have.

This predisposition can be assessed globally using the *Acceptance and Action Questionnaire* (AAQ; Hayes, Strosahl, et al., 2004; a copy is in appendix A and on the book CD). The original AAQ consists of nine items loading on a single factor. A revised version by Bond and Bunce (2003) consists of sixteen items and includes two subscales: The Willingness Scale consists of seven items assessing willingness to accept undesirable thoughts and feelings (items 3R, 4, 5, 7, 8R, 9R, 11R—item numbers followed by R are reverse scored). The Action Scale consists of nine items assessing whether individuals act in a way that is congruent with their values and goals (items 1, 2R, 6R, 10, 12, 13, 14R, 15R, 16). The original nine-item AAQ comprises items 1, 2R, 5, 7, 9R, 11R, 17R, 18, 19R. We include all nineteen items in appendix A so you can decide which version you'd prefer to score. Higher scores reflect more willingness/acceptance and action. Research thus far indicates that the AAQ has good psychometric properties (Bond & Bunce, 2003; Hayes, Strosahl, et al., 2004) and that it correlates with several other measures of negative affectivity and anxiety-related pathology (Forsyth, Parker, & Finlay, 2003; Hayes & Strosahl, 2004). Although the AAQ seems to work well as a measure of acceptance and willingness, it is still a relatively new measure. An expanded version (AAQ 2) is currently under investigation.

Another useful process and outcome measure is the *White Bear Suppression Inventory* (WBSI; Wegner & Zanakos, 1994; a copy is in appendix B and on the book CD). The WBSI measures people's tendency to suppress (i.e., not accept) and struggle with unwanted thoughts and feelings. This measure has been used extensively in laboratory and clinical settings to demonstrate the negative effects of experiential avoidance (e.g., Koster, Rassin, Crombez, & Nöring, 2003). Clinical studies involving people with various anxiety disorders such as obsessive-compulsive disorder (Smari, 2001) and specific phobias have shown that the WBSI is sensitive to measuring the effects of treatment. Items are scored by summing all individual responses (see Wegner & Zanakos, 1994, for more information on norms and interpretation).

The fifteen-item *Mindfulness Attention Awareness Scale* (MAAS; Brown & Ryan, 2003; a copy is in appendix C and on the book CD) assesses mindfulness across cognitive, emotional, physical, interpersonal, and general domains. Using a six-point Likert scale, individuals indicate how frequently they have the experience described in each statement, with high scores reflecting more mindfulness. Items are scored by summing all individual responses. A number of studies conducted by Brown and Ryan (2003) show that (a) the MAAS has good psychometric properties, (b) the scale differentiates people who practice mindfulness from those who don't, (c) higher scores are associated with enhanced self-awareness, and (d) following a clinical intervention, cancer patients showed increases in mindfulness over time that were related to declines in mood disturbance and stress.

Assessing Willingness as an Alternative to Control

Once patterns of control and avoidance of anxiety are identified and assessed, you will be positioned to address the more experiential aspects of an ACT approach to anxiety, which entails nurturing experiential willingness. Willingness is very much about fostering approach behaviors as an alternative to control and avoidance. Like hopelessness, willingness is not a feeling. It is not about wanting, putting up with, or tolerating. Willingness is both a stance toward life and an activity. It is about doing, and doing in the direction of what the client values and truly cares about. Willingness is the opposite of avoidance and means to show up and be open to experiencing life as it is. That is, one must be willing to experience what is and accept what cannot be changed in order to be positioned to change what can be changed; this is truly what ACT is all about.

Assessment of willingness is part of the process on the road to acceptance and value-guided action. In a sense, all three questionnaires described in the previous section provide assessments of willingness. These measures also are useful for assessing pre-post treatment effects and changes. In addition, the Daily ACT Ratings provide ongoing assessments of willingness. As a therapist, you can also assess your client's descriptions of an event, what they were thinking and feeling, and what they were willing to do. In the process, you will be helping your clients distinguish between clean and dirty discomfort. The former of these comes about simply as a consequence of living a life (e.g., the inevitable and sad loss of one's parents), whereas the latter involves suffering that is created by efforts to control or avoid the emotional and psychological pain that are normal consequences of living. Such assessments tend to be somewhat idiosyncratic and will most often occur in the context of metaphors, mindfulness, and other experiential exposure-like exercises.

Assessing Defusion

This facet of ACT builds upon what we have outlined previously in regard to the dark side of language. Much human suffering is related to cognitive fusion, a process that involves fusing with or attaching to the literal content of our private experiences. When fusion occurs, a thought is no longer just a thought, and a word is no longer just a sound; rather, we respond to words about some event as if we were responding to the actual event the words describe. Cognitive defusion means uncoupling or disentangling words and thoughts from the actual events that such words and thoughts refer to. The aim of defusion is to loosen a client's tendency to treat verbal evaluative processes of language as being equivalent with the actual experience that language refers to. The goal is to help clients create distance between what is and what their mind says that is. Simple descriptions of events, using "and" instead of "but," are part of this process and can be assessed directly. For instance, a client might say, "I want to go camping *but* I'm afraid of snakes" when a more accurate statement would be "I want to go camping *and* I am afraid of snakes."

Similarly, cognitive defusion seeks to undermine the fusion of evaluations with the actual experience. For instance, before treatment, the experience of a rapidly beating heart and dizziness is fused with the statement "I could be dying" or "I'm having a heart attack." These two thoughts are verbal evaluations of experiencing a rapidly beating heart, dizziness, and other physical sensations. If defusion is successful, a client would come to demonstrate a shift in evaluative statements about their experiences. Thus, they might say something like, "I feel my heart racing and dizziness and I'm having the thought that I may be dying of a heart attack." Likewise, a statement such as "I'm scared to get on a plane" would be defused to something like "I am having the feeling of being scared about getting on a plane." This component of therapy is not about simply replacing one thought with another thought or statement. Rather, it is about helping the client to approach their thinking and feeling as an observer and to describe how they think and feel from a self-as-context (observer) versus self-as-content perspective. In this sense, defusion techniques are also mindfulness techniques. Both function to help clients to become aware of what they are experiencing (e.g., thinking evaluative thoughts) while noticing the experiencing without judging it as good or bad.

At times, cognitive behavioral therapists mistake defusion in ACT as a form of cognitive restructuring. At the surface, they do indeed look similar because both seek to undermine and disentangle client evaluations of an experience from the actual experience. Defusion in ACT, however, is more radical than cognitive restructuring techniques. For instance, defusion is not aimed at correcting the erroneous assumption or prediction of persons with panic disorder that they will die during the next panic attack. Defusion is not about changing the content of the evaluation. Instead, defusion aims at having the client recognize and experience the evaluative thought for what it is: a thought, nothing more and nothing less. Its rightness or wrongness (its content) does not matter. What matters is that it is a thought that we can simply observe. The thought need not be evaluated, corrected, or struggled with. It comes and goes on its own accord. We simply have it *and* get on with doing what is important to us.

Fusion is a subtle and remarkably pervasive and insidious process. In fact, it is so overlearned and occurs with such high frequency that this habit is not easy to break and change. There have been a number of efforts to develop and utilize measures of defusion. In fact, some of the best process measures are in the defusion area. Most of these tend to be somewhat idiosyncratic (see Bach & Hayes, 2002), or standardized within a domain. An example of the latter is the Stigmatizing Attitudes Believability Scale (SAB; Nevada Practice Improvement Collaborative)—a measure of the believability of stigmatizing thoughts of substance abuse treatment providers toward their clients. The SAB, in turn, has been adapted to assess avoidance and defusion in persons undergoing a smoking cessation program (Gifford et al., 2004). The Automatic Thoughts Questionnaire-B (ATQ; Hollon & Kendall, 1980), augmented by item believability ratings, also may be used to assess defusion, as could the Thought-Action Fusion Scale (TAF; Shafran, Thordarson, & Rachman, 1996).

You will see that we have included measures to help you assess fusion and defusion in your clients. You may also wish to create other measures of defusion on your own as you go. This is relatively straightforward to do by simply adding "believability" ratings to lists of difficult thoughts in the specific domain being addressed. For instance, the thought "I need to get a handle on my anxiety and fear for me to have the life I want" could be rated in terms of how much the client believes this statement using a ten-point Likert-type scale anchored from 1 = not at all believable to 10 = completely believable. As defusion takes hold, your client ought to hold their thoughts and evaluative statements more lightly and be less inclined to believe in them and act because of them.

Assessing Values and Committed Action

This is ultimately the real prize and the guiding framework for an ACT approach to anxiety disorders. Thus, we have made values assessment a core feature of all treatment chapters. The aim of values assessment is to help clients identify valued life goals, then move in the direction of those values, and to commit to doing just that even in the face of anxious thoughts and feelings. Such assessments are relatively structured and straightforward. As a therapist, you help clients to clarify their own values over the course of treatment and then move in a direction toward meeting small goals that are part of valued living. We include several measures in the treatment chapters and on the enclosed CD to help you in this regard.

You will see that we do not limit values to circumstances related to anxiety. Values are much broader than that, and include domains that most of us typically associate with a good quality of life (e.g., family/relationships, work, social activities, play, education, spirituality, being a good citizen, and health and well-being, to name a few). The therapeutic task here is to clarify the direction of client values, while assessing client statements about valued ends and barriers to the achievement of valued directions (Wilson & Murrell, 2004). Most barriers for anxious clients involve anxiety-related thoughts and feelings, as well as strategies used to manage and control them. In chapter 11 we describe a number of mindfulness and other defusion techniques that therapists can use to help clients move with, rather than struggle with, these internal barriers. These techniques serve to illustrate that past solutions have not worked, that a direction in life depends on choices that are made, and that a life is made up of what people ultimately spend their time doing.

In our value work, we ask clients what they want their life to stand for—what really matters to them—and then we ask in what direction they are taking their feet. Where are they going? As Dahl (in press) points out, this distinction between valuing as a feeling and valuing as an activity is an important one because most clients do not separate these two aspects of valuing and simply assume that valuing is how they feel about a particular dimension or area in their lives. For instance, if they say that they value their career and working, then they should be doing just that: working. If they do not work, or do not put forth their best effort at work, then they do not value their career, regardless of how they feel about a career.

Values are not static or finite things; they are not goals that we can accomplish and be done with or destinations that we can reach. Values are a direction and must be lived out (Hayes, Strosahl, & Wilson, 1999). For instance, being a loving person or a good parent is an ongoing action, not something that we can finish while we are alive. Clarification of client values is similarly a process that helps generate a list of relevant goals that are important to the client. The goals, however, are not the values. Again, consider the value of being a good parent. One cannot complete this and tick it off in the same way one can complete and tick off a concrete goal. Goals are nonetheless important in this process, because it is the cumulative effect of such goals that, in the end, represents value-guided actions. Only a few of these goals can realistically become the focus of therapy. In fact, a client may not reach most of their goals by the end of treatment—and that is okay, because the client's journey does not end when therapy ends. Valued living takes a lifetime. As this process continues to unfold, and as long as clients stay on track in the direction of their value-guided goals rather than doing what their anxiety tells them to do, therapy has not failed. The same is true of making and keeping commitments. Here the issue is about making a choice to move one's hands and feet in the direction of valued goals, and to do so willingly and without defense. The reason for making the choice is that it makes sense to do so. The previous avoidance agenda will not get them to where they want to go. Remember the experiential avoidance loop in chapter 3. As commitment is about doing, it is typically assessed by whether the client did what they had set out to do.

As indicated, we provide several measures and worksheets in the treatment chapters (7 to 11) and have reproduced them for you on the enclosed CD. The Valued Directions worksheet is designed to help you and your client clarify relevant values and goals. For an individual with an anxiety disorder, moving in the direction of values involves a combination of anxiety exposure-type activities and behavioral activation. We have therefore designed three forms to assess client activities related to values: FEEL record forms, Weekly Valued Life Goal Activities, and the Goal Achievement Record. These forms specifically assess a client's progress in moving toward their goals, experiences during goal-related activities, and obstacles they encounter along the way.

Valued Directions Worksheet. Based on several value assessment forms published in Hayes, Strosahl, & Wilson (1999), we have designed a condensed and simplified Valued Directions Worksheet. You can find it at the end of chapter 9 and on the CD. This assessment tool is particularly useful for identifying what areas of life are important to a client and how satisfied they are with the quality and depth of their experience in those areas. In addition, clients are asked to come up with intention statements of how they would like to live their lives in areas of importance to them and identify what may stand in the way of pursuing their valued directions. Importantly, our questionnaire adds a quantitative goal-related activity measure by asking clients to indicate how often they have done something to move them forward in areas of importance to them during the last week. This measure in particular could be a very useful pre-post outcome measure because we would expect to see a noticeable increase in valued activities as treatment progresses.

FEEL Record Forms. Following activities that may have elicited fear or anxiety, we ask clients to complete FEEL forms. The acronym stands for Feeling Experiences Enriches Living. Using FEEL record forms (see chapter 10), clients record the intensity of the sensations they experienced, their level of anxiety, how willing they were to experience what they experienced, how much they struggled with their experience, and how much they tried to avoid it. All ratings are made on a 0 to 10 scale with 10 being the maximum rating.

Weekly Valued Life Goal Activities. We also ask clients to use a Weekly Valued Life Goal Activities form (chapter 11) to record their goal-related activities for each day of the week based on their commitments made in session. Clients record whether they engaged in the activities they committed to, how much time they spent on each activity, how much anxiety they experienced, how willing they were to have what they experienced, and how much they struggled with their experience at the beginning and end of each activity. Again, all ratings are made using the same 0 (low) to 10 (high) scale.

Goal Achievement Record. For each goal clients have set, you can keep track of their progress and achievement using the Goal Achievement Record (chapter 11). On this form, clients record the date they have set their goal and committed to it. They also record the activities necessary to achieve the goal, the date they committed to doing an activity, and the actual date on which they completed the activity.

Summary of Key Concepts

Human beings have a notoriously difficult time living in the present, and most human suffering is a direct consequence of this very problem. This chapter introduced acceptance and mindfulness as means to foster contact with present experiences as they are. This stance runs counter to the control and avoidance agenda that clients typically engage in to manage their anxiety-related thoughts and feelings. Acceptance is very much about choice—running into life, not away from it. It is about living life without defense, about choosing not to spend time in a needless and unproductive struggle with unpleasant thoughts and feelings, so as to live fully.

Acceptance opens the door to experience. It loosens the grip of verbal-evaluative self-talk that shuts clients off from contact with direct experience, and thus frees them to do things with their hands and feet that truly matter to them even if that means that their anxiety, worry, unpleasant thoughts, and histories come along for the ride. Young children are masters at being open to such experiential knowing—the first taste of ice cream, the first sunset, playing, and even direct pain—and only later do these experiences become tainted with evaluative processes. Such processes, and particularly cognitive fusion and experiential avoidance, diminish contact with the world and underlie various forms of human suffering. Anxiety-related problems are consequences of this process, which is why acceptance and mindfulness strategies open the door to living better without first having to feel better.

PART III

ACT TREATMENT
OF ANXIETY

CHAPTER 6

Core Treatment Components and Therapist Skills

We are coming to understand health not as the absence of disease, but rather as the process by which individuals maintain their sense that life is comprehensible, manageable, and meaningful, and their ability to function in the face of changes in themselves and their relationships with their environment.

—Aaron Antonovsky

In previous chapters, our intention was to lay the groundwork for this chapter and the remaining treatment chapters. This background is critical as you begin your journey of practicing ACT with persons suffering from anxiety disorders. Arguably, some of the earlier material is difficult, even counterintuitive, and requires that you—the therapist—make a commitment to rethinking some of the tried-and-true assumptions about psychopathology and psychotherapy. One of these, as the quote above emphasizes, has to do with what constitutes psychological wellness or, more broadly, a life lived well.

Hayes, Strosahl, and Wilson (1999) have stressed the importance of struggling with the conceptual and theoretical material that underlies good ACT therapy. We agree. In fact, if what we said in previous chapters came across as intuitively obvious to you, then we would suggest that you go back and reread it, grapple with its conceptual and applied implications, and attempt to relate it to your own experience and that of the clients with whom you have contact. There is no need to get it right away, so long as you commit to the process of understanding. To facilitate this process, our intention here is to provide a brief overview of the core components of an ACT approach to the treatment of persons suffering from anxiety and other emotional problems. In so doing, we also address therapist skills and competencies that underlie good ACT practice, described in detail by Strosahl, Hayes, Wilson, and Gifford (2004). The competencies we outline are, in some sense, aspirational, meaning that they describe a process of behaving in an ACT-consistent fashion. The competencies, therefore, are actions that therapists ought to do and work at doing better, not something they have or attain in an absolute sense. This is similar to the process of becoming a good writer. Most good writers are never satisfied with their writing. Instead, they are humbled by it, trying to do better the next time. The same is true of the process of living life well or becoming a good therapist. Both are processes that take a lifetime.

OVERVIEW

Abraham Maslow defined psychotherapy as the search for value. ACT similarly picks up on this theme. Within ACT, actions that get in the way of valued living are conceptualized as obstacles or barriers, and represent *the* problems that warrant clinical attention. Many such obstacles, as we have said, have to do with clients acting in ways to avoid unwanted private experiences. Such actions, in turn, can readily consume one's life. Fr. Alfred D'Souza came to a similar realization, and we share the following comment from him to illustrate that ACT is about fostering the development and growth of fully functioning human beings:

> For a long time it had seemed to me that life was about to begin—real life. But there was always some obstacle in the way. Something to be got through first, some unfinished business, time still to be served, a debt to be paid. Then life would begin. At last it dawned on me that these obstacles were my life.

Within ACT, we certainly do not want our clients to continue to do what has not worked for them, or to act in ways that are unworkable. ACT is about helping clients recognize that their personal histories, thoughts, feelings, and memories are not obstacles to living fully and richly. Instead, they are, in a real sense, part of a life lived well. The real obstacles to living a valued existence tend to be actions directed at not having aspects of our psychological experience. These actions, in turn, get in the way of living and result in needless suffering. An ACT approach to the treatment of anxiety disorders is very much about loosening the grip of such actions on our clients, thus creating space for clients to do what matters most to them. When the fight with anxious thoughts and feelings need not be fought, anxiety and fear are no longer obstacles to living. Ultimately, we hope that our clients' lives will come to be defined by doing more of what they consider worthwhile and what is meaningful to them and be less about trying to control, avoid, or escape from their fears and anxieties.

Focus of ACT for Anxiety Treatment

We noted early on that many obstacles to living are products of human language. We evaluate. We judge. We reflect. We plan. Such actions can be directed at ourselves, the actions of others, and the world in which we live. So much of human experience is laden with verbal-symbolic processes that it is difficult to imagine a nonverbal event in human beings. For instance, humans can quite literally beat themselves up in the present because of what they have done in the past or because of past events that may have occurred outside of their control (e.g., trauma, poor schooling, bad parenting). With the help of language, they struggle with emotional and psychological experiences that they do not wish to have (e.g., anxiety, fear, distressing thoughts, memories) and create doom and gloom about a future that has not yet happened. Acting solely on the basis of such verbally derived constructions, and not actual experiences, unedited and as they are, is both a natural human tendency and a potential trap. This natural tendency, when taken to the extreme, creates many problems in living.

Indeed, anxious clients spend a good amount of time engrossed in numerous battles to not have their unpleasant psychological and emotional experiences. This is both a trap and a fight that cannot be won. This trap, in turn, is what we have referred to as the dark side of language, and specifically the fusion of evaluative language with experience (i.e., the events that language refers to). You can think of this as a generalized tendency to react to one's own evaluations. This tendency, in turn, is often coupled with obvious (or subtle) forms of escape and avoidance so as to not have the negatively evaluated experience. Such actions, when rigidly and inflexibly applied, often get in the way of living and doing what matters most to clients suffering from anxiety disorders. An ACT-based treatment technology seeks to undermine the tendency for anxious clients to respond to their evaluations of the world and their private experiences in that world in a literal and inflexible way.

It is simply notoriously difficult to devote substantial portions of time and effort each day to avoiding and minimizing anxious feelings and thoughts, while also living life fully. Nonetheless, many clients with anxiety problems see such actions as sensible and logical solutions to their problems and expect something similar from psychotherapy (e.g., alleviation of symptoms = restoration of health = being able to live happily ever after). From an ACT perspective, the attempted solutions, however reasonable and sensible, are problems themselves and function to perpetuate anxiety-related suffering and human suffering more generally. For this reason, an ACT approach to the treatment of anxiety-related problems aims at fostering psychological flexibility, experiential acceptance, and ultimately movement in the direction of client values and goals.

ACT Is an Approach to Living Better

At the core, ACT is about helping suffering human beings live better, which means more fully, deeply, and meaningfully. It is about helping our clients use their hands, feet, mouths, and minds in the service of goals and values that they care about. It is about helping our clients make contact with what they truly care about and doing what is important to them. The treatment is not about getting rid of anxious thoughts and feelings, nor is it about teaching clients new or more elegant ways to control their anxiety. Such strategies are common elements of many cognitive behavioral therapies for anxiety problems and only make sense from the perspective that (a) anxiety is a problem, (b) anxiety is a cause of human suffering and other life problems, and (c) to live a life, one must control or reduce anxiety. An acceptance and mindfulness approach to anxiety treatment operates from a different stance:

- Anxiety is what it is, in many instances a perfectly adaptive response and in other instances a nuisance—either way, it is part of being a fully functioning human being.

- Anxiety is part of living rather than a cause of not living.

- To live a valued life, one must be willing to take the totality of human experience along for the ride.

Adopting this posture means that one need not struggle to manage anxiety first in order to live with meaning and purpose second. Rather, one can live with anxiety *and* have a life that is both rich and meaningful. The focus of an ACT approach to anxiety, therefore, is all about fostering the development of fully functioning human beings, with an eye on helping anxious clients live consistently with chosen values. Living life to its fullest, even in the face of difficulty and hardship, is what most persons ultimately associate with a life lived well. To do this, however, requires that clients give up old, unworkable strategies, and instead use their hands and feet in the service of living better, not simply feeling better. The procedures we describe in part 3 are designed to help foster such movement, and are truly about helping our clients spend their precious time each and every day doing what is important to them.

ACT Is Not a New Bag of Tricks

Magicians are renowned for their ability to reach into a bag of tricks and pull out a new illusion. The effectiveness of the illusion, however, depends not on the trick. Rather, it depends on the skill of the magician in the appropriate delivery of the trick to achieve the intended illusion. A magic trick in the hands of someone lacking skills in the art of illusion will likely not produce the intended effect. The same is true of the application of psychosocial treatment technologies, such as the approach we are describing here for those suffering from anxiety and other emotional disorders.

You will recall that ACT is an approach to the alleviation of human suffering and the promotion of human growth and value, one with a sound philosophical, conceptual, and empirical base. ACT also has a relevant treatment technology. Only recently has this technology appeared in the form of treatment manuals and guides (e.g., Hayes, Strosahl, & Wilson, 1999; Hayes & Strosahl, 2004). In chapters 7 through 11, we describe this technology in detail to facilitate your work with anxious clients.

One danger in specifying any treatment in manualized form is that one can lose sight of the approach and rationale for the treatment, and instead get bogged down in the application of the technology and treat the manual like one would a cookbook. We strongly urge you not to fall into this trap for two reasons. First, a technology-focused approach tends to reduce therapists and psychotherapy to the mere application of treatment techniques. Accordingly, therapists are nothing more than technicians. Increasingly, however, we are learning that effective psychotherapy depends on effective therapists, not simply the application of intervention technologies. In our view, you will be much more effective using the treatment technology we describe herein if you also keep your eyes firmly set on the processes you wish to target and the underlying rationale for doing so. Second, a technology-focused approach lends itself to excessive rule following. Rules are not necessarily bad, even in a psychotherapy context. Yet, we know from countless studies that rule-governed behavior tends to result in insensitivity to present contingencies, especially those that may contradict the rule. In a therapy context this means that, by focusing solely on applying the treatment technology just so, therapists may become inflexible and insensitive to the unique needs of clients and the clinical moments that arise during therapy.

The effectiveness of any treatment technology depends to a great extent on the effectiveness of its delivery. This, in turn, requires a thorough understanding of the strategic rationale for use of the technology (i.e., what do you intend to accomplish by using a particular intervention component?), as well as skill in its appropriate delivery. Throughout the treatment sections, you will find descriptions of the techniques and procedures, but also a good bit of information about the conceptual rationale for using them. Take time to understand the rationale for the intervention components we describe, and work to tailor the intervention to the unique concerns and needs of your clients. This individualized approach is good practice anyway, and ought to help you work effectively and meaningfully with your anxious clients using an ACT approach. Remember, ACT is not a bag of tricks!

CORE TREATMENT COMPONENTS AND THERAPIST STRATEGIES

As indicated in chapter 1, one of the best ways to describe the core treatment components of ACT is to break the ACT acronym up into its three functional components: **A**ccept, **C**hoose Directions, and **T**ake Action. In the following sections we provide you with an overview of how the major goals and components of ACT can be captured by this acronym. Apart from competency in understanding the core processes, therapists must also have sufficient technical knowledge in selecting and implementing interventions such as experiential exercises, metaphors, paradoxical strategies, behavioral tasks, and home-based practice. After describing each of the core components, we therefore also describe some competencies and skills that therapists should develop to deliver ACT effectively. There are several therapist postures and skills that are part of typical ACT intervention strategies. These therapist actions also are related to the three major treatment components. Because such postures are transparent, we simply list them under the three core ACT themes in table format. We provide more detailed instructions and examples to guide you in the delivery of specific techniques in the treatment chapters (7 through 11) that follow.

Accept What You Have and Cannot Change

Recall that acceptance is an active process. It is not about passive resignation, nor is it about giving up. Rather, acceptance is about acknowledging and connecting with who we are (the whole package) while recognizing aspects of our lives that can and should be changed and those that need not or cannot be changed. Acceptance is important within ACT because it provides a context for living in and within the world that runs counter to the struggle and control agenda that anxious clients are all too familiar with. It makes space for doing something different than what has been done in the past. To live with purpose and meaning, clients need not first alter unwanted private experiences. Giving up the struggle to do so paves the way for fundamental life change and renewed focus on what can be changed. When clients accept where they are, resisting aspects of their psychological experience becomes unnecessary. Acceptance is an ongoing process that is nurtured and developed within ACT via the following strategies.

Developing Creative Hopelessness

Creative hopelessness is a process that comes early on within ACT. The aim is for the therapist and client to explore the client's former solutions to their problems, with an eye on how well they have worked (both in the short and long term) and whether they are workable at all. Remember, this is not about feeling hopeless. Rather, creative hopelessness is about helping clients make contact with the unworkability of former strategies and solutions to their anxiety-related problems. This process is creative and empowering because it makes space for clients to do something else that may be more workable, while also creating room for clients to act in a manner consistent with what they care about.

The more general objective of this phase is to undermine and weaken the dominance of what may sound like reasonable and socially acceptable solutions to problems (e.g., "Once I feel less anxious, then I will be able to have a more intimate relationship with my partner"), while clarifying how those former solutions are, in fact, problems themselves. In the process, the therapist addresses what the client wants, what the client has tried, and how well those efforts have worked. Therapists need to be mindful of strategies that denote subtle and obvious signs of unwillingness, struggle, and control of anxious thoughts and feelings. Therapists need to alert clients to the consequences of such actions in terms of the client's quality of life, values, and goals.

The following is a brief example of an excerpt from a therapist and client exchange during this stage of therapy. The focus is on understanding what this particular client has done to manage her social anxiety.

Therapist: You've been suffering from anxiety in social situations for some time. Can you tell me what you have tried to do to get over it?

Client: Well, I've tried so many things … I'm not really sure where to begin.

Therapist: How about during a typical week… Tell me some of things you tried last week.

Client: Normally, I just steer clear of people as much as I can. For instance, last week I went grocery shopping at 2 A.M. I also screened all of my phone calls so that I wouldn't get caught off guard not knowing what to say. I'm pretty messed up.

Therapist: How has this worked for you?

Client: Not well. It's hard to get things done when you constantly have to dodge and weave around other people. I feel like such a freak [tearfully]. It is affecting my schoolwork, my job, my whole life. God, I'm twenty-five and haven't had a close relationship with someone other than my family.

Therapist: So, a good part of your day is spent steering through a maze of people so as to avoid…?

Client: Being embarrassed, saying something stupid, and then getting all nervous and panicky. I just want to feel better.

Therapist: So, if I hear you right, you've tried several reasonable strategies to cope with your anxiety. Now, what does your experience tell you about how well these strategies are working for you? Are they helping you live the life you want to have?

Client: Well, sometimes they work, but then the anxiety comes right back again. If I could only get a handle on my anxiety, then I think I would be able to be more normal.

Therapist: Is this what you want out of therapy? A way to control your anxiety, a way to be more normal and like other people?

Client: Yes. I want to be like most other people ... you know, normal.

Therapist: So, if I hear you correctly, you have tried a number of strategies to get a handle on your anxiety, and most of them have not really worked. It also sounds like your mind tells you all sorts of things ... like you are being watched, you might do something embarrassing, that you are a freak, that your life is messed up, that most people aren't like you, and so on. These thoughts or concerns keep coming back to haunt you despite your best efforts to overcome them. And, you are here with me right now still feeling miserable. I'd like you to consider the possibility that the sensible strategies you have tried up this point may never work the way you want them to work. Your mind is telling you they will, but what does your experience tell you about everything you have tried up to this point to get a handle on your anxiety and your life? Is it working? Is this the way you want to live your life?

Client: No, that's why I am here. I feel really stuck.

Creative hopelessness is an ongoing process that is designed to undermine the dominance of evaluative language and its relation with actions that on the surface seem reasonable, but ultimately keep the client stuck and miserable. If done appropriately, creative hopelessness should leave clients with a sense that what they have been doing will not work and cannot work, while also fostering a willingness to abandon the old change agenda and do something new. That new direction as well as the willingness to do something new are the creative parts of hopelessness. The tendency for clients to justify their own behavior in cognitive and emotional terms is also explored early on, as well as throughout treatment. The same is true of efforts to control, suppress, or eliminate unwanted anxious thoughts and feelings. The believability of reasons as causes for action and inaction are addressed via strategic use of therapeutic metaphors and paradoxical statements.

Undermining Reason Giving and Literal Thinking

Recall that many anxious clients tend to justify their own behavior in cognitive and emotional terms. "I cannot fly in planes because I might panic" and "I cannot go out with friends because I might be embarrassed" are but two examples of reasons that implicate undesirable private events as causes of inaction. Such reasonable-sounding reasons usually implicate unwanted thoughts, feelings, physical sensations, and memories as causes and are supported by family, friends, teachers, employers, and the larger social community. Not surprisingly, many anxious clients come to believe their reasons and feel compelled to act accordingly. Consequently, it makes perfect sense for anxious clients to try to control or eliminate the unwanted causes that are connected with inaction or action. Thus, to be able to fly in a plane, one must first get a handle on the panic. This is the more general system that an ACT approach seeks to undermine.

Defusion strategies that weaken the literal meaning of language and its connection with the self and behavioral actions include use of metaphor, stories, and paradoxical statements (e.g., the only way to change is to first accept what *is*). Metaphors are nothing more than stories. Because they cannot be taken literally, they allow clients to make experiential contact with an aspect of their experience that may be frightening for them to contact directly. In so doing, they help create distance between the client and how they are approaching their anxiety, while also opening the door for new solutions to emerge. Studies have shown that figurative metaphorical language is emotionally more meaningful, and hence more likely to impact a person's overt behavior, than straightforward rational-logical talk (Hayes & Wilson, 1994; Samoilov & Goldfried, 2000). Similarly, in a study with preschool children comparing metaphorical with literal relaxation instructions, we found that the children unequivocally preferred metaphors over literal instructions (Heffner, Greco, & Eifert, 2003). This may also be one of the reasons why, for centuries and across different cultures, authors have used fairy tales to teach values ("the moral of the story") to children and adults instead of simply telling their audience what to do or refrain from doing.

The therapeutic goal of defusion strategies is not to confuse clients. Rather, the intent is to weaken the fusion of language, experience, and behavioral actions, particularly when it involves thoughts and feelings that cannot and need not be changed in order to live a life with meaning and purpose. In a sense, the goal is to weaken the dominance of what the mind says "is" or "ought" to be, and instead allow the client to experience directly and fully what is, for what it is, while doing what matters to them. Clients are not their disorders. Anxiety is not bad. One can live richly and meaningfully with a full range of psychological and emotional content.

Experiencing Anxiety with Acceptance

Experiencing anxiety from a kind, open, and accepting posture is probably the last thing that any anxious person would come to expect from a psychosocial intervention. Yet, this posture is precisely the stance that an ACT approach to the treatment of anxiety problems seeks to establish. Acceptance, you will recall, is antithetical to the struggle and control agenda that anxious clients know all too well by the time they enter therapy. At the core, acceptance represents a deliberate and courageous stance on the part of a client to approach aspects of their psychological experience (the good, the bad, and the ugly) as they are, fully and without defense. The goal is not to create priestly clients, but to create fully functioning human beings who are intimately in contact with the world of their experience. Acceptance is about experiencing what is, for what it is, while not acting on the experience to change it—particularly when the experience cannot and need not be changed. Somewhat paradoxically, this stance allows clients to be where they are and who they are, and thus defuses the tendency to do something about their thoughts and feelings.

Please note that developing and nurturing acceptance is an ongoing learning process that requires a good deal of experiential practice and commitment. Mindfulness techniques, including experiential exposure-like exercises, are included throughout the treatment sections as a means to help clients learn to be with anxious thoughts and feelings in an accepting and willing manner and to foster an acceptance posture more generally. As we have stressed, acceptance of anxiety is itself not a therapeutic goal, but a process that frees clients to work toward living consistently in the direction of valued goals.

Table 1 lists a number of therapist strategies and behaviors that can foster the development of greater acceptance and willingness. We have adapted this table from a more comprehensive list provided by Strosahl et al., 2004. These skills are related to inducing creative hopelessness and undermining experiential control, fostering defusion of language from experience, and developing an observer self that is focused on making contact with the present moment in a nonjudgmental fashion.

TABLE 1. THERAPIST (T) STRATEGIES FOR DEVELOPING ACCEPTANCE AND WILLINGNESS

Undermining Experiential Control

- T helps client detect emotional control strategies and examine direct experience instead.

- T helps client make direct contact with paradoxical effect of emotional control strategies.

- T detects client emotional control attempts in session and teaches clients also to detect them.

- T uses concept of "workability" to help clients evaluate costs of experiential avoidance and control efforts.

- T communicates that client is not broken, but is using unworkable strategies.

- T actively encourages client to experiment with giving up the struggle for emotional control and suggests willingness as an alternative.

- T helps client investigate relation between levels of willingness and sense of suffering.

- T helps client make experiential contact with cost of being unwilling to reach valued life goals.

- T uses exercises and metaphors to help client contact willingness—the action—in the presence of difficult material.

- T identifies client's emotional, cognitive, behavioral, or physical barriers to willingness.

- T structures graded steps or exercises for client to practice willingness.

- T models willingness in the therapeutic relationship.

Undermining Cognitive Fusion

- T helps client defuse experience from evaluations and directs attention to the present moment.

- T actively contrasts what the client's mind says will work with what the client's *experience* says is (not) working.

- T uses language tools (e.g., get off "buts"), metaphors, and experiential exercises to create a separation between the client's actual and conceptualized experience.

- T uses various exercises, metaphors, and behavioral tasks to reveal the "hidden" properties of language that can serve as traps and blind alleys for the client.

- T suggests that "attachment" to literal meaning and evaluations of experiences makes willingness difficult to sustain.

- T helps client elucidate the client's own "story" and helps client make contact with the arbitrary nature of causal relationships within the story.

- T helps client make contact with the evaluative and reason-giving properties of the client's story (e.g., *no thing* matters).

- T detects "mindiness" and fusion (e.g., intellectualizing, evaluating, judging, reason-giving) in session and teaches the client to detect such mind games as well.

Developing Observer Self: Getting in Contact with the Present Moment

- T teaches client to just notice events with simple awareness and without evaluating content.

- T helps client separate self-evaluations from the self that evaluates (e.g., "thank your mind for that thought," calling a thought a thought, labeling thoughts or sensations).

- T employs metaphors and mindfulness exercises to help client make contact with self-as-context ("observer self").

- T helps client experiment with "having" and observing these experiences, using willingness as a stance.

- T detects client drifting into past and future, and models coming back to present moment.

Choose Valued Life Directions

The verbal-evaluative traps we have been describing all along, coupled with experiential avoidance and escape, tend to mask clients' ability to choose and follow a life direction that is important to them. An ACT approach is very much about removing these and other blinders to reveal what clients are capable of doing already—namely, defining a life direction (Wilson & Murrell, 2004; Dahl et al., 2004). In fact, when you strip away client concerns about the past, anxieties about undesirable emotional or cognitive content, distress about unwanted bodily states, and the like, what you are left with is a human being with a life that is not working. The overarching aim of ACT is to redirect attention and effort away from futile and costly goals (e.g., diminishing unpleasant thoughts or feelings) toward actions that define, in a real sense, what clients wish their lives to stand for. Everything that we describe within our treatment approach is, at its core, about helping clients clarify how they wish to live their lives, and helping them to do just that. Actions that get in the way of value-driven choices are, therefore, viewed as barriers to living and targets of our therapeutic efforts. These hooks or traps are assessed and brought out on the table throughout treatment, as they can readily get clients sidetracked and stuck back in the same old struggle and control agenda that ultimately brought them into therapy to begin with.

Table 2 lists some therapist strategies and behaviors related to helping clients choose and define their valued directions and their life goals related to such values (see also Strosahl et al., 2004). More details on specific techniques are provided in chapters 9 and 10.

TABLE 2. THERAPIST (T) STRATEGIES FOR CHOOSING AND DEFINING VALUED DIRECTIONS

- T helps client clarify valued life directions by means of values worksheet and other exercises (e.g., Valued Directions and Values Compass worksheets).

- T helps clients commit to what they want their lives to stand for and make therapy about *that*.

- ■   T teaches client to distinguish between values and goals.

- ■   T puts own therapy-relevant values in the room and models their importance.

- ■   T respects client values and, if unable to support them, finds referral or other alternatives.

Take Action

Choosing a valued direction is the first step on the road toward living well. It is an important and necessary step, but choosing is not enough. Ultimately, values are defined by what people do, not simply by what they say they want their lives to stand for. For instance, if a person values being a loving spouse, then we would expect that person to take actions that are consistent with loving behaviors toward their spouse. Saying "I love you" now and then is one such action, but it is not enough. We must show that we love others by what we do with our hands and feet. So many human actions can be plugged into this basic format. Values are defined, in a very real sense, by what we spend our time doing. Coming to terms with this truism can be a painful pill to swallow.

Alcoholics, for instance, exert an enormous amount of time and effort (and money) each day to obtain and ingest alcohol. In a sense, one could say that an alcoholic values drinking and the high that comes along with it. Their lives are consumed by it, and not surprisingly the life of the alcoholic typically suffers as a consequence. The struggle, control, and avoidance trap that many anxious clients find themselves in is similar in many respects to the life of the alcoholic. The lives of anxious persons tend to revolve around their anxieties, fears, and related physical sensations and thoughts, and particularly around not having them. *Judging by what most anxious clients do, one could say that they enter therapy with a life defined by the value of not having anxiety.* Here, it is important to note that anxious clients should not be faulted for acting in this manner. The problem is that the more important facets of their lives typically suffer as a consequence. No anxious client would wish their tombstone epitaph to read, "Jane spent twenty years of her life in the service of not having panic attacks, and died without winning the fight." The approach we describe is designed to help clients get their hearts and minds firmly fixed on what matters to them. This is why we first help clients clarify their values and how they want to live their lives. The second, more important objective is to help them start putting those words into action.

Recall that most value-guided action is not an all-or-none affair (i.e., you achieve it or you don't). Rather, valued living is about making a commitment to take small actions that are consistent with what one cares about. It does not matter whether values focus on being a good parent or a loving spouse, eating well, helping others who are less fortunate, taking care of the environment, or being a good neighbor or citizen. What is important is that clients take actions that move them in the direction of what they value, while recognizing that valued living is a process that has no clear end point.

Living consistently with values, therefore, often requires small actions each and every day. For clients with anxiety disorders, this almost invariably means engaging in behavior that they previously avoided because it was associated with anxiety. These actions, over time, add up to what most people would consider a life lived well. Our experience from working with clients tells us that, over time, anxiety will not be as much of an issue for clients anymore, either because it weakens in frequency or intensity as a result of "naturalistic," value-driven exposure exercises, and/or because it becomes less important to clients relative to the pursuit of goals.

Note that the commitment to engage in small actions on the road to valued living is itself a value. It implies caring and respect for oneself and the courage to live as one would wish to live. To facilitate such movement, behavioral activation is a key component in later sections of the treatment, and we encourage you to implement this approach with coaching, compassionate encouragement, and as much humor as possible. Remember that values are neither good nor bad. They are defined by actions. These actions will be idiosyncratic for each client you see in therapy.

Table 3 lists several therapist strategies and behaviors related to helping clients build patterns of committed action toward valued life goals and for maintaining such action in the face of setbacks and adversity (see also Strosahl et al., 2004).

TABLE 3. THERAPIST (T) STRATEGIES FOR BUILDING PATTERNS OF COMMITTED ACTION

- T helps client build an action plan based upon identified life values.

- T encourages client to take small steps and to look at the quality of committed action.

- T encourages client to move with barriers and to make and keep commitments.

- T uses exercises and nontraditional uses of language to reveal hidden sources of interference to committed actions.

- T integrates slips or relapses into the ongoing process of recommitting to future effective action.

CORE COMPETENCIES IN THE BASIC ACT THERAPEUTIC STANCE

In the previous section, we identified a number of specific competencies and skills that therapists should develop to deliver ACT effectively. The following section describes

basic therapist competencies and behaviors that characterize an ACT-consistent therapeutic stance (see also Strosahl et al., 2004). Like many treatment traditions, ACT
emphasizes the importance of therapist warmth and genuineness, but it also emphasizes
the importance of compassion. This stance is an especially important factor for good
ACT practice. It emerges quite naturally from the core understanding of human suffering from an ACT perspective. When we see our clients trapped by language and patterns of experiential avoidance, we also see ourselves and the traps that generate our
own pain. An "I and thou" perspective is the natural precipitant of this recognition. The
basic psychological stance of the ACT therapist involves being able to make contact
with the "space" from which ACT naturally flows, as well as modeling psychological
flexibility that we seek to help our clients to (re)gain.

What follows here is a summary of core competencies of an ACT therapeutic
stance as outlined by Steven Hayes, Kirk Strosahl, and Kelly Wilson in consultation
with a group of therapist trainers of ACT that we are a part of (a detailed account of
these competencies can be found in Strosahl et al., 2004). Though still in development,
the following features capture much of the essence of an ACT therapeutic posture and
what it means to do ACT therapy. These competencies and postures relate to the core
therapeutic processes, the effective delivery of ACT itself, and all stages and aspects of
the therapy. Therapists should make an effort to return to this section often, as it is
quite easy to fall back on a non-ACT-style therapeutic posture. We encourage you to
spend some time with the material that follows here. Think about it and apply it. Play
with it.

- Being Compassionate—*The therapist realizes that he or she is in the same soup as the
  client and speaks to the client from an equal, vulnerable, genuine, and sharing point of
  view. Consequently, the therapist takes a compassionate and humanizing stance toward
  the client's suffering and avoids criticism, judgment, or taking a one-up position.*

This is by far the most important point, and we cannot overemphasize its significance. It is easy to use the procedures outlined in this book from a dominating, controlling, one-up position rather than from a compassionate, caring, equal-level position.
For instance, therapists can easily slip into using metaphors in an examlike fashion by
testing whether the client "got it." This is not helpful, and clients sense that they are
being put on the spot and in a one-down position. If you sense a lot of resistance from a
client, then you are probably violating this most basic rule. ACT is not about convincing clients that your analysis is the correct one. It is not about replacing one set of beliefs
("Anxiety must be controlled") with another set ("Controlling anxiety doesn't work
and only makes things worse"). It is about making contact with suffering—one human
being to another—so as to help facilitate fundamental change.

- Applying Techniques in a Creative, Flexible Manner—*The therapist tailors interventions to fit the client's language and immediate life experience and avoids the use of
  "canned" ACT interventions. The therapist sequences and applies specific ACT interventions in response to client needs and experiences, and is ready to change course to fit*

those needs at any moment. For instance, new metaphors, experiential exercises, and behavioral tasks are allowed to emerge from the client's own experience and context.

This point is about flexibility and tailoring the intervention to fit the unique needs of your clients—a point we have stressed several times already. Metaphors, for example, are nothing more than stories that can help in not taking the mind literally. They should not be delivered in a canned fashion. Instead, embellish them, tweak them, and modify them as appropriate, depending on the client's responses to them. In fact, clients typically comment on metaphors by expanding or otherwise modifying them. This is a good sign that clients are actively engaged in therapy. Your task as a therapist is to run with such comments and modifications and spin them along the path your client points out to you. Do not fall into the trap of somehow correcting client changes and getting them to revert back to your version or the one you read in this book. Changes made by clients are probably reflective of their experience and, as such, are more valuable and powerful therapeutically than anything you could ever make up yourself.

- Modeling Acceptance and Willingness—*The therapist models acceptance of experience and willingness to hold contradictory or difficult ideas, feelings, memories, and the like without needing to resolve them.*

Many therapeutic traditions see resolution of internal conflict as a goal. Not so with ACT. It is quite natural for human beings to experience multiple contradictory or difficult ideas. Our natural tendency is quite often to seek some sort of resolution. This is unnecessary from an ACT stance. Recall that we are trying to foster experiential openness and willingness in our clients. As such, therapists should model what they are asking of their clients in session. This means that you let clients experience contradictory or difficult ideas for what they are, while resisting the temptation to resolve apparent conflicts for the client. These facets of human experience are quite normal. Difficult ideas need not be interpreted, fixed, or resolved. Help clients experience them for what they are.

- Focusing on Client Experience—*The therapist always brings the issue back to what the client's experience is showing, and does not substitute his or her opinions for that genuine experience.*

Opinions are simply another form of verbal evaluative behavior that can get in the way of experiential knowing. This is particularly important in the context of creative hopelessness, where one goal is to facilitate the client making contact with the unworkability of the change agenda. We want clients to contact fully the experience of their experience, unedited, as it is. We are aiming to foster psychological flexibility and less rule-governed behavior, while promoting more experiential, direct contingency-shaped behavior. Clients already have more than enough opinions about their experiences and what needs to be done about them. We do not need to add to that with more opinions.

- No Arguing, Persuading, or Convincing—*The therapist does not argue with, lecture, coerce, or attempt to convince the client of anything. If you find yourself attempting to change a client's mind, please stop, because you are not doing ACT.*

Remember that ACT is not about who is right or wrong and not about convincing the client that your analysis is somehow superior to the client's. It is not about replacing one rule ("Anxiety must be controlled") with another one ("I can be anxious and do what I want to do"). ACT is much more radical, and it aims at a more fundamental change. ACT questions the dominance of language and rules, particularly when they do not work for an individual. ACT is not about what you think as a therapist. It is about workability—what works for the client and what does not. It is about not buying into anyone's mindiness, including that of the therapist. This is why ACT therapists say seemingly odd things like, "Don't believe what I tell you" or "Don't listen to my mind." Instead, we want clients to pay attention to their own experiences, because all of the solutions are right there. So when you find yourself lecturing, or even arguing with your clients trying to convince them of anything, you are on the wrong track. Do not try to "sell" ACT—there is no need for that. Instead, return to the client's experience with past solutions and let them experience how well those solutions worked. Also, ask whether a particular solution that clients are considering now is likely to bring them closer to their life goals or farther away from them.

- No Explanations or "Cognitive Insight"—*The therapist does not generally explain the "meaning" of paradoxes or metaphors to develop insight.*

Remember that one goal of using paradox and metaphor is to loosen rigid and inflexible verbal regulation of client behavior. Explanations are simply more verbal behavior that can undermine the process of loosening verbal regulation. What we would like to see is a client relating to their experiences differently via paradox and metaphor. No detailed explanation of the metaphors is required for this to happen. It is sufficient for the therapist and client to discuss the client's reactions to the metaphor and its message for them. After clients see a point, it is also common to help them state it verbally. Insight, or a sense of distance and perspective, may come as clients discover that their quality of life is starting to improve when they don't always do what their mind tells them to do. However, such insight is not a requirement for meaningful change to come about.

- Therapist Self-Disclosure—*The therapist is willing to self-disclose about personal issues when it illustrates a therapeutic point.*

This point should be obvious to most seasoned therapists. Judicious use of self-disclosure helps to convey to the client that you, as a therapist, are human and hence suffer and at times struggle. This, by the way, may include disclosure about your experiences in session that occur as a function of what the client may say or do. For instance, you may experience certain thoughts or emotions as a function of what a client says or does in therapy. Depending on the context, it may be appropriate to acknowledge that experience as it is (e.g., "I am experiencing sadness in response to what you just said…"). Such disclosure can help foster a close therapeutic working relationship, while modeling the appropriateness of being honest and open about oneself and one's own experiences and personal history.

- ■ Focus on Clinically Relevant Behavior—*ACT-relevant processes are recognized in the moment and, where appropriate, are directly targeted in the context of the therapeutic relationship.*

It goes without saying that clients seek therapy because of problems they are having in the world outside of therapy. They do not normally seek therapy because of problems that occur in therapy. Nonetheless, it is easy for therapists to focus on problems clients are having outside of therapy, while failing to see clinically relevant behaviors and processes as they show up during therapy. Some client actions in session are clinically relevant and, when they occur, therapists should recognize and support them. The same is true of clinically relevant processes that you wish to influence. This approach is characteristic of Functional Analytic Psychotherapy (FAP; Kohlenberg & Tsai, 1991), and it is common for ACT therapists to use FAP methods to target clinically relevant behaviors that occur in session. Fusion, evaluation, avoidance, escape, and reason giving are a few general processes that will likely show up in session as you work with anxious clients. There is no better way to shape and influence such clinically relevant behavior and processes than doing so directly, gently, and in the moment when they occur during therapy (for a more detailed description of techniques, see Kohlenberg & Tsai, 1991).

OVERVIEW OF THE TREATMENT PROGRAM

Before outlining the treatment program in the chapters that follow, let us provide you with an overview of the goals and main components of the program on a session-by-session basis.

The ACT treatment program for anxiety disorders we outline in this book consists of twelve sessions lasting approximately one hour each. By placing the treatment in this twelve-session format, with suggested time limits for the various sections, we do not wish to imply that you must implement the program that way. Both number of sessions and the suggested time limits for sections are meant to be a guide. With some clients you might be able to move a bit faster, whereas with others you may need more sessions and more time to accomplish what you and your client need to do. There is nothing wrong with taking longer, and we caution you not to rush through the treatment. Humans are organisms with a history. The processes that are being worked on here have long histories of development that cannot be undone quickly or superficially. Also, short of a lobotomy, humans do not get rid of previously established automatic functions so much as they add new ones (Wilson & Roberts, 2002). It takes time for this new learning to occur and consolidate.

Session 1 seeks to provide clients with a general understanding of the nature and purpose of anxiety and what can make anxiety become disordered. The session also introduces clients to the active, experiential, and participatory nature of this treatment and its emphasis on living a rich and meaningful life rather than focusing on anxiety reduction.

Sessions 2 and 3 review and evaluate the strategies clients have used in the past to cope with anxiety. The goal is to undermine the client's anxiety control agenda and create an ACT-specific treatment motivation (creative hopelessness) by letting clients experience (a) the unworkability and futility of past avoidance and control efforts and (b) that nothing will change unless clients are willing to do something differently about and with their anxiety, and hence how they are living their lives. Session 3 introduces the notion of value-driven behavior as an alternative to managing anxiety.

Sessions 4 and 5 focus on acceptance and mindfulness as ways of learning to observe unwanted anxiety-related responses fully for what they are. The goal is to provide clients with more response options when experiencing anxiety—that is, to broaden the client's current narrow set of responses (e.g., escape, avoidance, suppression) so as to make responding more flexible. Clients also learn to differentiate what they can control from what they cannot control in their lives. Sessions 4 and 5 continue to develop and affirm valued living as an alternative to the anxiety management and control agenda. This alternative agenda functions to help clients focus on what really matters in their lives by choosing valued directions and by identifying specific goals as well as potential barriers. In sum, Sessions 1 through 5 are designed to create a more flexible acceptance-oriented context that sets the stage for the remaining treatment sessions, where clients learn to be and move with anxiety from a mindful observer perspective while engaging in value-driven action in their natural environment.

Sessions 6 and 7 introduce in-session experiential exposure exercises, defusion, value-guided action, and making commitments to move in valued life directions. In-session exposure exercises are designed to let clients practice mindful observation, acceptance, and cognitive defusion in the presence of anxiety-related responses. They are to be done initially in a safe environment with the guidance of the therapist. Cognitive defusion techniques do not target the content or validity of clients' negative evaluations (of themselves, their reactions, thoughts, histories, etc.), only the process of evaluating itself. That is, these techniques teach clients to respond to their experience as it is rather than to the evaluation of their experience. The goal of these in-session exercises is to foster a new stance when anxiety-related responses show up while engaging in real-life client-chosen activities that move them in the direction of their values. Anxiety reduction is not a stated goal. It is, however, likely to occur as a by-product of in-session and between-session exercises.

The remaining portions of treatment (Session 8 and beyond) focus on movement forward and doing. Behavioral activation is used here to assist clients in doing what matters most to them, with particular focus on making and keeping value-guided commitments, as well as moving with barriers to valued action. Although our treatment program differs in several important respects from the mindfulness-based cognitive therapy program for depression developed by Segal and colleagues (2002), one of the core skills to be learned in the ACT program is very similar to theirs: how to step out of and stay out of self-perpetuating and self-defeating emotional, cognitive, and behavioral avoidance routines:

> Letting go means relinquishing involvement in these routines, freeing one-self of the aversion driving the [routines]—*it is the continued attempts to escape or avoid unhappiness, or to achieve happiness, that keep the negative cycles turning. The aim of the program is freedom*, not happiness, relaxation, and so on, although these may well be welcome by-products. (Segel et al., 2002, p. 91)

Summary: ACT as a Core Process Approach

There is a clear link between ACT components and core clinical processes and targets for treatment. For this reason, we reemphasize that ACT is not another or more sophis-ticated bag of tricks that contains lots of nifty techniques such as cute metaphors and playing with Chinese finger traps. It is fundamentally different because its choice of treatment targets is based on identified dysfunctional processes that underlie anxiety disorders and psychological suffering more generally. Rather than narrowly focusing on symptom reduction and control, ACT instead focuses on life-expanding targets: weak-ening experiential avoidance and client efforts to reduce or control their anxiety, loos-ening the dominance of verbal and evaluative forms of behavior, promoting psychological and experiential flexibility, and fostering actions that move clients in the direction of their values. This is what ACT therapists mean when they say in an uncan-nily simple fashion, "ACT treatment is not about anxiety symptoms—it's about life and what the client wants it to stand for."

CHAPTER 7

Psychoeducation and Treatment Orientation

Session 1

Your life is a sacred journey. And it is about change, growth, discovery, movement, transformation, continuously expanding your vision of what is possible, stretching your soul, learning to see clearly and deeply, listening to your intuition, taking courageous challenges at every step along the way. You are on the path ... exactly where you are meant to be right now... And from here, you can only go forward, shaping your life story into a magnificent tale of triumph, of healing, of courage, of beauty, of wisdom, of power, of dignity, and of love.

—Caroline Adams

GOALS AND THEME

Session 1 has four goals: (1) to establish good rapport with clients; (2) to provide clients with a general understanding about the nature and function of anxiety; (3) to introduce clients to the active, experiential, and participatory nature of this treatment; and (4) to gently introduce value-driven action in real life as the primary treatment goal, while being sensitive to the goals of clients which, at this stage, probably still focus on anxiety reduction and symptom control.

This first session is designed to lay the groundwork for what will come. A good portion of it is devoted to developing rapport and dispelling common misconceptions about fear, anxiety, and psychotherapy more generally (e.g., anxiety is bad, psychotherapy is about fixing symptoms). Anxiety and fear are adaptive in many circumstances, and they need not be monsters. They are part of the totality of human experience and only become monsters, and hence disordered, when we act to avoid and escape from them. It follows that the goal of this treatment is about living a rich and meaningful life, fully and without defense.

Therapy is framed as an opportunity to learn and practice new and more flexible ways of responding when experiencing anxiety. The basic idea is for clients to learn ways of no longer letting anxiety be an obstacle to doing what they want to do. Accordingly, the therapist commits to making treatment all about what clients really care about and what matters most in clients' lives—it is about helping clients accept what needs to be accepted and change what can be changed to make meaningful changes and life improvements.

Session Outline

1. Introductory Information (5 min.)

2. Initial Problem Discussion (5 min.)
   - Ratings of Distress and Disablement form

3. Nature and Function of Normal Fear and Anxiety (15 min.)
   - What Are Fear and Anxiety?
   - What Is the Purpose of Anxiety—Is It Good for Anything?
   - Are Anxiety and Fear Dangerous?
   - How Pervasive Are Problems with Anxiety and Fear?

4. How Has Anxiety Become a Problem in the Client's Life? (10 min.)

5. Treatment Focus/Goal and Therapist Commitment (10 min.)

6. Acquisition of New Skills Through Direct Experience (5 min.)

7. Centering Exercise (5 min.)

8. Rationale for Experiential Life Enhancement Exercises (5 min.)

   ■ Experiential Monitoring Forms

9. Session Materials and Handouts

   ■ Ratings of Distress and Disablement form

   ■ Living in Full Experience (LIFE) form

   ■ Daily ACT Ratings form

Agenda

1. Introductory Information (5 min.)

Spend a few moments with general introductions and procedures, covering the following issues:

■ Initial discomfort is natural and usually subsides as the client becomes familiar with the process of therapy.

■ All information will be kept confidential, although you are obligated to inform when a client poses a danger to self or others; also indicate whether sessions will be audio- and videotaped for purposes of supervision and training.

■ Provide client with twenty-four-hour emergency numbers.

2. Initial Problem Discussion (5 min.)

At this point, the therapist should refer to the information gathered from the client's initial contact or intake form and ask them what primarily brought them to therapy. Ask clients about the area of fear and anxiety that is currently most distressing and disabling and has been a major concern for at least a month. Ask clients to describe a recent episode of fear or panic attacks, phobic anticipation or worry about events in the future, and avoidance or escape behavior in relation to the episode. Avoid lengthy symptom descriptions or presentations of the history of their disorders.

Discuss each of the main anxiety domains (social phobia, post-traumatic stress disorder, panic disorder/agoraphobia, generalized anxiety disorder, specific phobias, obsessive-compulsive disorder) with your clients using lay descriptions of the major anxiety disorders rather than the *DSM* labels. Focus on how much they are distressed by each one and how much each one interferes with their life functioning, using the 0 to 8 scale shown below (the form is also available on the enclosed CD). Facilitate client ratings of distress and disablement by prompting them to consider issues such as how much of the day they are preoccupied with a specific set of anxiety problems, how much their daily life is influenced by anxiety problems, how much they are prevented from doing what they want to do because of anxiety, and how frequently they experience acute anxiety and fear in relation to each area of anxiety. Therapists should write the numeric ratings on the form rather than handing it to clients.

RATINGS OF DISTRESS AND DISABLEMENT

0	1	2	3	4	5	6	7	8
Not at all		Mildly		Moderately		Strongly		Extremely

Domain	Distress (0–8)	Disablement (0–8)
Social Anxiety	_____	_____
Post-traumatic stress disorder	_____	_____
Panic disorder/agoraphobia	_____	_____
Generalized anxiety disorder	_____	_____
Obsessions and compulsions	_____	_____
Specific phobias	_____	_____

3. Nature and Function of Normal Fear and Anxiety (15 min.)

The purpose of this section is to help clients understand the nature and function of normal anxiety and what can make anxiety become "disordered." Therapists should explain to clients that this early part of therapy will be fairly "educational," meaning that you will be talking and explaining a lot and looking for input from the client as you go along. Below we only summarize the information to be covered in this section. Please refer to chapter 2 for a more detailed account of these topics.

Start by asking the client to describe what fear, or being afraid, is like for them. Here you will be looking for three components that we think of as comprising the emotions fear and anxiety, namely physiological sensations (e.g., heart flutters, sweating, dizziness, blurred vision, shortness of breath, tension), cognitive aspects (or what clients think when they are afraid), and overt behavior (i.e., what clients do during and immediately following an episode of fear or anxiety, such as escape or avoidance). For a more detailed account of this "triple-response mode" view of anxiety, see Eifert and Wilson (1991).

What Are Fear and Anxiety?

Recall that fear is characterized by an abrupt and acute surge of the sympathetic branch of the autonomic nervous system, accompanied by wide-ranging and intense physiological sensations (e.g., increased perspiration, rapid heartbeat, breathlessness, dizziness) and a powerful action tendency to fight or flee from perceived or real environmental and bodily signs of threat or danger (see Barlow, 2002). Fear is a present-oriented mood state that occurs in response to real or imagined danger or threat. In many circumstances, fear is perfectly adaptive because it motivates and mobilizes us to take action. Anxiety, by contrast, is a future-oriented mood state that is accompanied by anxious apprehension, worry, and heightened and sustained activity of the sympathetic nervous system (e.g., increased muscle tension, chest tightness). We are typically anxious about something that may happen in the near or distant future.

Use the client's descriptions of their fear and anxiety experience to outline the difference between fear and anxiety. Have them take an example of their fear and turn it into anxiety and vice versa. For instance, a panic attack is a good example of fear, whereas worry about a future attack represents anxiety. The response one might experience while recalling a traumatic memory may be close to fear, whereas worry that the memory might resurface again characterizes anxiety. Worry about a house fire is anxiety, whereas being in your home while it is burning to the ground is fear. The reaction to seeing a bear in the woods is fear, whereas worrying about the possibility of seeing a bear in the woods at some later date is anxiety.

What Is the Purpose of Anxiety—Is It Good for Anything?

Most clients with anxiety problems will have a hard time thinking about the purpose of anxiety, let alone answering the question of what it may be good for. After all, anxiety is aversive, and aversive events cause suffering, right? Your client's own pain and suffering over their anxiety will tell them as much. So they may rightly ask, how could anxiety be good for anything?

Take a moment to explore the practical benefits of anxiety and fear. Ask clients whether they can think of instances in their lives where they or someone close to them experienced fear and this reaction, in turn, helped them stay alive, safe, and out of trouble. Most clients will be able to remember at least one of those situations. If not, you can give one or two examples from your own life. The examples will probably show that fear made them take some type of defensive or offensive action when their health or safety appeared to be threatened. This can help clients discover that responding to real threats with fear, and at times anxiety, allows appropriate action. Both tendencies have worked well for us as individuals and as a species because without such fear-induced actions, we would probably not have survived.

Also, the beneficial effects of moderate amounts of anxiety and worry have been known for a long time (Yerkes & Dodson, 1908). These emotions help motivate us to respond to real and potential threats, and to take action to manage our day-to-day lives (e.g., health, job, future tasks/plans). In this sense, fear and anxiety are motivational. Note also that the three components of fear and anxiety (physical sensations, thinking, and doing) are not unusual or disordered—we feel, think, and do things all the time. It would be hard to imagine living without these three aspects of human experience.

Are Anxiety and Fear Dangerous?

To address the common question of whether anxiety and fear are dangerous, return to the discussion on the adaptive benefits of fear and anxiety. Though the temptation may be great, do not simply reply with no to this question and move on. Remember that most clients have come to view anxiety and fear as dangerous in some way. For this reason, it is important to reiterate that there is nothing disordered about emotions such as anxiety and fear. They are perfectly adaptive and are not dangerous by themselves. We all have the human potential within us to be extremely anxious, fearful, and sad. We also have the potential to be joyous, full of life, and at peace with ourselves and the world we live in.

Anxiety and fear typically become dangerous if we are unwilling to experience them, and thus live in the service of our avoidance of this facet of what it means to be a fully functioning human being. Hence the danger of anxiety and fear is not that we have them or that we have too much of them. Anxiety and fear become dangerous when we let such emotions rule our lives. As a consequence, we fail to live. We compromise what is truly important in our lives. And, we let anxiety and fear come to define who we are and what we are about.

How Pervasive Are Problems with Anxiety and Fear?

Many clients with anxiety disorders feel that they are alone with their problems. Therapists should therefore point out that anxiety disorders are among the most prevalent psychological disorders, affecting as much as 25 percent of the general population at some point in their lifetime (Eaton, Dryman, & Weissman, 1991; Kessler et al., 1994). Inform clients that we typically learn the processes that contribute to such disorders (i.e., avoidance, escape, control tendencies to manage unpleasant emotions) early on in life. For instance, as kids we learn to avoid touching a red-hot stove because it hurts. We may have learned this the hard way or by listening to our parents or caregivers warning us about the consequences.

We are socialized to use physical and psychological pain and suffering as reasonable reasons for our behavior and that of others. For instance, it is acceptable to miss a day at work or school for feeling ill. We also learn to apply the very same management strategies to our thoughts, memories, and emotions that are unpleasant or painful. Yet, those sensible strategies of dealing with the hot stove and other sources of real harm and pain do not work well when applied to our emotions. We cannot avoid feelings of anxiety and fear in the same way that we keep our hands away from the hot stove. Ask clients whether they can turn their emotions on or off in the same way that they can move their hand on or off a hot stove. Ask clients whether they can make themselves feel one way or another just because they want to. Ask clients whether they have noticed that their feelings go with them no matter where they run to. Could it be that we cannot escape or avoid our feelings of anxiety, apprehension, and insecurity because they are simply part of us? Remember, "You can run, but you can't hide from yourself!"

4. How Has Anxiety Become a Problem in the Client's Life? (10 min.)

At this point, therapists should bring the discussion to the important question of what can make normal anxiety problematic or disordered. Rather than simply explaining the issue to clients, we suggest letting clients explore how anxiety or fear has become a problem in their own lives. Ask clients to look for one obvious example of how anxiety-related avoidance has become a problem in their lives, and how such avoidance may have narrowed their life space (what they do). Consistent with the model we outlined in chapters 3 to 5, ask clients to evaluate patterns of avoidance that are designed to prevent them from feeling anxious or afraid or to prevent them from thinking about anxious or disturbing thoughts, as well as any action following anxiety and fear that is geared to manage such thoughts and emotions. Below is a short clinical excerpt illustrating avoidance of the possibility of experiencing anxiety and the consequences of such avoidance for the client.

Therapist: Can you tell me about a recent example where you experienced strong feelings of anxiety?

Client: Well, the other day my friends asked me to go out with them to see a new movie. I really wanted to go, but then I got all anxious about being in a dark movie theater with lots of people.

Therapist: So, it sounds like you really love movies and that seeing movies is important for you.

Client: Oh yes, I am sort of a movie buff.

Therapist: I also get this sense that you didn't end up going out to see the movie. Am I right?

Client: Yup. I told them that I wasn't feeling well—like a cold. I wasn't really sick or anything like that, but they bought the story.

Therapist: What did you end up doing that night?

Client: I stayed home alone feeling miserable about myself and why I can't just be like other, normal people.

Therapist: Hmm … so even though you were not sick, you ended up spending the night feeling "sick."

Client: [*long pause*] Yes, this is usually what happens to me.

At some point during such discussions, clients typically say that their biggest problem is that they simply have too much anxiety and that this anxiety is paralyzing them. Therapists should not argue with clients about this (or indeed any other) issue. Instead, you could agree that too much fear or anxiety can indeed impede one's ability to take productive action. Even animals don't do much under extreme fear. Yet there is one important difference between humans and animals that has to do with language. Humans, unlike other animals, can get caught up in a struggle with their own emotions in an effort not to have them. This creates a whole set of additional problems that animals do not have because they are not verbal beings.

This struggle takes much effort, and effort directed at struggling to minimize or prevent anxiety and fear is effort not invested in other valued life activities. Humans end up avoiding people, places, activities, and situations that might lead to anxious and fearful feelings. They may even use and come to rely on substances to minimize the occurrence of such feelings. Humans also will escape from situations during unpleasant emotional states. Thus, when humans quite literally live a life focused on trying not to have anxiety and fear—the unwanted bodily sensations, thoughts, past memories, and worries about the future—we begin to talk about the shift from normal anxiety and fear to disordered anxiety and fear.

This may also be an opportune time to let your client know that there are many people out there who regularly experience panic attacks or high levels of anxiety in various settings but who do not develop panic or another anxiety disorder. Studies have found that these people do not get caught up in a struggle with their anxiety. They also do not devote increasingly larger portions of their life energy and space to the task of avoiding or getting rid of anxiety. They have learned to let their anxiety be *and* continue to live their lives and do what is really important to them.

At this point, therapists need not delve any further into these issues. The focus of this discussion should simply be on what the client is doing to manage anxiety and fear, and as a consequence what they are not doing by way of living fully and consistently with what they truly care about in their life. In Sessions 2 and 3, there will be time to examine in greater detail additional examples of how efforts to control anxiety have worked and what effect they have had on the client's life, including more subtle patterns of avoidance and escape. This analysis serves as a stepping-stone to explore alternative ways of dealing with anxiety by letting go of the agenda that anxiety needs to be dealt with, that symptoms need to be gotten rid of, or that there is a quick solution or cure.

5. Treatment Focus/Goal and Therapist Commitment (10 min.)

At some point in this session, clients will invariably ask, "What about my anxiety? Will it ever go away, or can you at least help me reduce it or control it?" *We strongly recommend that therapists do not say things like, "Our goal is not anxiety reduction and symptom control."* Such a statement would almost certainly be inaccurate from the client's perspective and is not consistent with ACT. At this stage, the client's goal probably *is* still anxiety reduction and symptom control, so therapists cannot simply say that anxiety control is not "our" goal. Although you are planting important seeds in this session about how anxiety control efforts have backfired in the client's life, it is essential that clients have a chance to experience fully the costs and futility of anxiety control and avoidance efforts. This is indeed the very purpose of the numerous experiential exercises in the next few sessions. Simply telling clients what is not *your* goal could seriously alienate and overwhelm clients at this early stage and result in dropout.

Instead of ruling out anxiety control and reduction—which incidentally may very well occur even if it is not targeted—therapists should frame therapy as an opportunity for clients to learn and practice new and more flexible ways of responding when they experience anxiety. The basic idea is for clients to learn ways of no longer letting anxiety be in the way of doing what they want to do. Using the example of having to practice to learn any new skill (e.g., playing an instrument, playing sports), tell clients that new learning can only occur though experience, not through talking or thinking. Accordingly, you will guide clients through this process of experiencing their fear, worries, and anxiety for what they are rather than what their mind tells them they are. Any questions and discussion about treatment goals is a good opportunity for you as a therapist to state your treatment values and make a commitment to the client right in this first session. For example, "Jane, I want treatment to be all about what you really care about and what matters most in your life. I will do whatever I can to help you accept what needs to be accepted and change what you can change to make improvements and meaningful changes in your life … the place that matters most to you!"

Let clients know that apart from doing exercises in the session, the major component of treatment is for them to engage in activities and exercises at home and elsewhere between sessions. In-session exercises are merely designed to help prepare clients for making important life-enhancing improvements outside of session, where it really counts—in their daily lives! These exercises are focused opportunities for clients to do something different from what they have been doing; namely to face what their mind and body are doing during fear and anxiety in a gradual fashion so as to learn new ways of responding to their own responses. Incidentally, we do not use the term *homework* because it has negative connotations (i.e., having to do it, usually because someone other than the student or client requests that it be done). Instead, we prefer to refer to such assignments as *experiential life enhancement exercises*. Point out to clients that such exercises are not arbitrary but will involve activities that are designed to bring them closer to goals that are really important to them. The client is ultimately responsible for making the choice to do such exercises and is more likely to do so if they are perceived as freely chosen and consistent with what matters to them.

Inform clients that treatment is highly experiential and that their success will depend on how much they put into it. This point may require some elaboration, particularly for clients who are unfamiliar with psychotherapy or are seeking solutions where they can take a passive role and be "fixed" by the therapist. Relying on over-the-counter and prescription medications is an example of this passive process. Medications, when taken appropriately, act on our bodies to do what they are designed to do. They require little effort to bring about the desired effects, apart from the act of taking the medication.

Yet there are no medications that can produce a full, rich, and meaningful life. ACT is about changing how clients relate with themselves, including their fears, anxieties, and worries. It is about living better. To get there requires commitment and effort. Indeed, commitment to treatment is critical. Issues will come up that are difficult for your clients. They may even feel a bit worse for a time, before getting better. After all, your clients probably know deep down that things are not working. Otherwise they would not be in the room with you. What you are asking clients to do is choose to give treatment a chance and to suspend their agenda of "getting cured" and getting rid of symptoms. You are not asking clients to will anything. They need only be willing to play the unique deck of cards that life has dealt them (Linehan, 1993).

6. Acquisition of New Skills Through Direct Experience (5 min.)

This is a tough one for clients to grasp at first, so a few examples will be helpful. One easy example is learning how to ride a bike. Most of us have learned how to ride a bike. How exactly did we do that? Did we learn to ride by hearing someone describe how to ride a bike, watching a video, or reading a book? For most of us, the answer on all three counts would be no. Rather, riding a bike required direct hands-on riding experience on a bicycle, and good riding required many hours of practice and a willingness to fall and get scratched up, bumped, and bruised along the way. And when we fell, we got right back on and tried again. There is no other way to learn how to ride a bike than through such direct experience—and even experienced riders continue to fall once in a while. There are many other examples in life that more or less follow this principle (e.g., learning to hit a baseball, swim, drive a car, be a good parent, teacher, employee, or friend). There is no substitute for direct experience in such cases.

Words alone are no replacement for direct experience with the world. For example, hearing about a beautiful sunset on a windswept beach, with the sounds of birds and the smell and feel of a gentle sea breeze on one's face is good, but does not compare to the experience of actually being there on the beach at that moment. This, of course, assumes that we are fully present with our direct experiences as they are, even now during therapy. Being present is difficult given the fast-paced lives that many of us lead nowadays. Take, for example, eating a meal while reading or watching the TV, taking a morning shower while thinking about what you will wear and what you have to do that day, driving while talking on a cell phone, and so on. If the goal is eating, experiencing a relaxing shower, or the experience of driving, then do each by itself without doing anything else. Otherwise each activity is diminished because you are not fully present with those events and those events alone.

Tell clients that you would like to start each session with a mindfulness or focusing ("centering") exercise. The purpose of these exercises is to help them be more ready for new experiences and become better at just noticing what they experience. In this first session, you could finish with such an exercise.

7. Centering Exercise (5 min.)*

This little exercise will help clients focus on where they are right now and why they are here. This exercise should take about five minutes to complete. Just like with any other exercise or activity, before you start, ask clients whether they are willing to do it. We suggest that therapists read the instructions to clients in a slow and soft fashion.

1. Go ahead and get in a comfortable position in your chair. Sit upright with your feet flat on the floor, your arms and legs uncrossed, and your hands resting in your lap. Allow your eyes to close gently [pause 10 seconds]. Take a couple of gentle breaths: in … and out—in … and out. Notice the sound and feel of your own breath as you breathe in [pause] and out [pause 10 seconds].

2. Now turn your attention to being inside this room. Notice any sounds that may occur inside the room [pause] and outside [pause 10 seconds]. Notice how you are sitting in your chair [pause 10 seconds]. Focus on the place where your body touches the chair. What are the sensations there? How does it feel to sit where you sit? [pause 10 seconds] Next, notice the places where your body touches itself [pause 10 seconds]. Notice the spot where your hands touch your legs. How do your feet feel in the position that they are in? [pause 10 seconds] What sensations can you notice in the rest of your body? If you feel any sensations in your body, just notice them and acknowledge their presence [pause 10 seconds]. Also notice how they may, by themselves, change or shift from moment to moment. Do not try to change them [pause 10 seconds].

3. Now let yourself be in this room. See if you can feel the investment of you and I in this room—what we are here for [pause 10 seconds]. If you are thinking this sounds weird, just notice that and come back to the sense of integrity in this room. Be aware of the value that you and I are

* We gratefully acknowledge the suggestions by Kelly Wilson and Amy Murrell (University of Mississippi) for the wording of this centering exercise.

serving by being here [pause 10 seconds]. See if you can allow yourself to be present with what you are afraid of. Notice any doubts, reservations, fears, and worries [pause 10 seconds]. See if you can just notice them, acknowledge their presence, and make some space for them [pause 10 seconds]. You don't need to make them go away or work on them [pause 10 seconds]. Now see if for just a moment you can be present with your values and commitments. Why are you here? Where do you want to go? What do you want to do? [pause 10 seconds]

4. Then, when you are ready, let go of those thoughts and gradually widen your attention to take in the sounds around you [pause 10 seconds] and slowly open your eyes with the intention to bring this awareness to the present moment and the rest of the day.

8. Rationale for Experiential Life Enhancement Exercises (5 min.)

It is useful to initiate some form of self-monitoring between this first session and the next. Self-monitoring serves several functions for both the therapist and client. For the therapist, self-monitoring assignments allow assessment of progress in therapy, and provide a better window on a client's daily experiences in and within the world outside of therapy. Resulting data can be summarized quantitatively (e.g., via charts, frequencies, means) and more qualitatively for the client. From the client's perspective, self-monitoring can help make patterns of experiential avoidance and inaction more obvious. Just as we want our clients to show up in therapy, we also want them to show up in their daily lives. Outside the session, self-monitoring and experiential exercises function to promote showing up by increasing contact with patterns of inaction that are getting in the way of valued living and life experiences that are of value to the client. It is, therefore, important to end this first session with a clear rationale for self-monitoring and experiential life enhancement exercises. Both forms introduced at the end of this session are also on the CD and used throughout the entire treatment.

Experiential Monitoring Forms

Living in Full Experience (LIFE).   We designed a worksheet—Living in Full Experience (LIFE)—that can be used to monitor and track contexts where anxiety and fear show up, associated experiences (thoughts, physical sensations, and behaviors), client willingness to have those experiences, and how the client's reactions to them are compromising and interfering with their values and goals. The acronym LIFE is not accidental; it's a deliberate effort to frame this exercise in terms of what really counts: living. It is best that you go over this form with the client before the end of the session. Ask them to complete this form shortly after every episode where unwanted thoughts, sensations, or feelings occur. Provide enough copies so that multiple daily episodes can be documented. Tell the client that you would like to see their records at the beginning of the next session and those that follow. Ask the client for permission to do so—make it their choice as part of their commitment to therapy.

Daily ACT Ratings.   Also ask clients to complete the Daily ACT Ratings form at the end of every day by making a rating on a scale from 0 (not at all) to 10 (extreme amount) of how upset and distressed over anxiety clients were that day, how much effort they put into making anxious feelings or thoughts go away that day, to what degree they would consider that day be part of a vital, workable way of living, and how much they engaged in behaviors that are in accord with their values and life goals. These ratings will be collected throughout treatment as a process and outcome measure rather than a therapeutic tool. We expanded this rating form and adapted it for clients with anxiety disorders from a shorter Daily Willingness Diary introduced by Hayes, Strosahl, and Wilson (1999).

LIVING IN FULL EXPERIENCE—THE LIFE FORM

A Life Enhancement Exercise

Date: _____ / _____ / _____   Time: _____ A.M./P.M.

Check off any sensations you experienced just now:

☐ Dizziness   ☐ Sense of unreality   ☐ Feeling of choking
☐ Breathlessness   ☐ Sweatiness   ☐ Nausea
☐ Fast heartbeat   ☐ Hot/cold flashes   ☐ Neck/muscle tension
☐ Blurred vision   ☐ Chest tightness/pain   ☐ Detachment from self
☐ Tingling/numbness   ☐ Trembling/shaking

Check what emotion best describes your experience of these sensations (pick one):

☐ Fear   ☐ Anxiety   ☐ Depression   ☐ Other: _____

Now rate how strongly you felt this emotion/feeling (circle number):

0	1	2	3	4	5	6	7	8

Mild/Weak   Moderate   Extremely Intense

Now rate how willing you were to have these sensations/feelings without acting on them (e.g., to manage them, get rid of them, suppress them, run from them):

0	1	2	3	4	5	6	7	8

Extremely Willing   Moderate   Completely Unwilling

Describe *where you were* when these sensations occurred: _____
_____

Describe *what you were doing* when these sensations occurred: _____
_____

Describe *what your mind was telling you* about the sensations/feelings: _____
_____

Describe *what you did* (if anything) about the sensations/feelings: _____
_____

If you did anything about the sensations or feelings, *did it get in the way of anything* you really value or care about? If so, describe what that was here: _____
_____
_____

DAILY ACT RATINGS

Life Enhancement Exercise Record Form

At the end of each day, please make a rating for each of the following four questions using the scale below. Ratings for each question can range from 0 (not at all) to 10 (extreme amount):

| 0 | 1 | 2 | 3 | 4 | 5 | 6 | 7 | 8 | 9 | 10 |

None / Not at all   Extreme amount

Suffering: How upset and distressed over anxiety were you today overall? _____

Struggle: How much effort did you put into making anxiety-related feelings or thoughts go away today (for example, by suppressing them; distracting yourself; reassuring yourself or seeking reassurance from someone else)? _____

Workability: If life in general were like today, to what degree would today be part of a vital, workable way of living for you? _____

Valued Action: How much have you engaged in behaviors (actions) today that accord with your values and life goals? _____

Day	Suffering 0–10	Struggle 0–10	Workability 0–10	Valued Action 0–10
Monday				
Tuesday				
Wednesday				
Thursday				
Friday				
Saturday				
Sunday				

CHAPTER 8

Creating an Acceptance Context for Treatment

Sessions 2 & 3

It's like you're surfing... The same wave that can be a source of pain,
can be a beautiful flowing grace and source of power.
It's all a matter of how you respond to it.

—Trey Anastasio

Session 2
Evaluating the Workability and Costs of Past Control Efforts

GOALS AND THEME

This session seeks to induce creative hopelessness as a motivational enhancement component to normalize human suffering and to prepare the client for treatment. During this early phase of treatment, the therapist explores with clients the workability of the various strategies they have used to cope with anxiety and to reduce suffering. The purpose of creative hopelessness exercises is to let the client experience that, despite putting forth tremendous effort, their problems have remained. The therapist instills a sense of hopelessness, which is "creative" if clients are willing to do something different and let go of futile efforts to control unwanted thoughts and feelings. If clients start focusing on changing what they can change, their situation in life may improve. The key is to let go of the struggle with oneself instead of adding more strategies to reduce or control anxiety. Many clients have difficulty grasping what letting go means in practical terms and what letting-go behavior looks like. A practical aspect of letting go is to learn to observe anxiety-related experiences mindfully rather than by struggling with, or attempting to eliminate, such experiences. This theme is introduced with a metaphor and a mindfulness exercise.

Session Outline

1. Centering Exercise (5 min.)

2. Review of Daily Practice (5 min.)
   - Review Daily ACT Ratings

3. Review of Patterns and Costs of Avoidance (25 min.)
   - Patterns and Workability of Avoidance
   - Costs of Avoidance
   - Develop Creative Hopelessness

4. Observing Rather Than Reacting to Anxiety (20 min.)
   - Acceptance of Thoughts and Feelings Exercise

5. Life Enhancement Exercises (Home)

- Daily practice of Acceptance of Thoughts and Feelings exercise (at least 20 min.)

- Continue monitoring anxiety and fear-related experiences using the LIFE form

- Complete worksheet: What Have I Given Up for Anxiety This Week?

- Complete Daily ACT Ratings form

6. Session Materials and Handouts

- Acceptance of Thoughts and Feelings exercise instructions (two sets)

- Acceptance of Thoughts and Feelings practice form

- Living in Full Experience (LIFE) form

- Worksheet: What Have I Given Up for Anxiety This Week?

- Daily ACT Ratings form

Agenda

1. Centering Exercise (5 min.)

Begin the session with the centering exercise described at the end of Session 1.

2. Review of Daily Practice (5 min.)

First, review the LIFE form briefly, discussing the anxiety-related experiences clients had and any instances of clients engaging in behavior to manage unpleasant sensations and feelings. Also discuss costs associated with such management (i.e., whether that behavior got in the way of something clients value or care about) and client willingness to experience unwanted internal events. Finally, review Daily ACT Ratings and ask clients whether they have any questions regarding the last session and provide brief answers.

3. Review of Patterns and Costs of Avoidance (25 min.)

Therapists can begin this review by asking what clients typically do when they experience anxiety. The purpose is to identify patterns of experiential avoidance and/or experiential control efforts at the cognitive, emotional, and behavioral levels, and to identify the life-constraining costs of avoidance and control.

Patterns and Workability of Avoidance

The purpose of this discussion is to reveal ways in which clients feel "stuck." Start by asking clients to describe things they have tried in the past to eliminate anxiety. Go through some specific examples of what clients have done. For instance, they may have tried to relax or distract themselves, breathe differently, take pills, reassure themselves, argue with their thoughts or worries, or talk to other people. Are there things that they have not tried? The goal here is to gather as much information as possible about major strategies (more, less, better) that the client has tried in the past and may be doing now.

The next step is to help clients evaluate how these methods to manage their anxiety have worked. Has avoidance worked? Has escape worked? Has distraction worked? The purpose of this discussion is to review the workability of past solution attempts. It is not about whether these efforts were right or wrong. It is about whether they have worked for the client. The authors of the first ACT treatment manual for anxiety (Hayes, Wilson, Afari, & McCurry, 1990) suggested to tell clients something like:

> You have tried to do everything that can logically be done, tried all the obvious techniques. And none of them are working. If it is true that, in your experience, anxiety has not responded to your quite logical attempts to get rid of it, then something is wrong here. Could it be that your very efforts to solve the problem are actually part of the problem? What has always looked like a solution may not be a solution—it may actually be part of the problem.

Hayes and colleagues (1990) point out that clients may react by defending what they have done in the past because this exercise attacks their beliefs about the solutions to their problems, and by implication, their sense of self. It is important for therapists not to get caught up in the content of what clients say—no arguing, no attempts to convince the client of anything. Instead, return to the simple question about whether the strategies have worked for them. This, by the way, includes the act of defending what they have done about their anxiety with you in session. If the client makes a response implying that a particular strategy has worked, the therapist should *gently* point out that if this was the solution, why are they here?

In a dialogue of that nature, clients may feel blamed by the therapist for their predicament. As we indicated in chapter 6, it is imperative that a therapist not slip into a one-upmanship role with clients or attempt to logically convince them of a particular point of view (the therapist's). We recommend that therapists explore attempted solutions to manage and control anxiety nonjudgmentally, with both eyes squarely on how they have worked in both the short and long term. Therapists should model compassion and show empathy by affirming all the hard work and effort clients have put into past control attempts, and should communicate understanding about clients' reasons for engaging in such attempts. Remember that, in the short term, such strategies typically provide some partial or full relief of anxiety and fear. However, just as living a valued, rich, and meaningful life is a process made up of numerous small moments, the cumulative effect of such short-term anxiety management strategies is often long-term suffering.

Costs of Avoidance

The purpose of this discussion goes beyond evaluating the effectiveness of control and avoidance efforts to reduce and manage anxiety. The discussion must also identify the very personal costs of these efforts for clients in terms of restricting and limiting their lives. In this context, and again a bit later on in this section, you may draw upon experiences the client listed on the LIFE form. Crucial questions to ask clients are:

- What have been the long-term costs of your avoidance patterns?

- What have you given up as a consequence of managing your anxiety or worries?

- What has happened to your life over time? Have you done more or less with your life?

- Have your options increased or has your "life space" narrowed over time?

- What would you do with your time if it were not spent trying to manage anxiety, fear, unsettling thoughts, memories, and the like?

Develop Creative Hopelessness

The discussion of past experiential avoidance and control efforts is likely to reveal that the old solutions have not worked. The discussion might also reveal that these efforts have come at considerable personal costs. Hopelessness is a state where clients feel and experience that past solutions have not worked, and will not work in the future, because they cannot work. Hopelessness is about experiencing that past anxiety management strategies have not worked, not giving up or giving in to despair. The therapist therefore should affirm a client's fears about the hopelessness of current solutions while firmly resisting the temptation to console or motivate clients by reassuring them that "things will get better."

Therapists may be reluctant to encourage hopelessness because it appears to contravene the generally held therapeutic tenet that therapists should provide clients with hope. Paradoxically, this is exactly what creative hopelessness does. It provides such hope, however, not by means of cheap reassurance but through honest feedback. Helping clients experience they have been caught in a self-defeating struggle is important and does not mean despair for the client; such hopelessness is creative because it allows for new things to emerge (cf. Hayes, Strosahl, & Wilson, 1999). What makes hopelessness creative is the emphasis on the hopelessness of *past* solutions and that these e *solutions* are hopeless, not the client. This emphasis implies that there is hope if the client chooses to adopt a different approach when anxiety shows up.

Here is a simple, true-to-life story to illustrate this perspective. Sally was out driving one afternoon and noticed that she was running low on gas. So, she stopped at the nearest convenience store, filled her car with gasoline, and headed inside to pay the cashier. Ahead of her was another man doing the same. He arrived at the door before Sally and pushed on it to get inside. Sally waited patiently behind. The man pushed and pushed on the door to get in, but the door would not open. Sally could hear the man huffing and puffing in frustration, and then watched him knock on the door, figuring that the door was locked from the inside. Sally looked past the man and noticed many people inside and a sign on the door. The sign read PULL. No amount of pushing against the door, even if unlocked from the inside, would open it. Sally then approached the man and kindly suggested that he might try something different: pulling, instead of pushing. Sure enough, the door opened and both walked inside to pay for their gasoline. Creative hopelessness is very much about helping the client to experience with kindness and compassion that pushing against anxiety does not work and a different response may be all that is needed.

The Child-in-a-Hole Metaphor

The purpose of this metaphor is to let clients experience the hopelessness of their struggle with anxiety and that it may be time to adopt a fundamentally different strategy when anxiety shows up. The basic idea here is to show that "more of the same" does not work. The purpose of this metaphor is to plant important seeds for subsequent interventions and break down old assumptions and unrealistic expectations about therapy. Specifically, it attempts to let clients experience that therapy cannot provide them with better control over their anxiety. The clients' situation is unlikely to improve if the therapist tries to teach them the same types of control efforts they have used in the past without success. For instance, if clients have tried to reassure or distract themselves without success, then it would not be helpful for you, as a therapist, to use similar strategies again.

Imagine a happy child running through a wide-open field. We often think that this is how life is supposed to be: fresh and carefree. Try to imagine this scene vividly. Now, in a sad twist of fate, imagine the child running through the field and falling into a hole. It's a hole named anxiety. It wasn't the child's fault—it just happened. The perfect life is now imperfect. The child struggles and struggles to climb out of the hole, but there is no escape. If climbing won't work, there must be another way out. She thinks to herself, "Maybe digging is the way out." So, the child squats down on her hands and knees and starts to dig. She digs and digs and digs … and keeps on digging. Yet after all this digging, where is the child? She looks around, and she is still in the hole. So she tries to dig much harder and faster, thinking, "Maybe it will work if I just work harder at it." After a while, she stops and looks around again. And where does she find herself? She is even deeper in the hole. All this effort and hard work. And what is the result? The hole has only gotten deeper and wider, and she is more scared and frustrated.

Is this your experience? Clearly, the problem is not lack of effort. Just like the child who gave all she had to dig herself out, you've tried everything, too: you've used the distraction dig, the relaxation dig, the positive thinking dig, the seeing-a-therapist dig [insert other strategies the client has used]. Yet all this effort has not paid off. In fact, the effort is only creating a bigger problem. Perhaps the whole approach of digging is hopeless, and it doesn't matter whether you use your hands, your mind, relaxation, or the help of other people. The bottom line is, you're still digging, and that only gets you deeper into the hole.

Client:	Perhaps you could show me or teach me a better way to get myself out of here?
Therapist:	Actually, I don't have a better way of digging, and even if I did, what does your experience tell you? Would that help you? After all, you'd only be digging better, and end up deeper in the hole.
Client:	So are you telling me there is no way out of my anxiety hole, and I should just give up?
Therapist:	Please do not believe what my mind or your mind tells you. Just look at *your experience* and examine what that tells you. I know your mind is telling you that you must find a better way of digging. Your mind has also told you to relax, to stay at home, to use positive thinking, and so on. Has it helped you when you listened to your mind and did those things?
Client:	Sometimes those things have worked a bit, but ultimately they have been pretty useless. That is why I had really hoped you could help me. After all, you're the expert.
Therapist:	Actually, I think *you're* the expert when it comes to *your experience*. Nobody knows that better than you. The crucial question for you is, Whom do you trust now? Your mind or your experience? Which of those two voices do you think will steer you closer to the life you want to be living?
Client:	I'm not sure. I only know I'm pretty far away from where I want to be.
Therapist:	I'd love to spend some time exploring with you where you want to be. So perhaps your job right now is not to figure out how to get out of the hole. After all, you have been doing this all along. You can't do anything until you stop digging, and free your hands to use them for other activities. That is a very difficult and bold thing to do. Letting go of digging looks as though it will doom you to stay in the hole forever. Your best ally is your own pain, and your knowledge based on experience that no form of digging has

worked. Have you suffered enough? Are you ready to give up digging and do something else? Can you allow yourself to simply be in the hole?

Blaming Versus Response-ability

Clients sometimes respond to the hole metaphor by asking whether you think they are to blame for their predicament. The hole metaphor makes it clear that it is not their fault that they are in this hole. As in the case of the girl wandering through the field, it doesn't really matter how she fell into the hole—it just happened. This is one of the cards that life has dealt her. So the important thing is to accept that she is in the hole *and* that digging hasn't worked. Blaming is useless because it serves no purpose and does not work. Will self-blame get the girl out of the hole? Lack of motivation is not the problem either. She has done everything she could and worked very hard. So who's to blame is not the issue. Ask your clients, "Is blaming taking you closer to or further away from where you want to go"?

What is important to realize is that clients are responsible in the original sense of the word: *response-able*. It means clients are able to respond and can choose between different types of responses. The first thing for them to do is to let go of digging. Describe being response-able as a great gift because it means there *are* things that clients can do to improve their current life situation. They cannot choose the sensations that come up in their body or the thoughts that their minds serve up. Often they cannot choose what life may offer them. What clients can choose is what they do with their hands and feet to improve their lives.

Now is a good time to return to the LIFE form from last week. Ask the client to share life experiences where they found themselves in a hole with their anxiety and fear. What did they do about it? Did they use one or more ways of digging to manage it and how did that work for them? What were the costs? Did they end up blaming themselves or others as a consequence?

Feeding-the-Anxiety-Tiger Metaphor

Apart from showing that avoidance efforts have not worked, the feeding-the-anxiety-tiger metaphor is a powerful illustration of the ultimate cost of control efforts. Hayes and colleagues (1990) originally described this metaphor to show clients that they cannot control anxiety by trying to appease it (e.g., by giving in to what it seems to demand). It also shows how increasingly larger portions of the client's resources and life space get eaten up by efforts to control and avoid anxiety.

It seems you have been dealing with your anxiety the way someone might who lives with a hungry baby tiger. Although the tiger is just a baby, he is scary enough, and you think he might bite you. So you go to the fridge to get some meat for him so he won't eat you. And, sure enough, throwing him some meat shuts him up while he's eating the meat, and he leaves you alone for a while. But he also grows just a little bigger. So the next time he's hungry, he's just a little bigger and more scary, and you go to the fridge to throw him more meat. Again, you feed him to keep him at bay. The problem is that the more you feed him, the bigger he gets, and the more frightened you feel. Now eventually that little tiger is a big tiger, and he scares you more than ever. So you keep on going back to the fridge to get more meat, feeding and feeding him, and hoping that one day he will leave you alone. Yet the tiger doesn't leave—he just gets louder and more scary and hungry. And then one day you walk to the fridge, you open the door, and the fridge is empty. At this point, there is nothing left to feed to the tiger ... Nothing? ... Except *you!*

You've got anxiety monsters out there that look as though they could swallow you whole. When the emotional and bodily discomfort and disturbing thought monsters show up, you keep hoping that, if you feed them, they will go away. You keep hoping that if you trade in your life flexibility just a little bit more, eventually the anxiety monster will leave you alone. Does your experience tell you that this has ever really happened? Is there anything that indicates that it is going to happen?

To make this metaphor personally relevant for clients, ask them to consider examples of how they have fed the anxiety monsters in their own lives. If a client has difficulty coming up with examples (e.g., staying home alone to avoid having a panic attack), you can offer a few examples based on the client's in-session comments or their responses to the LIFE form.

4. Observing Rather Than Reacting to Anxiety (20 min.)

It is likely that clients will again ask what it is that they should do or do differently. At this stage, it is important to tell them not to change anything, and to just focus on observing how they are responding to their anxiety when it occurs, and to take note of how well that works. Go back to the notion that the skills for dealing with anxiety without more "digging" can only be acquired through direct experience—just like learning how to ride a bike. For this reason, the following mindfulness exercise is particularly useful because it helps clients just notice what is going on inside of them without getting involved with trying to change their experience.

Acceptance of Thoughts and Feelings Exercise*

Mindfulness exercises that focus on breathing are a core part of traditional Buddhist teachings and practice (e.g., Chödrön, 2001). We have adapted the following exercise from more generic versions (Davis, Eshelman, & McKay, 2000; Kabat-Zinn, 1990; Segal et al., 2002) for the purposes of this anxiety treatment program. In this

---

*   We are grateful to Joanna Arch for her insightful comments on this section and her suggestions for wording and conducting this mindfulness exercise.

exercise, we focus on the breath because internal sensations such as thoughts, worries, bodily sensations, and feelings are constantly shifting and changing—just like our breathing. The goal is for clients to practice paying attention to a single focus, the breathing, and to allow other internal events, such as thoughts, feelings, and sensations, to come and go in their minds. Clients may also experience that no matter how bad an internal experience seems, it neither lasts forever nor can it do any physical harm. If they pay attention to it, they will see how it changes from moment to moment, how it comes and goes on its own, without any effort on our part.

Tell clients that mindfulness exercises are a way to learn that we cannot choose what comes into our minds and what we feel. We can only choose what we pay attention to and *how* we pay attention to internal events. The goal is for clients to notice any thoughts and images and their emotional responses to such thoughts and images, just as they are. Encourage clients to bring some compassion and kindness to their private experiences by not arguing or struggling with them and instead accepting them without judging them as good or bad. This is a concrete way of learning that anxiety is not the enemy. Simply noticing bodily sensations without trying to manage them is a difficult skill for individuals with anxiety disorders to learn, because it differs from the past control struggles they have engaged in when feeling anxious. So learning this new skill will require regular daily practice.

Right before starting the exercise, remind clients that the purpose of this practice is to learn to observe and make them better at feeling. Its aim is not to make them feel different, better, relaxed, or calm; this may happen or it may not. Instead, the goal of this practice is for the client to, as best they can, bring a compassionate, kind awareness to each breath, to any sensations they detect, and to any thoughts or worries that come into their mind. During the pauses in the exercise, feel free to remind clients to "gently focus on the breath" as often as seems natural, to help bring clients back to the exercise if and when their minds wander off. Some clients initially experience some difficulty understanding the instructions and following them. Remind them that they will become better at doing it with continued practice. The exercise itself should take about fifteen minutes to complete. We suggest that therapists read the instructions to clients in a slow and soft manner. The instructions for the exercise are also on the book CD.

---

1. First, I would like to ask your permission to do another experiential exercise. Are you willing to do that? [Get clients' permission and then move on.]

2. Go ahead and get in a comfortable position in your chair. Sit upright with your feet flat on the floor, your arms and legs uncrossed, and your hands resting in your lap (palms up or down, whichever is more comfortable). Allow your eyes to close gently [pause 10 seconds].

3. Take a few moments to get in touch with the movement of your breath and the sensations in your body [pause 10 seconds]. Bring your awareness to the physical sensations in your body, especially to the sensations

of touch or pressure, where your body makes contact with the chair or floor [pause 10 seconds].

4. Now, slowly bring your attention to the gentle rising and falling of your breath in your chest and belly. Like ocean waves coming in and out, your breath is always there. Notice its rhythm in your body [pause 10 seconds]. Notice each breath. Focus on each inhale ... and exhale [pause 10 seconds]. Notice the changing patterns of sensations in your belly as you breathe in, and as you breathe out [pause 10 seconds]. Take a few moments to feel the physical sensations as you breathe in and as you breathe out [pause 10 seconds].

5. There is no need to try to control your breathing in any way—simply let the breath breathe itself [pause 10 seconds]. As best you can, also bring this attitude of generous allowing and gentle acceptance to the rest of your experience. There is nothing to be fixed, no particular state to be achieved. As best as you can, simply allow your experience to be your experience, without needing it to be other than what it is [pause 15 seconds].

6. Sooner or later, your mind will wander away from the breath to other concerns, thoughts, worries, images, bodily sensations, planning, or daydreams, or it may just drift along. This is what minds do much of the time. When you notice that your mind has wandered, gently congratulate yourself—you have come back and are once more aware of your experience! You may want to acknowledge briefly where your mind has been (*Ah, there's thinking* or *there's feeling*). Then, gently escort your attention back to the sensation of the breath coming in and going out [pause 10 seconds]. As best you can, bring a quality of kindness and compassion to your awareness, perhaps seeing the repeated wanderings of your mind as opportunities to bring patience and gentle curiosity to your experience [pause 15 seconds].

7. When you become aware of bodily sensations and feelings, tension, or other intense sensations in a particular part of your body, just notice them, acknowledge their presence, and see if you can make space for them [pause 10 seconds]. Do not try to hold on to them or make them go away [pause 10 seconds]. See if you can open your heart and make some room for the discomfort, for the tension, for the anxiety, just allowing them be there [pause 10 seconds]. Is there enough space in you to welcome in all of your experience? [pause 15 seconds]

8. Watch the sensations change from moment to moment. Sometimes they grow stronger [pause 10 seconds], sometimes they stay the same

[pause 10 seconds], and sometimes they grow weaker—it does not matter [pause 10 seconds]. Breathe calmly in *to* and out *from* the sensations of discomfort, imagining the breath moving in *to* and out *from* that region of the body [pause 10 seconds]. Remember, your intention is not to make you feel *better* but to get better at *feeling* [pause 15 seconds].

9. If you ever notice that you are unable to focus on your breathing because of intense physical sensations of discomfort in your body, let go of your focus on the breath and shift your focus to the place of discomfort. Gently direct your attention *on* and *into* the discomfort and stay with it, no matter how bad it seems [pause 10 seconds]. Take a look at it. What does it *really* feel like? [pause 10 seconds] Again, see if you can make room for the discomfort and allow it to be there [pause 10 seconds]. Are you willing to be with whatever you have? [pause 15 seconds].

10. Along with physical sensations in your body, you may also notice thoughts about the sensations and thoughts about the thoughts [pause 10 seconds]. You may notice your mind coming up with evaluative labels such as "dangerous" or "getting worse." If that happens, you can thank your mind for the label [pause] and return to the present experience as it is, not as your mind says it is, noticing thoughts as thoughts, physical sensations as physical sensations, feelings as feelings—nothing more, nothing less [pause 15 seconds].

11. To help you experience the difference between yourself and your thoughts and feelings, you can name thoughts and feelings as you notice them. For instance, if you notice you are worrying, silently say to yourself, "Worry ... there is worry," just observing worry and not judging yourself for having these thoughts and feelings [pause 10 seconds]. If you find yourself judging, just notice that and call it "Judging ... there is judging" and observe that with a quality of kindness and compassion [pause 10 seconds]. You can do the same with other thoughts and feelings and just name them as *planning, reminiscing, longing,* or whatever you experience. Label the thought or emotion and move on [pause 10 seconds]. Thoughts and feelings come and go in your mind and body. You are not what those thoughts and feelings say, no matter how persistent or intense they may be [pause 15 seconds].

12. As this time for formal practice comes to an end, gradually widen your attention to take in the sounds around you ... notice your surroundings [pause] and slowly open your eyes with the intention to bring this

awareness to the present moment and into the upcoming moments of the day.

After completing the exercise, therapists should ask clients how they experienced the exercise and briefly discuss any comments, questions, or concerns. Therapists can weave into this discussion some basic points about mindfulness and acceptance. You will want to counteract any attempts by clients to misuse acceptance and this exercise as tools to control or reduce anxiety. Also remind clients that they will become better at being mindful observers with continued practice and that the stance entailed in this exercise is the basis for important exercises in subsequent treatment sessions. It is therefore critical that clients practice it regularly at least once a day at home and keep a daily record of their practice using the form at the end of this chapter and on the CD. The instructions for the exercises are also on the CD. Ask clients whether they are ready to commit to doing these exercises on their path of becoming a better observer and a full participant in life.

5. Life Enhancement Exercises (Home)

- Practice the Acceptance of Thoughts and Feelings exercise once a day for at least 20 minutes and complete the practice form after each practice. Give clients a copy of the instructions to take home.

- Continue monitoring anxiety and fear-related experiences using the LIFE form.

- Complete the worksheet: What Have I Given Up for Anxiety This Week?

- Complete the Daily ACT Ratings form.

Explain to clients that the purpose of the new worksheet, What Have I Given Up for Anxiety This Week?, is to have them make contact with what they are giving up in the service of anxiety between sessions on a daily basis (the worksheet is at the end of this chapter and on the CD). This exercise is designed to let clients experience the costs associated with their efforts to manage and avoid anxiety. Such costs may include giving up opportunities to do things that matter to them and activities that clients could have done had they not been sidelined by control and avoidance strategies.

Session 3
Creative Hopelessness:
Making Space for New Solutions

GOALS AND THEME

The first goal of this session is to establish control efforts as the problem, not the solution. The therapist further nurtures creative hopelessness by letting clients experience the unworkability of previous avoidance and control efforts and that nothing will change unless they change how they approach anxiety. A related message is that "*You are not hopeless—only your past solution attempts are!*" The first step in a new direction is to let go of past solution attempts. This letting go, in turn, makes room for new possibilities. Through in-session exercises, clients have the opportunity to experience that letting go of their struggle and doing things that go against the grain could be an option for them.

If anxiety reduction is not a stated goal of this program, then clients may rightly wonder, what is the ultimate goal? For this reason, we introduce the notion of value-driven behavior as an alternative to managing anxiety. Clients learn that moving in the direction of chosen values and living a full life is what this treatment is about and what makes the hard therapy work worthwhile.

Session Outline

1. Repeat Acceptance of Thoughts and Feelings Exercise (15 min.)

2. Review of Daily Practice (5 min.)
   - Review Acceptance of Thoughts and Feelings exercise and Daily ACT Ratings

3. Control Is the Problem—Letting Go Is the Alternative (20 min.)
   - The Chinese Finger Trap Exercise
   - Tug-of-War with the Anxiety Monster Exercise

4. Value-Driven Behavior as an Alternative to Managing Anxiety (20 min.)
   - Review LIFE form and What Have I Given Up for Anxiety This Week? worksheet
   - Choosing Valued Directions

- Values Make the Hard Work Worthwhile

- What Matters Most in Your Life?

- The Epitaph Exercise: What Do You Want Your Life to Stand For?

5. Experiential Life Enhancement Exercises (Home)

- Daily practice of Acceptance of Thoughts and Feelings exercise (at least 20 min)

- Continue monitoring anxiety and fear-related experiences using the LIFE form

- Complete worksheet: What Have I Given Up for Anxiety This Week?

- Complete Daily ACT Ratings form

- Complete one or two Write Your Own Epitaph exercise worksheets

6. Session Materials and Handouts

- Acceptance of Thoughts and Feelings practice form

- Living in Full Experience (LIFE) form

- Worksheet: What Have I Given Up for Anxiety This Week?

- Daily ACT Ratings form

- Write Your Own Epitaph exercise worksheet (two copies)

- Three Chinese finger traps: two for use in session and one to give to client to take home (available at party supply and novelty shops or through the Internet: www.supercoolstuff.com, then search for finger traps)

- Bath towel for tug-of-war exercise

Agenda

1. Acceptance of Thoughts and Feelings Exercise (15 min.)

Begin the session by repeating the Acceptance of Thoughts and Feelings exercise that was introduced and assigned for home practice in Session 2. Evaluate progress and difficulties during the in-session practice, and praise client efforts and willingness to do the exercise.

2. Review of Daily Practice (5 min.)

Review the client's daily practice of the Acceptance of Thoughts and Feelings exercise, paying attention to any lack of compliance for reasons of lack of willingness, lack of commitment, or high fearfulness. Reiterate the rationale for home practice. Defer review of the LIFE form and What Have I Given Up for Anxiety This Week? form until the final part of the session that deals with value-guided behavior as an alternative to managing anxiety.

3. Control Is the Problem—Letting Go Is the Alternative (20 min.)

This treatment component addresses the problems associated with the use of experiential avoidance strategies. It continues to be important for clients to experience that past solution attempts involving experiential avoidance are not solutions but problems themselves. One of the goals of Session 2 was to show clients that past attempts to avoid experiencing anxiety have not worked for them. The goal of this session is to expand upon this theme. The metaphors and exercises in this session allow clients to make experiential contact with the unworkability of old anxiety avoidance and control solutions and how these strategies have resulted in considerable personal costs.

As in the previous session, it is important that therapists resist the temptation to rescue clients from their felt hopelessness by consoling and reassuring them that "things will get better." The hopelessness that clients may experience at this stage is not the emotion of despair. Rather, it is the experience that past solutions are hopeless and will not work. As Hayes, Strosahl, and Wilson (1999) put it, the experience of hopelessness is bittersweet—both sad and hopeful, painful and empowering. It feels open, spent, sober, humble, and courageous. Such a state is likely to be beneficial and motivating ("creative") because it allows clients to experience the unworkability of their self-defeating experiences straight on and unedited. This experience allows for new and fundamentally different ways of relating with anxiety to emerge.

At this stage, it is not necessary to be specific as to what this new approach might look like. The goal of these exercises is to let clients experience that (a) letting go of the struggle is an option; and (b) whatever they may do differently in the future must be *fundamentally* different from what they have done in the past. It may even be the complete opposite of what they have done before.

The Chinese Finger Trap Exercise

A Chinese finger trap is a tube of woven straw about five inches long and half an inch wide. First, you must slide both index fingers into the straw tube, one finger at each end. If you attempt to pull the fingers out, the tube catches and tightens, causing discomfort. The only way to regain some freedom and space to move is to push the fingers in *first* and *then* slide them out. The purpose of this exercise is to let clients experience how doing something seemingly counterintuitive ("leaning into one's anxiety") may be a better solution than persisting with the same old solutions that have not worked. The Chinese finger trap is a metaphor for moving *toward* suffering in order to lessen it and heal from it. We have adapted this exercise from the metaphor described by Hayes, Strosahl, and Wilson (1999), who present the metaphor to clients in verbal form. Based on the results of a study we conducted (Eifert & Heffner, 2003), we suggest allowing clients to act out the metaphor with an actual finger trap so that they may experience the effects of their actions. This experiential component is in line with the action-oriented nature of behavior therapy and could serve to enhance the credibility and effectiveness of the metaphor. Following the exercise, give clients an extra finger trap to take home.

The goal of this exercise is to let clients discover that attempting to reduce and control essentially uncontrollable sensations, while understandable and seemingly logical (like pulling out of the finger trap), only creates more problems: the harder you pull, the more the trap tightens, resulting in less room to move and even more discomfort. In contrast, doing something counterintuitive, such as pushing the fingers *in* rather than *out* and leaning into the discomfort, effectively ends the struggle. It gives the client more space to move and do other things. Doing the exercise together with the client is a good way to illustrate that we are all in this boat together and that clients are not alone in the way they attempt to deal with their struggles.

Give clients a finger trap and use one yourself. First, ask clients to slide in both index fingers, one finger at each end of the tube. After you fully insert your fingers, ask clients to try to get out of the finger trap. They are likely to do so by attempting to pull their fingers out. If they do that, ask them what they notice. They will experience and report some discomfort as the tube squeezes their fingers and reduces circulation. They might also voice some worry that they might be stuck inside the finger trap for the rest of the session. They may experience some confusion because pulling out of the tube seems the most obvious, natural way to escape. Yet it doesn't work, and they are definitely stuck if they simply just go on pulling. Use the following dialogue as an example of how to individualize this exercise to specific client responses, suggestions, and comments as you and the client work through the exercise.

Therapist: Pulling out is a very natural and seemingly logical reaction to free yourself from the finger trap, but what happens when we do that? [Hold up your finger trap and encourage the client to try pulling out again.]

Client: It doesn't work. I'm stuck.

Therapist: I notice that, too. Our fingers only get caught more tightly, creating more discomfort and less room to move.

Client: So how do we get out of here?

Therapist: Perhaps getting out is not the main issue. The good news is that there *is* an alternative that does work, insofar as it gives you some space and room to move. To get there, however, you have to approach this situation differently. What could that approach be?

Client: I am not quite sure. There has to be some kind of trick that will do it and get me out of here. Perhaps I need to pull in a different way.

Therapist: Okay, why don't you go ahead and do that and see what happens.

Client: It doesn't work either. I am still stuck.

Therapist: So am I. Let me give you a hint. We have to do something that goes against the grain and doesn't seem to make sense at first. Instead of pulling out, we could push our fingers *in*. Let's try that instead and see what happens. [Therapist models gently leaning into the tube.]

Client: Well, I can move now, but I still can't get out of the trap. I'm still in it.

Therapist: So am I. We might not get out of the trap, but as you noticed, pushing the fingers in definitely gave you more space to move around. It seems like leaning into the tube gives us more wiggle room. What if we didn't need to get out of the finger trap at all? What if we just created some more space for us to have what we have, to experience what there is to be experienced?

Client: That sounds weird and scary—and I don't like it.

Therapist: I understand that you do not like and would want to get away from things that scare you like your [insert some of client's worst fears]. But what happens when you keep on pulling away from what you have? The harder you pull away from your anxiety, the more the trap tightens, and the more stuck you are. Trying to get rid of your anxiety, trying to reduce it when it's there, trying not to have it come back when it happens to be gone—what has all this pulling and controlling done to your life? Has it created more space for you to do what really matters to you, or has it taken over more and more of your life?

Client: Well, what I have done certainly hasn't helped much or solved any problems. So tell me, what should I do instead?

Therapist: I am not quite sure, but when you look at these finger traps, pulling away doesn't seem to work, does it? Yet doing something counterintuitive, pushing your fingers *in* rather than *out*, has given you space and new options to make moves. Perhaps doing something that goes against the grain is a way of getting yourself unstuck from where you are with your life right now. What could you do that would go against the grain?

The finger trap exercise is powerful. It is powerful precisely because it provides direct experience with our instinctive and often well-intentioned solutions to our problems and shows us how often these turn out not to be solutions at all. In fact, these so-called solutions may create even bigger problems than the ones they were designed to address. As Tim Dunn wrote in his book (no longer available) *How to Escape the Chinese Finger Trap: A Manual for Changing*:

> In the end, all attempts to escape the fact that life contains suffering are doomed. A gloomy philosophy, you say? Not entirely bleak, I would respond. Because, THERE IS AN EXIT. Don't try to escape it. Go towards it. Seek out what hurts and frightens you. It is mindlessly pulling away from pain and mindlessly seeking pleasure that causes people to greatly increase the troubles that life brings them. [cited by Hand-Boniakowski, 1997]

Dunn suggests that hope lies not in escape or avoidance. Instead, real hope comes about when we head toward suffering and embrace it with compassion and kindness. Only then will suffering have less of a stranglehold on our happiness. By embracing suffering, clients relax the weave of the trap that they have built for themselves, and can begin to escape from its hold on them and live their lives fully.

Tug-of-War with the Anxiety Monster Exercise

The notion of doing something counterintuitive and letting go of the struggle is likely to be quite alien to clients. In fact, they may be frightened by this notion. Also, clients often have trouble understanding what statements like "let go of your struggle" mean. We therefore recommend using an additional metaphor, tug-of-war metaphor. Similar to the finger trap exercise, this metaphor suggests letting go of a struggle by doing something opposite to what people typically do in a struggle. Interestingly, a woman with agoraphobia came up with this metaphorical story during ACT therapy and told it to Steven Hayes (Hayes et al., 1990).

After a brief verbal introduction of the tug-of-war metaphor, we recommend acting this metaphor out too. Give clients a bath towel and ask them to play tug-of-war with you in your newfound role as "the anxiety monster." If they attempt to pull the anxiety monster over, the monster simply pulls back. Acting out this exercise lets clients physically experience how much energy and focus it takes to keep the anxiety monster in check. Also, we have found that almost all clients will grab the towel with both of their hands when you hand it to them. This is a very graphic illustration for clients because it shows how anxiety, and the efforts of fighting it, have left their hands tied up in the fight and no longer free to do other things in life. Incidentally, therapists need not worry about ending up in a fight with their clients. We have found that clients fully recognize and stay within the boundaries of the playfulness of the situation!

Therapist:	It seems like your situation is like being in a tug-of-war with an anxiety monster. You hate the monster because it is so big and powerful. In between you and the monster is a pit, and so far as you can tell it is bottomless—an abyss. If you lose this tug-of-war, you will fall into the abyss and be destroyed. The anxiety monster will have won. You don't want this to happen, so you fight back. You pull and pull, but the harder you pull, it seems the harder the monster pulls back—and all the time it seems you are pulled a bit closer to the edge of the pit. So how can this fight ever end?
Client:	Either I win by pulling harder than the anxiety monster *or* the anxiety monster wins by wearing me out and I'm gone—kaput!
Therapist:	Can you see how you are using both of your hands to keep the monster in check? Also look at your feet. They're pretty much tied in one position. What else can you do with your hands and feet while you're doing that?
Client:	Just about nothing. I am stuck fighting.
Therapist:	I notice your eyes are focused on the towel, too. What are you thinking?
Client:	I'm wondering what your next move will be.
Therapist:	So your mind, hands, and feet are all tied up in the struggle with anxiety?
Client:	Yes, they pretty much are, and that is even more frightening than the anxiety itself. It seems I have nothing left to work with.
Therapist:	You could indeed spend all your energy fighting anxiety monsters until the end. But there is a different way, which is perhaps hard to think of while you're so busy fighting: *You could simply drop the rope!* The hardest thing to see is that your job here is not to win the tug-of-war. Your job is to drop the rope! Just imagine, what would happen if you refused to fight anymore and just dropped the rope? Are you willing to let go of the rope now and see what happens?
Client:	*[after letting go of the rope]* The fight is over and my hands are free.
Therapist:	Isn't that great? And where am I—the anxiety monster?
Client:	You're still there. You probably fell on the floor when I dropped the rope on you.
Therapist:	I *am* still here *and* the fight is over. And you're right, I did fall down. But that won't stop me from getting up and shouting at you, "Hey, pick up the

rope. What's wrong with you?" What do you do then? [therapist dangles the towel in front of the patient]

Client: I guess I have to listen, and I could pick up the rope—but I don't have to pick it up, right?

Therapist: That is indeed a choice you have: You don't have to pick up the rope! Just remember though, I am still here in the room with you, and I am still shouting at you. I am not dead and gone.

Client: I wish you were!

Therapist: I understand. So you can't make me go away. What is it then that you *can* control?

Client: I cannot shut you up. The only thing I can do is *not do* what the monster tells me to do.

Therapist: That is your choice. You do not have to do what the monster tells you. You can't make it shut up, as much as you'd like to silence it. Yet you also need not fight it or do whatever else it tells you to do. By the way, take a look at your hands and your legs now. Did you notice that they are free now? You are free to do all sorts of things that really matter to you now because you're no longer caught up in the fight with the anxiety monster.

---

4. Value-Driven Behavior as an Alternative to Managing Anxiety (20 min.)

At this point, clients will inevitably ask, "So, what do I do next?" Consistent with what we have said about creative hopelessness, you may be tempted to respond with something like, "I don't know what you should do," or "There is really nothing that can be done." Yet these responses are not genuine. You will likely have some ideas about what might be done to help a client get unstuck and move forward. The exercises in this and the previous session will have helped clients explore the unworkability of past change efforts and let them contact the experience of unworkability fully, without defense and avoidance, so as to create space to move in the direction of creative workability. So, when clients ask, "What am I to do?" you might respond by saying something like "There is no simple answer as to what exactly will work for you. What we don't want to do is go down the same old road where you got stuck in the first place. Perhaps it is time that we explore what it is that you really want to do. What is it that you care about most?"

Choosing Valued Directions

Begin the discussion on choosing values by referring back to the feeding-the-anxiety-tiger metaphor. Trying to appease and manage anxiety (e.g., by giving in to the various avoidance and escape behaviors that it seems to demand) has led to a loss of increasingly larger portions of the client's resources and psychological space. The anxiety thoughts and panicky feelings clients experience are like a monster growing inside. Each time clients give in to what panic, anxiety, fear, and worries ask them to do, they inadvertently feed the monster and make it grow bigger and bolder. Feeding the anxiety monster won't make it calm and friendly in the long term. Ask clients, "Who is in control here? Who is choosing? Is it you or is it a monster called anxiety or panic?"

Feeding the anxiety monster has moved clients away from valued life directions and put living a valued life on hold. Tell clients that the remaining sessions are primarily devoted to reclaiming their lives. Whereas until now we have emphasized what clients cannot control (their internal experiences), we now focus on what clients can control with their hands and feet. A typical question ACT therapists might ask is, "In what valued direction are your feet currently taking you?" (Hayes & Wilson, 1994). Clients truly are in control and have the power to choose the direction they want their lives to take. At this point, the therapist could get up and walk around the room and point to their feet and legs to demonstrate that clients are in control of where their feet are taking them. They do not have to devote their time, energy, and lives to feeding the anxiety monster. Most importantly, they need not wait until they have "mastered" their anxiety, and have gotten rid of all the symptoms and problems associated with it, to move on with their lives.

Therapists can make this discussion more concrete by reviewing a few examples from the What Have I Given Up for Anxiety This Week? form clients completed at home and discussing the consequences and costs of anxiety management as related to living a full and valued life. You should also review last week's LIFE form and focus on any instances of clients engaging in behavior to manage unwanted sensations and feelings. Again, point out costs associated with such management (i.e., whether that behavior got in the way of something clients value or care about).

Values Make the Hard Work Worthwhile

Clients often wonder why their therapist is talking about values in a treatment program for anxiety disorders. Tell clients that when they first entered therapy, their focus was on managing or getting rid of anxiety. This hasn't worked in their lives. Instead, it has created more problems and solved very few of them. The purpose of the mindfulness exercises is to let them experience that they can observe aversive thoughts and feelings *and* approach situations that often got in the way of pursuing valued activities. The purpose of these exercises is to give clients skills that could be helpful as they start doing things that they really care about.

Tell clients that the last part of this session, and indeed the rest of the treatment, is about learning that they deserve to live a full life, and that you'll be helping them find a path and commit to a plan that will lead them in that direction. As a therapist, you make a commitment to help your client explore and move toward their chosen values and goals in a systematic way so they can reclaim their lives. In the process, your clients may rediscover, or perhaps discover for the first time, what is most important to them. The following brief metaphor, adapted from Heffner and Eifert (2004), may help illustrate this process for your clients.

> Think of life as a walk through a corridor with many doors. You [the client] have the power to choose which doors to open and enter. One of those doors is labeled "anxiety," and you have chosen the anxiety door for so long that you may have lost sight of other options that are available to you. This session and the exercises at home will give you alternatives to explore. You can venture out and open up other doors. You can also choose to stay inside the anxiety room. What choice do you want to make? When you stay locked behind the anxiety door, what will that do to your life? Here is one of the most important questions for you: Do you want to be free of anxiety or panic, or do you want to have your life back? Now is the time to muster the courage to explore other doors in your life corridor. Think about your life. Besides anxiety, what other doors can you open?

In the past, clients have spent their energy trying to manage their anxiety almost as if anxiety management were their occupation. Now they can think about how they can use their energy in a different way, such as being a trusted friend, a student, an athlete, a loving sister, brother, partner, or parent, or by starting a more fulfilling career, rekindling a hobby, or doing whatever else their heart desires. Heffner and Eifert (2004) used the following brief metaphor to help illustrate this point:

> Your life energy is a gift. You can think of it as being like a hammer. Just as you can use a hammer to build or to destroy, you can also focus energy on committing yourself to leading a full life, or waste your energy by trying to control the uncontrollable. Either way, anxiety will be with you.

What Matters Most in Your Life?

One way to get into a discussion of exploring values and living a full life is to ask clients what is really important to them. What really matters to them, and what do they care about? Some clients find it difficult to focus on what matters to them because their mind tells them anxiety control is what matters, precisely *because* anxiety appears to be the main barrier to doing what really matters to them. So, ask them whether they have ever wondered what their lives would be like if the anxiety monster did not rule them. For instance, what would be different if they didn't have panic attacks, experienced less anxiety, or had fewer worries? What kind of things would they do or like to do if that were so? You may also ask the following: If you only had today to live, what would you do with the time you had left on this earth?

The Epitaph Exercise: What Do You Want Your Life to Stand For?

The purpose of this powerful exercise, adapted from Hayes, Strosahl, and Wilson (1999) and Heffner and Eifert (2004), is to help clients clarify their values and make contact with what they care about. Is it conquering their anxiety or living a valued, rich life? Therapists should give the client a copy of the epitaph worksheet, which is at the end of this chapter and on the book CD.

Imagine that one day this will be the headstone on your grave. Notice that the epitaph has not yet been written. What inscription would you like to see on it that will capture the essence of your life? What is it that you want to be remembered for? What would you like your life to stand for? What do you want to be about? Take this sheet with you and give yourself some time to think about this really important question. If you find an answer—or more than one—just write it down on the lines on "your" tombstone. This may seem like another strange and perhaps somewhat scary exercise. If you stick with it and complete it *and* feel a bit queasy, it will help you get in touch with what you want your life to stand for.

This is not really a hypothetical exercise. What you will be remembered for—what defines your life—is up to you. It depends on what you *do now*. It depends on the actions you take that are consistent with what you care about. This is how you can determine the wording of your own epitaph. Now, I make no promises that people will build a Lincoln-type memorial for you at the end of your life. Yet if you persistently move in your valued directions, chances are that people will write more on your tombstone than "Here lies [insert the client's name]—she conquered panic disorder" or "Here lies [insert the client's name]—he finally stopped worrying" [individualize to fit client's main presenting problem].

What does it mean that people never mention those items on tombstones? Could it mean that the goal you have been working extremely hard to achieve is ultimately not going to matter much in the grand scheme of things? An important question to ask yourself now is, Are you doing things to be the type of person you want to be? If not, *now* is the time to live the life you want and do the things that are most important to you. Each minute you spend at home trying to not have panic [individualize and insert client's worst fear] is a minute away from doing what really matters most to you.

Valued living is a lifelong process in which roadblocks and barriers arise. Each day you live is a day to move in a valued direction *and* take your painful thoughts and feelings with you. In a way, we write our own epitaph by the choices we make and actions we take each and every day. So once again, what do you want your epitaph to say when you're no longer alive? It is one of the most important questions that we ask you in this program.

Before moving on, we wish to point out that there is another way this exercise can be done. You can give clients two copies of the epitaph worksheet. First, you ask clients to write their own epitaph as if they died today. The epitaph should focus on everything clients have done in the service of not having anxiety. For instance, a person with panic and agoraphobia might write the following:

I spent the last eight years homebound for fear of my panic. I have visited my doctor dozens of times to manage my anxiety. I have refilled countless prescriptions for medication. I have been unable to work for the past several years and have few friends outside of my immediate family. I have not gone to the beach all this time. I have not watched a sunset from a mountaintop since I was in high school. I haven't felt the cool breeze of a warm summer evening on my face for a long time. My life has been about not having panic and I leave this earth having been enslaved by this goal and not having conquered it.

Then you ask clients to complete the second worksheet with what they want out of life and what they want their lives to stand for. Both tombstones can then be compared and discussed in the next session.

5. Experiential Life Enhancement Exercises (Home)

■   Practice the Acceptance of Thoughts and Feelings exercise once a day for at least 20 minutes and complete the practice form after each practice

■   Continue monitoring anxiety and fear-related experiences using the LIFE form

■   Complete the worksheet: What Have I Given Up for Anxiety This Week?

■   Complete the Daily ACT Ratings form

■   Complete one or two Write Your Own Epitaph exercise worksheets

ACCEPTANCE OF THOUGHTS AND FEELINGS

Life Enhancement Exercise Practice Form

In the first (left) column, record whether you make a commitment to practice the Acceptance of Thoughts and Feelings exercise that day and include the date. In the second column, record whether you actually practiced, when you practiced, and how long you practiced. In the third column, record whether you used a tape or not. In the fourth column, write down anything that comes up during your practice and that you would like to talk about at our next meeting.

Commitment: yes/no Date:	Practiced: yes/no When practiced? How long (min.)?	Tape/CD: yes / no	Comments
Saturday: Date:	Practiced: yes / no Time: A.M./P.M. Minutes:		
Sunday: Date:	Practiced: yes / no Time: A.M./P.M. Minutes:		
Monday: Date:	Practiced: yes / no Time: A.M./P.M. Minutes:		
Tuesday: Date:	Practiced: yes / no Time: A.M./P.M. Minutes:		
Wednesday: Date:	Practiced: yes / no Time: A.M./P.M. Minutes:		
Thursday: Date:	Practiced: yes / no Time: A.M./P.M. Minutes:		
Friday: Date:	Practiced: yes / no Time: A.M./P.M. Minutes:		

WHAT HAVE I GIVEN UP FOR ANXIETY THIS WEEK?

Life Enhancement Exercise Record Form

The purpose of completing this exercise and record form is to let you examine on a daily basis how costly managing your anxiety is for you. What are you giving up in order to manage, reduce, and avoid anxiety? What opportunities to do things that you like or that matter to you are you trading in to control and manage anxiety? What are you missing out on?

In the first (left) column, record the situation or event that triggered your anxiety, concerns, or worries. In the second column, write down your anxiety, bodily sensations, thoughts, concerns, or worries. In the third column, record what you actually ended up doing to manage your anxiety. In the fourth column, record what effect your efforts to control or reduce your anxiety had on you. For instance, how did you feel afterward? In the fifth (right) column, write down the consequences and costs associated with your efforts to manage your anxiety. What did you give up or miss out on?

Situation/Event	Anxiety/Concern	Anxiety Control Behavior	Effect on You	Costs
Example: was invited to go out with some friends	Example: was afraid of having a panic attack	Example: stayed at home and watched TV	Example: felt lonely, sad, and angry with myself for being so weak	Example: lost out on a good time with my friends; missed an opportunity to deepen friendships

WRITE YOUR OWN EPITAPH
"WHAT DO I WANT MY LIFE TO STAND FOR?"

An Experiential Life Enhancement Exercise

Here Lies

CHAPTER 9

Acceptance and Valued Living as Alternatives to Managing Anxiety

Sessions 4 & 5

Trying to fix ourselves is not helpful because it implies struggle and self-denigration. Lasting change occurs only when we honor ourselves as the source of wisdom and compassion. It is only when we begin to relax with ourselves that acceptance becomes a transformative process. Self-compassion and courage are vital. Staying with pain without loving-kindness is just warfare.

—Pema Chödrön

Session 4
Mindfulness, Acceptance, and Choosing Valued Directions

GOALS AND THEME

This session has three goals. The first goal is to introduce clients to acceptance and mindfulness as a skillful way of approaching our various life experiences. Clients learn to observe anxiety-related thoughts and feelings without evaluation or judgment and without holding onto, getting rid of, suppressing, or otherwise changing what they experience. Clients learn to assume an observer perspective in relation to their anxiety-related feelings and thoughts via the Acceptance of Anxiety exercise. The exercise encourages willingness to make full contact with the experience of anxiety and provides clients with a tool for doing so. The larger goal is to undermine the tendency to react to anxious thoughts and sensations so as not to have them, including avoiding situations where anxiety may show up. The second goal is to help clients differentiate what they can control from what they cannot control in their lives. The third goal is to affirm valued living as an alternative agenda to managing anxiety. Based on the epitaph exercise and what clients want their lives to stand for, therapists help clients explore more specific values and identify goals by means of the Valued Directions worksheet to be completed by clients at home.

Session Outline

1. Review of Daily Practice (5 min.)

   ■ Review Acceptance of Thoughts and Feelings exercise and Daily ACT Ratings

2. Learning to Accept Anxiety with Mindfulness (25 min.)

   ■ The Nature of Acceptance and Mindfulness

   ■ Acceptance of Anxiety Exercise

   ■ Acceptance Is Not a Clever Fix for Anxiety

3. Controlling Internal Versus External Events (10 min.)

   ■ The Polygraph Metaphor

4. Exploring Values (15 min.)

   ■ Making a Commitment

   ■ Valued Directions Worksheet

   ■ Values Versus Goals

5. Experiential Life Enhancement Exercises (Home)

   ■ Daily practice of Acceptance of Anxiety exercise for at least 20 minutes

   ■ Continue monitoring anxiety and fear-related experiences using the LIFE form

   ■ Complete Daily ACT Ratings form

   ■ Complete Valued Directions worksheet

6. Session Materials and Handouts

   ■ Acceptance of Anxiety exercise instructions (two sets)

   ■ Acceptance of Anxiety practice form

   ■ Living in Full Experience (LIFE) form

   ■ Daily ACT Ratings form

   ■ Valued Directions worksheet

Agenda

1. Review of Daily Practice (5 min.)

Review the client's daily practice of the Acceptance of Thoughts and Feelings exercise and Daily ACT Ratings. Defer review of the LIFE form and Write Your Own Epitaph worksheet until you discuss values later in the session.

2. Learning to Accept Anxiety with Mindfulness (25 min.)

Instead of the usual centering exercise, begin this session with a brief 5-minute introduction to clarify the nature of acceptance and mindfulness. This introduction should be followed by a 15-minute Acceptance of Anxiety exercise.

The Nature of Acceptance and Mindfulness*

Please refer back to chapter 5 for a more detailed discussion on the nature of acceptance and mindfulness. Below is only a summary of the main points that therapists should convey to clients.

Acceptance means letting go of fighting the reality of having fear and anxiety. This means willingness to experience anxious thoughts, memories, sensations, and feelings as they are, without acting to avoid or escape from these experiences and the circumstances that may give rise to them, and without acting solely on the basis of what their mind may say about the meaning of these events (e.g., "I'm losing control," "I must be dying or going crazy," "I can't do XYZ because I am too anxious"). Point out to clients the close relation between acceptance, willingness, and life goal–related behavior. Linehan (1993) defined willingness as accepting what is, together with responding to what is, in an effective and appropriate way. It is doing what works and just what is needed in the current situation or moment. Experiential acceptance is a willingness to experience anxiety-related thoughts, feelings, memories, and physiological reactions so that clients can participate in activities that they deem important and meaningful (Orsello et al., 2004).

These definitions make it very clear that acceptance and willingness are not feelings. They are a stance toward life and are very much about behavior and action. Stress that acceptance within the context of anxiety does not imply passive resignation ("giving up"), inactivity, or diminished personal responsibility. On the contrary, mindful acceptance creates space for clients to think and feel their thoughts and emotions rather than continuing to resort to automatic, habitual ways of responding. Let clients know that the mindfulness and acceptance exercises in this program are designed to help them broaden their behavioral repertoire and increase flexibility in responding (Wilson & Murrell, 2004)—they are literally meant to increase their response-ability.

When discussing these notions with clients, point out that acceptance does not mean approving or condoning their experience (past or present). It is simply about acknowledging and experiencing what is there. What makes mindfulness exercises so useful for clients is that they encourage observing without evaluation or judgment and without getting rid of, suppressing, or otherwise changing what they experience. Point out that such observation without judgment and with compassion is "acceptance behavior" or "skillful experiencing" of life in the present moment. This is actually an active response—just not in the way we usually think of being active (as in running, fighting, struggling, etc.). Mindfulness exercises teach clients to allow private events such as thoughts and emotions to come and go, simply sitting with and noticing them *as they are* in the present moment (Greco & Eifert, 2004).

The ultimate goal of mindfulness is happiness in terms of freedom from unnecessary suffering. Suffering occurs when we push psychological pain away and do things to escape from experiencing it. Recall how Marsha Linehan (1993) defines suffering as

---

*   We acknowledge with gratitude Joanna Arch for her contributions to this section and her suggestions for wording and conducting the acceptance exercises.

"pain plus nonacceptance." Painful feelings of sadness and anxiety turn into suffering when we do not accept them and when we struggle to get rid of them. This leads us to become sad about being sad and fearful of having fear. Emphasize to clients that this is the type of suffering that mindfulness seeks to end and the type of freedom from suffering that mindful acceptance holds out for them. In this sense, the goal of mindfulness goes beyond acceptance of anxiety. Through mindfulness exercises, clients can gradually teach their mind to be less reactive, gain insight into how it works for and against them, and develop flexibility in responding to their mind. The goal is to develop a place of calm beneath the storm, to promote health and vitality, and to foster caring kindness toward themselves and others.

Acceptance of Anxiety Exercise

We adapted and tailored the Acceptance of Anxiety exercise to individuals with anxiety disorders from a more general set of acceptance exercises introduced by Segal and colleagues (2002) for use with depressed persons. At first, many clients are horrified by the notion that they should accept their anxiety, so explain to clients that accepting anxiety does not mean liking or wanting anxiety. It means dropping the rope and willingly making space for it when it is there—simply because it is there anyway. It means learning to see anxiety as it is (i.e., a jumble of uncomfortable feelings and physical sensations in the body) not as what their mind tells them it is (i.e., something dangerous, intolerable sensations that must be defeated, a sign that disaster is about to strike).

Tell clients that this exercise contains some elements from the Acceptance of Thoughts and Feelings exercise but focuses more explicitly on awareness of anxiety-related thoughts and bodily sensations and staying with such experiences until they no longer pull on the client's attention. The exercise is about actively making space for anxiety-related thoughts, feelings, and other experiences by allowing or letting them be rather than rushing in to fix or change them (Segal et al., 2002). When clients let anxiety be—simply noticing and observing whatever is already present—they begin to create space for it, thereby opening up a fundamentally different way of being with their anxiety experience. This exercise is critical because it specifically teaches clients new skills that foster a new way of relating with anxiety-related aversive bodily sensations, thoughts, and feelings. Such experiences will likely show up in future sessions and in real-life situations as clients move forward on their path toward valued life goals. We suggest that therapists read the instructions to clients in a slow and soft manner. The instructions for the exercise are also on the book CD.

---

1. In our previous exercises, we have used the breath as the focus of attention. When the mind wandered off and started focusing on thoughts, worries, images, or feelings, you were asked to notice these thoughts and feelings and then gently redirect attention back to your breath. In this exercise, we actively and openly invite into our awareness bodily sensations and unwanted thoughts, worries, and images so that you may learn

to approach them in an accepting and compassionate way. Just like in the finger trap and tug-of-war exercises, this exercise encourages you to *lean into* anxiety rather than fight it. Leaning into anxiety means creating a space for you to feel your emotions and think your thoughts, experiencing them as they are, rather than what your mind tells you they are. It also provides you with space to do things with your life that you may have put on hold for a long time. Are you willing to do an exercise to help you do that? [Wait for client's permission and then move on.]

2.   Go ahead and get in a comfortable position in your chair. Sit upright with your feet flat on the floor, your arms and legs uncrossed, and your hands resting in your lap (palms up or down, whichever is more comfortable). Allow your eyes to close gently [pause 10 seconds].

3.   Take a few moments to get in touch with the physical sensations in your body, especially the sensations of touch or pressure where your body makes contact with the chair or floor. Notice the gentle rising and falling of your breath in your chest and belly. There is no need to control your breathing in any way—simply let the breath breathe itself [pause 10 seconds]. As best you can, also bring this attitude of allowing and gentle acceptance to the rest of your experience. There is nothing to be fixed. Simply allow your experience to be your experience, without needing it to be other than what it is [pause 10 seconds].

4.   It is natural for your mind to wander away to thoughts, worries, images, bodily sensations, or feelings. Notice these thoughts and feelings, acknowledge their presence, and stay with them [pause 10 seconds]. There is no need to think of something else, make them go away, or resolve anything. As best you can, allow them to be ... giving yourself space to have whatever you have ... bringing a quality of kindness and compassion to your experience [pause 10 seconds].

5.   Allow yourself to be present to what you are afraid of. Notice any doubts, reservations, fears, and worries. Just notice them and acknowledge their presence, and do not work on them [pause 10 seconds]. Now see if for just a moment you can be present with your values and commitments. Ask yourself, Why am I here? Where do I want to go? What do I want to do? [pause 15 seconds]

6.   Now focus on a thought or situation that has been difficult for you. It could be a particular troubling thought, worry, image, or intense bodily sensations [pause 10 seconds]. Gently, directly, and firmly shift your attention on and into the discomfort, no matter how bad it seems [pause 10 seconds]. Notice any strong feelings that may arise in your

body, allowing them to be as they are rather than what you think they are, simply holding them in awareness [pause 10 seconds]. Stay with your discomfort and breathe with it [pause 10 seconds]. See if you can gently open up to it and make space for it, accepting and allowing it to be [pause], while bringing compassionate and focused attention to the sensations of discomfort [pause 15 seconds].

7. If you notice yourself tensing up and resisting what you have, pushing away from the experience, acknowledge that and see if you can make some space for whatever you're experiencing [pause 10 seconds]. Must this feeling or thought be your enemy? [pause 10 seconds] Or can you have it, notice it, own it, and let it be? [pause 10 seconds] Can you make room for the discomfort, for the tension, for the anxiety? [pause 10 seconds] What does it really feel like—moment to moment—to have them? [pause 10 seconds] Is this something you *must* struggle with or can you invite the discomfort in, saying to yourself with willingness, "Let me have it; let me feel what there is to be felt because it is my experience right now"? [pause 15 seconds]

8. If the sensations or discomfort grow stronger, acknowledge their presence, stay with them [pause 10 seconds], breathing with them, accepting them [pause 10 seconds]. Is this discomfort something you *must* not have, you *cannot* have? [pause 10 seconds] Even if your mind tells you that you cannot, can you open up a space for it in your heart? [pause 10 seconds] Is there room inside you to feel that with compassion and kindness toward yourself and your experience? [pause 15 seconds]

9. Apart from physical sensations in the body, you may also notice thoughts coming along with the sensations, and thoughts about the thoughts. When you notice any such thoughts, also invite them in . . . softening and opening to them as you become aware of them [pause 10 seconds]. You may also notice your mind coming up with evaluative labels such as "dangerous" or "getting worse." If that happens, you can simply thank your mind for the label [pause 10 seconds] and return to the present experience as it is, not as your mind says it is, noticing thoughts as thoughts, physical sensations as physical sensations, feelings as feelings—nothing more, nothing less [pause 15 seconds].

10. Stay with your discomfort for as long as it pulls on your attention [pause 10 seconds]. If and when you sense that the anxiety and other discomfort are no longer pulling for your attention, let them go [pause 15 seconds].

11. Then, when you are ready, gradually widen your attention to take in the sounds around you in this room [pause 10 seconds]. Take a moment to make the intention to bring this sense of gentle allowing and self-acceptance into the present moment [pause 5 seconds], and when you are ready, slowly open your eyes.

Acceptance Is Not a Clever Fix for Anxiety

After completing the exercise, ask clients how they experienced the exercise and discuss any comments, questions, or concerns. Therapists can also weave into this discussion some more points about the nature and purpose of mindful acceptance.

As we outlined early on, clients may use mindfulness as yet another control strategy to get relief from anxiety. Briefly point out that it is essential that clients not use mindfulness and other exercises in this program as clever ways to combat or fix their anxiety. This may work in the short run, but it is a step back to the old, unworkable control agenda. Hence, therapists should pay careful attention when clients talk about their experiences with mindfulness exercises. Examine whether clients are using such exercises to control or manage anxiety. For instance, it is fine when clients report that they find themselves better able to allow anxiety-related thoughts and feelings to be rather than fighting them or pushing them away. Here clients are making progress toward being more accepting of their experience.

On the other hand, when clients report positive changes (e.g., symptom relief) as a result of having used the mindfulness exercises, they link acceptance to positive feeling outcomes. In such instances, clients may be attempting to use mindfulness as part of the "doing/driven" mode to achieve the goal of relaxation or anxiety relief, which has little to do with mindful acceptance (cf. Segal et al., 2002). Remind clients that "acceptance is so important because its opposite is too risky. An unwillingness to accept negative feelings, physical sensations, or thoughts [because they are aversive] is the first link in the mental chain that can rapidly lead to the reinstatement of old, automatic, habitual, relapse-related patterns of mind" (Segal et al., 2002, p. 223).

Also emphasize that mindfulness and acceptance ultimately occur in the service of committed action. Hence, acceptance is a more skillful way for them to relate to anxiety by acknowledging its presence, allowing it to be and making space for it as it is, so that they can move forward with their lives. Acceptance empowers them to do what they really want to do *and* experience whatever they may experience along the way. It will also be important to reiterate this purpose when providing the rationale for exposure exercises in subsequent sessions.

3. Controlling Internal Versus External Events (10 min.)

The purpose of this section is to discuss with clients the contingencies that govern controllability. Ask clients whether they have heard of the serenity creed: Accept with serenity what you cannot change, have the courage to change what you can, and develop the wisdom to know the difference. Although many clients will have heard of it and agree with it, they simply do not know what they *can* change and what they *cannot* change in their life. Living the creed is difficult. We suggest the following text as a possibility for discussion.

The metaphors and exercises in this section are designed to help you to recognize what you can and cannot control, and to distinguish one from the other. Being able to make this distinction will help you better understand why anxiety became a problem for you, and it will point you in the direction of what to do and not to do. By now you already know that distracting yourself or telling yourself [use examples from client's experience or LIFE form] has not really worked to control your anxiety and worries. Yet there is a good reason why you keep on doing this type of thing. The reason is that taking control does work well in certain situations. For example, if you had this chair in your room and you no longer liked it, you could get rid of it by getting up, taking it, and throwing it into the garbage [therapist stands up, goes to a chair in the room, and hints at throwing it away]. Once it is gone, it's much like the saying "Out of sight, out of mind." [Ask clients to come up with similar examples on their own, and discuss them briefly.]

These and other examples involve situations where you really are in control. The important question is, what makes these situations controllable? They all involve objects or situations in the outside world—the world outside the skin. Getting rid of things you don't like in the outside world often *is* possible and has worked well for you.

Now what about controlling your thoughts and feelings? Can you also get rid of them or change them? By distracting yourself or using positive affirmations, you may feel better at first. But does it last? Do the worries, concerns, memories, and fears come back after a while? Do you recognize this pattern? Unlike old chairs that stay away after you toss them away, your thoughts and feelings keep coming back. The problem here is that what works well in the external world just does not work well in our internal world of thoughts and feelings. Here we are not in charge—our bodies and minds seem to march to their own tune. Yet, we often deal with our thoughts and feelings in the same way we deal with clothes we don't like or the chair we wish to throw away. If we don't like what we think and feel, we want to throw out those thoughts and feelings. And it just doesn't work.

The Polygraph Metaphor

At this point, remind clients of the finger trap and tug-of-war exercises. The purpose of these exercises was to demonstrate that control efforts do not work and that clients have the option of ending their struggle by letting go and doing something counterintuitive; that is, something different from what they have done in the past. The polygraph metaphor (Hayes, Strosahl, & Wilson, 1999) is therefore particularly suited for clients with anxiety disorders because it illustrates the paradoxical effects of attempting to control and reduce anxiety-related responses and how such efforts can backfire. Such control efforts typically are ineffective, and often make matters worse. In a sense, the polygraph metaphor illustrates the vicious cycle of anxious apprehension, bodily sensations, catastrophic evaluations of such sensations, and panic (Barlow, 2002).

Imagine you are hooked up to the best and most sensitive polygraph machine that's ever been built. Because this polygraph is incredibly effective in detecting anxiety, there is no way you can be aroused or anxious without the machine detecting it. Now here is your task: All you have to do is stay relaxed—just stay calm. If you get the least bit anxious, however, I will know it. I know you really want to stay relaxed. So I want to give you a special incentive to succeed. I will hold this revolver to your head [point your finger to your own temple and gesture about it going off]. If you just stay relaxed, I won't shoot. In fact, I will even give you $100,000! But if you get nervous—and remember, this perfect polygraph will notice that immediately—I'm going to have to kill you. So, just relax!

Therapist:	What do you think would happen in this situation?
Client:	I don't think I could do it, but what about you? Could you do it or help me do it?
Therapist:	I don't think I could do it either. The tiniest bit of anxiety would be terrifying. We'd be going "Oh, my God! I'm getting anxious! Here it comes!" We're dead.
Client:	I thought I was the one with the problem. Why can't *you* do it?
Therapist:	Because none of us can stay calm with a gun pointed at our head. If I were in that situation, I'd get shot, too. So it's not that you are somehow broken and need to be fixed by me. We're in this together.
Client:	Are you saying there is nothing we can do or control?
Therapist:	I'm not saying that at all. What if I had told you, "Get rid of that painting on the wall or I'll shoot you," instead of telling you to relax? You probably would have taken down the picture and given it away, and everything would be fine. That is how the world outside the skin works. We can change and control things by doing stuff with our hands and feet. But if I simply told you, "Relax, or I'll shoot you," what would happen?
Client:	I guess I'd get quite nervous and would get shot if there really was a gun.

Therapist: The harder you'd try, the more nervous you'd get because you would be able to tell it wasn't working. So why does it not work? What's the difference between getting rid of a picture on your wall and staying relaxed?

Client: Well, I can get rid of the picture by literally throwing it away with my hands, but I can't get inside my brain and change what's going on there. That's why I have tried talking to myself—you know, trying to calm myself down.

Therapist: How has that worked in your experience?

Client: Sometimes a bit, but not for long and certainly not as much as I would like it to.

Therapist: It is interesting that you mention your brain, because it is actually the command center of the perfect polygraph, and you're already hooked up to it. Your nervous system is better than any polygraph and will detect any anxiety you have. Now, in your situation, you've got something pointed at you that is even more threatening than any gun: the workability of your life. So what do you get when you notice anxiety and hold that powerful workability gun to your head and say, "Relax"?

Client: I'm getting shot! This is what my life feels like, and it's definitely not what I want.

Therapist: Perhaps we should be looking more closely at what it is that you do want. I mean what really matters to you deep down—and what it is that you can get.

Apart from illustrating the paradoxical effects of attempting to control and reduce anxiety-related responses, the polygraph metaphor helps clients experience the difference in how control works for most things in the external world versus how control works against us when applied to aspects of the private world. Conscious, deliberate, purposeful control works great in the manipulable world, where the following rule applies: "If you don't like it, figure out a way to get rid of it, and then get rid of it." This type of control, however, does not work with emotions, feelings, memories, worries, and bodily sensations. In fact, when control is applied to unpleasant thoughts and emotions, it tends to give us more of the very experiences we do not want to have. In such cases, deliberate control is not a solution; it becomes part of the problem or even *the* problem. Again, remind clients, "You can run but you can't hide. You simply cannot avoid yourself and what is happening inside of you. These experiences define what is uniquely human about you. To act against them is to act against your very being."

Any references to values in these discussions plant an important seed for future sessions and are a good transition to the next treatment section. Recall that valued living often gets pushed out of the way as anxious clients struggle to manage fear, panic, worries, and so on. Continued practice and work with the LIFE form serves to identify and emphasize these personal costs. In the last part of this session, we begin exploring values—something clients do have control over.

4. Exploring Values (15 min.)

Making a Commitment

This is an important emotional and potentially very motivating moment in therapy. First, review last week's LIFE form and focus on any instances where engaging in behavior to manage anxiety-related feelings and thoughts was associated with short- or long-term costs. Then move on to the epitaph exercise and discuss the client's experience with this exercise. If clients have identified one or more core values, the therapist can ask clients whether they are willing to take a stand and commit to these values.

Therapist:	I want you to connect with this statement on your epitaph and what you really intend to have in your life. Are you willing to stand up, look me in the eye, and tell me what is most deeply true about you, what you'd want your life to be about if you weren't living a life in the anxiety box?
Client:	I am not sure whether I will get out of the box, but I do know what I want in life.
Therapist:	Okay, then please stand up, look at me, and tell me: *what do you want to be about?*
Client:	I want to be a loving partner, independent, and a great architect.
Therapist:	*[keeping eye contact with the client]* Then I want what we do together to be about that! *[pause]* You can have that.

The discussion of what clients want their lives to stand for and their subsequent commitment to these values is a good basis for a more specific discussion of values and goals. Some clients initially are confused as to what therapists mean by "values." A simple way to describe values is to refer to them as parts of life that are important to most people. We categorize values into domains or areas: family, friends, romantic relationships, leisure, education, career, citizenship, health, and spirituality. Although we list domains separately, most domains overlap. For example, the value of education can lead to a career, and your career can lead to meeting new friends.

The epitaph exercise and other value-related exercises often make people sad when they realize how much of their lives they put on hold in the service of managing or avoiding anxiety. This is a good opportunity to reassess the client's agenda. Until now, this agenda typically has been, "I will only be able to move on with my life after my anxiety symptoms are lessened or controlled." Therapists can encourage clients to use these life directions as both a guide and a justification for the hard work of treatment. Whenever therapists notice, or clients report, attempts at symptom alleviation, therapists should ask clients whether these attempts move them toward or away from life goals. Again, the issue is not whether control or acceptance behavior is the "better" strategy—the question is what behavior works and helps clients move toward their chosen life directions.

Valued Directions Worksheet

Therapists should briefly explain how to complete the Valued Directions worksheet provided at the end of this chapter and on the book CD. It is a somewhat lengthy form that incorporates the ten life domains examined in the Valued Living Questionnaire (Wilson & Groom, 2002) and parts of the value worksheets presented in our ACT anorexia workbook (Heffner & Eifert, 2004) and in the book by Hayes, Strosahl, and Wilson (1999). It is essential that clients complete this worksheet at home and bring it back to the next session because the identified directions will be used to construct a Life Compass and identify barriers to moving in those directions. This exercise also will become the focus of exposure exercises in subsequent treatment sessions. So ask clients whether they are 100 percent willing to make a commitment to complete this worksheet for the next session.

Values Versus Goals

One of the most common problems we encounter when we ask clients about their values is that they confuse values with goals. For instance, a client may say, "I want to be less anxious" or "I want to be more at peace with myself." Both statements sound like values, when they are really goals. One could regard being less anxious and more at peace as emotional goals. Essentially, being more calm or at peace is an outcome, a result that may (or may not) happen *after* we start moving toward our values. Values are a direction. They must be lived out (Hayes, Strosahl, & Wilson, 1999). They are what you do.

Goals are destinations. Goals are actions that people can tick off and complete—you've done it or not (e.g., losing ten pounds, taking a vacation, getting a degree, mowing the lawn). Once we reach a goal, the work is done, and we are finished. For example, getting married is a goal. Once that ring is on your finger, your goal is achieved. Values are lifelong journeys. One can answer the question "Am I done yet?" for goals, but not for values. They have no end point. Instead, they direct us throughout life. For example, the value of being a loving, devoted partner is not complete the moment you say "I do." Being a loving, devoted partner is something you must constantly keep on working toward, and there is always room for improvement. Also, reaching a particular goal (getting married) is just one of many steps in a valued direction (being a loving partner).

Although values and goals are not the same, they are related. Also, different values can underlie the same goal. For instance, most college students pursue the same goal: They want to graduate from college. They have reached this destination or goal when they have the degree certificate in hand. Different values may underlie the goal of a college education. Some people want to earn a degree because they value learning and education. Others value being financially secure, and earning a degree is a step toward a higher income. Others value friendship, and college is a way to meet new people and make friends. You can then ask clients to examine their own behavior and identify the values that underlie their goals. Ask them to think of one or two goals they have set for themselves. To determine the value that underlies the goal, they can ask themselves, "Why am I doing this?" "What am I trying to accomplish in my life with this goal?" "Where am I heading with this?"

5. Experiential Life Enhancement Exercises (Home)

- Practice of the Acceptance of Anxiety exercise for at least 20 minutes daily, and complete the practice form after each practice. Give clients a copy of the instructions to take home.

- Continue monitoring anxiety and fear-related experiences using the LIFE form

- Complete the Daily ACT Ratings form

- Complete the Valued Directions worksheet

ACCEPTANCE OF ANXIETY

Life Enhancement Exercise Record Form

In the first (left) column, record whether you made a commitment to practice the Acceptance of Anxiety exercise that day and include the date. In the second column, record whether you actually practiced, when you practiced, and how long you practiced. In the third column, record whether you used a tape or not. In the fourth column, write down anything that comes up during your practice and that you would like to talk about at our next meeting.

Commitment: yes/no Date:	Practiced: yes/no When practiced? How long (min.)?	Tape/CD: yes / no	Comments
Saturday: Date:	Practiced: yes / no Time: A.M./P.M. Minutes:		
Sunday: Date:	Practiced: yes / no Time: A.M./P.M. Minutes:		
Monday: Date:	Practiced: yes / no Time: A.M./P.M. Minutes:		
Tuesday: Date:	Practiced: yes / no Time: A.M./P.M. Minutes:		
Wednesday: Date:	Practiced: yes / no Time: A.M./P.M. Minutes:		
Thursday: Date:	Practiced: yes / no Time: A.M./P.M. Minutes:		
Friday: Date:	Practiced: yes / no Time: A.M./P.M. Minutes:		

VALUED DIRECTIONS

Below are areas of life that some people value. We are concerned with your quality of life in each of these areas. One aspect of quality of life involves the importance you put on different areas of living. First rate the importance of each area by circling a number on a scale of 0, 1, or 2. Not everyone will value all of these areas, or value all areas the same. Rate each area according to *your own personal sense of importance*. If you rated an area as unimportant (0), move right on to rate the importance of the next area. If you rated an area moderately or very important (1 or 2), make a rating of how satisfied you are with the quality and depth of your experience in this area of life. Then rate how often you have done something to move you forward in this area during the last week. After completing your ratings, write down your intention of how you would like to live your life in that area (e.g., what is most important to you in that area?) Always leave the second line (barriers) blank. We will discuss them and complete those lines in the next session.

Family (other than marriage or parenting): *How do you want to interact with your family members? What type of sister or brother do you want to be? What type of son or daughter do you want to be?*

How important is this area to you?

 0 = not at all   1 = moderately   2 = very important

Overall, how satisfied are you with the quality and depth of your experience in this area of life?

 0 = not at all   1 = moderately   2 = very important

How often have you done something to move you forward in this area during the last week?

 0 = no action   1 = once or twice

 2 = three or four times   3 = more than four times

Intention: _____

Barriers: _____

Intimate Relationships (e.g., marriage, couples): *What is your ideal relationship like? What type of relationship would you like to have? What kind of partner do you want to be in an intimate relationship? How would you treat your partner?*

Importance:	0 = not at all important	1 = moderately important	2 = very important	
Satisfaction:	0 = not at all satisfied	1 = moderately satisfied	2 = very satisfied	
Actions (last week):	0 = no action	1 = once or twice	2 = three or four times	3 = more than four times

Intention: _____

Barriers: _____

Parenting: *What type of parent do you want to be? How do you want to interact with your children?*

| Importance: | 0 = not at all important | 1 = moderately important | 2 = very important |

| Satisfaction: | 0 = not at all satisfied | 1 = moderately satisfied | 2 = very satisfied |

| Actions (last week): | 0 = no action | 1 = once or twice | 2 = three or four times | 3 = more than four times |

Intention: _____

Barriers: _____

Friends / Social Life: *What type of friend do you want to be? What does it mean to be a good friend? How would you behave toward your best friend? Why is friendship important to you?*

| Importance: | 0 = not at all important | 1 = moderately important | 2 = very important |

| Satisfaction: | 0 = not at all satisfied | 1 = moderately satisfied | 2 = very satisfied |

| Actions (last week): | 0 = no action | 1 = once or twice | 2 = three or four times | 3 = more than four times |

Intention: _____

Barriers: _____

Work / Career: *What do you value about your work? Financial security? Intellectual challenge? Independence? Prestige? Getting to interact with other people? Helping people? What type of work would you like to do?*

| Importance: | 0 = not at all important | 1 = moderately important | 2 = very important |

| Satisfaction: | 0 = not at all satisfied | 1 = moderately satisfied | 2 = very satisfied |

| Actions (last week): | 0 = no action | 1 = once or twice | 2 = three or four times | 3 = more than four times |

Intention: _____

Barriers: _____

Education / Training: *Why is learning important to you? Are there any skills you'd like to learn?*

Importance: 0 = not at all   1 = moderately   2 = very important
                        important   important

Satisfaction: 0 = not at all   1 = moderately   2 = very satisfied
                         satisfied   satisfied

Actions (last week):   0 = no   1 = once or   2 = three or   3 = more than
                        action   twice   four times   four times

Intention: _____

Barriers: _____

Recreation / Fun: *What type of activities do you enjoy? What type of activities would you really like to engage in? Why do you enjoy them?*

Importance: 0 = not at all   1 = moderately   2 = very important
                        important   important

Satisfaction: 0 = not at all   1 = moderately   2 = very satisfied
                         satisfied   satisfied

Actions (last week):   0 = no   1 = once or   2 = three or   3 = more than
                        action   twice   four times   four times

Intention: _____

Barriers: _____

Spirituality: *This domain is about faith and spirituality rather than organized religion. Why is faith important to you? If this is important in your life, what is it that makes this so important?*

Importance: 0 = not at all   1 = moderately   2 = very important
                        important   important

Satisfaction: 0 = not at all   1 = moderately   2 = very satisfied
                         satisfied   satisfied

Actions (last week):   0 = no   1 = once or   2 = three or   3 = more than
                        action   twice   four times   four times

Intention: _____

Barriers: _____

Citizenship / Community Life: *What can you do to make the world a brighter place? Are community activities (e.g., volunteering, voting, recycling) important to you? Why?*

Importance: 0 = not at all   1 = moderately   2 = very important
                              important   important

Satisfaction: 0 = not at all   1 = moderately   2 = very satisfied
                              satisfied   satisfied

Actions (last week):   0 = no   1 = once or   2 = three or   3 = more than
                              action   twice   four times   four times

Intention: _____

Barriers: _____

Health / Physical Self-Care: *What issues related to health and physical well-being do you care about (e.g., sleep, diet, exercise)? Why and how do you take care of yourself?*

Importance: 0 = not at all   1 = moderately   2 = very important
                              important   important

Satisfaction: 0 = not at all   1 = moderately   2 = very satisfied
                              satisfied   satisfied

Actions (last week):   0 = no   1 = once or   2 = three or   3 = more than
                              action   twice   four times   four times

Intention: _____

Barriers: _____

Session 5
Moving Toward a Valued Life with an Accepting, Observing Self

GOALS AND THEME

The major goal of Session 5 is to prepare clients for subsequent in-session and between-session exposure exercises and to link those exercises to the client's values and goals. Previous exercises have already laid the necessary groundwork. At this point, clients should have developed some rudimentary skills for observing anxiety in a mindful, accepting way. Several exercises in this session are designed to facilitate further development of an accepting observer perspective (self-as-context). In so doing, clients will gain additional practice distinguishing between experiences they have (thoughts, emotions, and physical sensations) and the person having them. Clients also learn that they have a choice. They can choose to observe and accept their anxiety for what it is, or choose to react to it in a way that has limited their options and their lives.

Using the Valued Directions worksheet as a guide, begin by helping your client complete the Life Compass by focusing attention on specific values, goals, and barriers to achieving those goals. Clients and therapists should then compare the importance of identified values with how much time clients have recently devoted to these values. A discussion of the discrepancy between importance and consistency ratings will identify some common barriers to movement in valued directions. This exercise serves an important motivational function for exposure exercises in subsequent treatment sessions, and provides the context for such exercises.

Session Outline

1. Centering Exercise (5 min.)

2. Review of Daily Practice (5 min.)

   - Review daily practice of Acceptance of Anxiety exercise and Daily ACT Ratings

3. Self as Context Versus Content (20 min.)

   - Playing Volleyball with Anxiety Thoughts and Feelings

   - The Chessboard Metaphor and Exercise

   - Anxiety News Radio Metaphor

4.   Life Compass—The Ultimate Reason for Exposure (25 min.)

   - Review LIFE form

   - Review Valued Directions worksheet

   - Complete Life Compass

5.   Experiential Life Enhancement Exercises (Home)

   - Daily practice of Acceptance of Anxiety exercise at home for at least 20 minutes

   - Continue monitoring anxiety and fear-related experiences using the LIFE form

   - Complete Daily ACT Ratings form

   - Rewrite Life Compass based on in-session discussion

6.   Session Materials and Handouts

   - Acceptance of Anxiety practice form

   - Living in Full Experience (LIFE) form

   - Daily ACT Ratings form

   - Life Compass form (2 copies)

   - Chessboard with two teams of players

   - Printout of Anxiety News Radio metaphor text (if possible, also paste text on the front and back of an index card for client to take home)

Agenda

1. Centering Exercise (5 min.)

Begin the session with the centering exercise described at the end of Session 1.

2. Review of Daily Practice (5 min.)

First, briefly review Daily ACT Ratings and the client's daily practice of the Acceptance of Anxiety exercise, paying attention to any lack of compliance for reasons having to do with unwillingness, lack of commitment, or high fearfulness. Defer reviewing the Values Assessment worksheet and LIFE form until you introduce the Life Compass later in the session.

3. Self as Context Versus Content (20 min.)

The idea of a self that is context as opposed to a self that is defined by its content (what is in it or what it is made of) is quite abstract and difficult to grasp, even for professionals. Self as context is a stance toward oneself and the world. Here the self is not the experience but simply provides the context for experience. Clients often have a hard time grasping this concept and the notion of an *observer self*. The observer self simply observes experience without taking sides (e.g., "good" or "bad"). The metaphors and exercises in this session are designed to help clients experience that they are not the content of their experience. They are the context for their experiences. The metaphors also bring out the behavioral implications of being an observer: Clients can make choices that are different from those they made in the past.

Start the discussion by pointing out that most people (not just clients) find it difficult to grasp the idea that we are not our experience; that is, we are not our thoughts, our worries, our bodily sensations, our feelings, our histories. These experiences are a part of us. They come and go. We do not own them. We cannot hold on to them if we like them. We cannot make them go away if we dislike them. Also, one thought does not define us more than another thought. The content, and perhaps social desirability, of our experiences may change over time. Yet, a "good" thought ("I am confident") is not more like us than a "bad" thought ("I'd like to hit this man"). Either thought is no better or worse than any other thought. Much like a house provides the context (e.g., rooms with walls, floors, and ceilings) for people to live in along with all their furniture and other belongings, the self (with the brain and the rest of the body) provides the context for our experiences to occur (Hayes, Strosahl, & Wilson, 1999). The house basically remains the same regardless of who lives in it, what furniture is in it, and whether its walls are painted white or red. And as far as we know, the house probably doesn't care much about who lives in it, what people do in it, what they think or feel, or what furniture its inhabitants may put in it. The house just provides the space or context for all of that living to occur.

Playing Volleyball with Anxiety Thoughts and Feelings

We first used this metaphor in the context of an ACT treatment program for anorexia (Heffner & Eifert, 2004). Below is an adaptation for use with clients with anxiety disorders.

Throughout a volleyball match, both teams strive to keep the ball in action, back and forth from one side of the court to the other and never letting the ball hit the ground. Each time the ball is about to sail across the net to one side of the court, a player in the front row jumps up to block it with her bare hands. Behind the blocker are five other players strategically positioned to keep the ball in motion. If the ball is not blocked, a player in the back row dives to the ground with her arms stretched out to pop the ball into the air, as another teammate is set up to deliver a mighty spike to send the ball back to the other side. All the while, each player stands alert and ready, trying to read the opponents in anticipation of their next move.

The strategy of volleyball is a way of describing how you are responding to anxiety-related thoughts and feelings. Imagine that a volleyball match is going on inside your mind. Instead of volleying a ball back and forth, the teams inside your head are volleying thoughts about you. Much like competitive volleyball, which is not exactly the fun leisure activity you play on a nice day at the beach, your anxiety-related thoughts seem intense and forceful. And just when you thought they might be taking a rest, they are right back in your face, challenging you and yelling at you to take them on.

On one side of the court is Team A (Anxiety). Team A serves up the following thought: *If you go to the mall tomorrow, you're going to have a horrific panic attack. This could be the big one you've always been afraid of!*

Team S (Struggle) is ready for action, diving to the ground to prevent that thought from touching down: *Wait a minute. I have gone before and I can do it again.*

At this point, Team A keeps the ball in motion: *That's what you think now, but when you get there, I am going to be so big that you'll just run and leave as quickly as you can. I'm going to yell right into your face and tell you to get out of that place. You might not even get out in time and just end up lying on the floor with people staring at you.*

Across the net, the thought goes, with Team S ready for the return: *I am going to ask my friend to come with me. She can help me if things get out of control.*

Before that thought crosses the net, Team A blocks it with: *But she can't really help you. When I attack you, you have no chance of beating me—no matter who is with you. I am in control here, in case you hadn't noticed it.*

Then, Team S powers back with: *Well, at least I can try to beat you.*

And so the game goes on and on. As soon as Team Anxiety serves up an unsettling thought, Team Struggle responds to that thought by somehow arguing with it. Have you noticed how this volleyball competition of thoughts and feelings seems to go on in your head?

Ask clients to think of examples of mental volleyball they have been playing with anxiety-related thoughts and feelings. For clients with GAD or OCD, you can use the activity of worrying or struggling with intrusive thoughts as perfect examples of mental volleyball.

After discussing a few examples of how your client plays mental volleyball, you can present an additional metaphor that suggests the possibility of responding differently by taking a different perspective. Fighting with anxiety has become a firmly ingrained habit for most clients. So the idea of *deliberately* observing rather than *mindlessly* participating in a struggle with anxiety is likely to be quite foreign to them. The following chessboard metaphor illustrates that clients do have an option that is different from struggling. The chessboard metaphor was first described by Hayes, Strosahl, and Wilson (1999) and can be applied in a flexible way to address fighting with internal events such as thoughts, feelings, memories, and physical sensations. Instead of choosing to be a member of Team A or Team S in the volleyball game, clients can choose to be the chessboard instead of being a player on either the black team or the white team. In fact, they *are* the board already—it's just that they have never before taken this perspective.

The Chessboard Metaphor and Exercise

Rather than presenting this metaphor verbally, we prefer to use an actual chess board with two teams of players on it. Using a real board with players should help increase the experiential salience of the metaphor and make it more concrete. Also, even if people don't know anything about the rules of chess, they will get the general idea of the game if you demonstrate how players knock each other off the board and try to outsmart each other through various maneuvers.

Look at this chessboard. It's covered with different-colored pieces—black pieces and white pieces. They work together in teams: The white pieces fight against the black pieces and vice versa. You can think of your thoughts and feelings and beliefs as these pieces; they also hang out together in teams. For example, "bad" thoughts, memories, and feelings like anxiety hang out on one side (the "dark team"), whereas the "good" pieces (e.g., thoughts expressing self-confidence, feelings of being in control, etc.) hang out on the other side of the board. They all move toward members of the other team in an effort to defeat the other side—to take over the opposing team's space on the board, and ultimately the whole board. So, when the dark knight of the anxiety team attacks, you get up on the back of the white queen, ride into battle, and knock the dark knight out by doing or thinking something to defeat the dark knight. [Therapist can literally knock a few players off the board.]

Therapist:	Is this the end of this war? Is the anxiety team gone and defeated?
Client:	No, one of the other guys will step forward and try to knock me down.
Therapist:	It seems like there are a lot of anxiety players left on this board, just patiently waiting for their chance to attack you.
Client:	It sure feels like that. But if I fight back using smart tactics and maneuvers, can't I eventually take them all out? I mean, eventually all the anxiety thoughts and feelings should be dead and gone.
Therapist:	I can see your point. Looking back at your experience, has this ever happened in your struggle with anxiety?
Client:	I wish it had. I guess I wouldn't be here then. Perhaps I'm just not smart enough.

Therapist: Or perhaps this is not at all about being smart? Something in *this* game is different from an actual chess game. If we were playing a real chess game, I would be in charge of one team and you would be in charge of the other. I would never know your strategy and next move and you would never know mine, because we are two different players. If you were to use a clever strategy and make the right moves in that situation, you could actually beat me for good. When it comes to the chess game against your anxiety, however, a tricky problem arises that ensures that you can never win that game. The two opposing teams are really one team, and there is only one player in this game: *you.* The thoughts on both sides of the board are *your* thoughts and feelings. They both belong to you. You support them with your board. No matter which side wins, one part of you will always be a loser. You can never win a competition where your own thoughts compete against each other. If you side with one particular team, huge portions of yourself are your own enemy. It's like waging a war against yourself. This is a game you just cannot win.

Client: And the game is very tiring, too.

Therapist: This war game surely sucks up a lot of life juices. You are fighting to win the war against anxiety, trying to knock off enough of those pieces so that you eventually dominate them. Except in this game, you can't ever seem to win the battle. Although you can knock down the black pieces temporarily, you can't ever knock them off the board for good. They keep coming back to life no matter what you did to strike them down beforehand. So the battle goes on, every day, for years. You feel hopeless and sense that you can't win, and yet you can't stop fighting. And as long as you're on the back of that white horse or queen, fighting is the only choice you have.

[*This is a good time to introduce a new perspective—one that clients probably have not contemplated before.*]

Therapist: Let's step back and think about what is really going on here. What if I told you that those chess pieces aren't you anyway? Can you see who else you would be? [Respond to all client answers; ultimate answer is, "You are the board."] Within this game, what would happen to all the pieces if there were no board?

Client: They'd just go away. We couldn't play. Without the board, there is no game.

Therapist: Yes, it seems like the role of the board is to let it all happen. If you're the pieces, however, the outcome of the game is very important; you've got to beat that anxiety as if your life depends on it. But if you're the board, *it doesn't matter if the war stops or not.* The game may go on, and it doesn't make any difference to the board. As the board, you can see all the pieces, you can hold them and have them played out on you, and you can simply watch all the action. And the board doesn't care which team seems to be winning or losing. Same thing with the volleyball game: Instead of siding with Team A or S, you could be the volleyball court and simply look at the action.

Client: Is that why we've been doing these mindfulness exercises?

Therapist: Well, they are a way of getting in touch with the part of you that is the volleyball court and the chessboard. You can simply watch what is going on, and you don't need to respond to anything. For instance, the volleyball court is merely there and watches and holds all of the players, the net, and the ball. The court does not care who wins or loses. The court does not worry about the outcome and will continue to be there after the game is over, as different players come and go. Occasionally, the players pounce and dive on the court, and it is possible that the court will suffer some scuff marks and poundings.

Client: It seems like I have quite a few of those.

Therapist: And it is okay to feel that pain. The fact that you, the court, sometimes experiences pain is just a reminder that being an observer is easier said than done. As you observe your thoughts and feelings, you notice that some of them are painful and scary. You may not like what you think or feel, and you may wish you felt differently. However, your thoughts and feelings—all of them—are a part of you. They are not *you*, but they are all a part of you. If you choose to be the court and the board, you are an impartial observer who watches the games take place; you need not be a player with a stake in the outcome of each game.

Anxiety News Radio Metaphor**

The chessboard and volleyball metaphors serve to illustrate the notion that we need not fight and struggle with our experience—we can choose to observe and accept instead. Perhaps an even simpler way of summarizing this ACT principle is that we can choose what we pay attention to. This choice is humorously illustrated in the Anxiety News Radio metaphor. The text of this metaphor is also on the book CD. Though most

---

**   We are grateful to Peter Thorne, a British clinical psychologist, for sharing this metaphor with us and allowing us to use it in this book. We are also grateful to Steven Hayes for the rewording of "Just So Radio."

metaphors used throughout this book should not be read verbatim, we suggest that you print both parts of this metaphor on the front and back of an index card and read it verbatim to the client in the voice of a radio news anchor. At the end of the session, clients can then take the index card home or put it in their pocket, purse, or briefcase and refer to it later as they see fit.

ANXIETY NEWS RADIO (WANR): "This is Anxiety News Radio, WANR, broadcasting inside your head twenty-four hours a day, seven days a week. Wherever you are, the signal will reach you. When you wake in the early hours, we'll be there to make you aware of all the unhappy aspects of your life, even before you get out of bed. Let us take over and control your life. Anxiety News Radio is compelling listening, and guess why! It's the news station you've grown up with, and now it comes to you automatically, 24/7. Pay attention! Anxiety News Radio knows what's best for you and we want you to buy our products. We advertise only what is most disturbing and distressing to you personally. So don't forget that, and remember, if you should forget us and ACT without seeking permission, then we'll broadcast all the louder. Remember, what you think and feel inside your skin can be really awful, so you should stay tuned to this station to know what to think and how to control it."

JUST SO RADIO (WJSR): "Wake up! Anxiety News Radio is just a station—you can tune in, or you can tune out! One thing is guaranteed though, whatever the time of day, you'll hear the same old stuff on WANR. If that's been really helpful to you, then go ahead, tune in and stay tuned. That would make sense. If not, then tune in more often to Just So Radio. We bring you the news of actual experience, in the moment—all live, all the time. *Actuality is our business!* We give it to you straight—as it is, not as your mind says it is. In contact with the world outside and inside the skin, you can experience what it is to be human, and it's entirely free! We can guarantee that experiencing what's inside the skin—exactly as it is—will never damage you, but it just might bring you joy. Just So Radio brings you information about how things are, not how you fear they might be. Just So Radio invites you to step forward and touch the world, just as it is, and to touch your life, just as it is. We get louder the more you listen to us. So, stay tuned. Give us a fair trial, and if not convinced by your own experience (please don't take our word for it) then WANR—Anxiety News Radio—is still there on the dial."

Our colleague, Peter Thorne, who provided the Anxiety News Radio metaphor, also shared an interesting comment with us from one of his clients with an anxiety disorder. She told him that she'd gotten tired of listening to Anxiety News Radio long before she came into therapy. However, it had never occurred to her that she didn't have to stay glued 24/7, slavishly believing all the broadcasts inside her mind. The idea that she could tune into more helpful sources of information out there in her world of actual real-life experience was a helpful new direction for her.

4. Life Compass—The Ultimate Reason for Exposure (25 min.)

Return to the discussion on values by first reviewing last week's LIFE form and focusing on any instances of clients engaging in behavior to manage anxiety-related feelings and thoughts and how such behavior may have interfered with what clients really care about or wanted to do.

Next, take out a Life Compass form and tell clients you will be using the information from their Valued Directions worksheet to complete the Life Compass (Dahl et al., 2002). Explain that the person in the middle of the compass is the client, surrounded by ten life domains. This is a good opportunity to help clients clarify or simplify any value statements. Sometimes clients find it easier to refer to these value statements as intentions—that is, how they would like to live their life in that area. Ask clients to copy the intention statements from the worksheet into the life compass for areas they rated as at least moderately important. What is most important to them in that area? Then ask clients to copy their importance rating from the worksheet to the "i" box connected to each value. The next step is to examine how much their current behavior is in accord with these importance ratings.

We have gone all around your life compass and looked at how important each dimension is for you, and you have written your intentions in each area that matters to you at least moderately. Now please think about your activities in the past week. We can call your activities your "feet." In this past week, how consistent were your feet with these intentions, the ones you just wrote down? How consistent have your actions been with your intentions? In other words, how actively have you been working toward those intentions? I am not asking about your ideal in each area or what others think of you. I just want to know how you think you have been doing during the past week. So for each intention, rate how often have you done something to move you forward in this area during the last week. Use the same activity rating scale as on the Valued Directions Worksheet (0 = no action, 1 = once or twice, 2 = three or four times, 3 = more than four times). Write your ratings in the "c" box next to the "i" box connected to each value. These ratings will give you an idea of how consistent your behavior has been with your values.

[*The next step is to compare how well intentions and behavior have matched. Are clients doing things that are important to them? It is quite likely that there will be discrepancies between importance and consistency ratings. This means that clients have identified their values but are not moving in a direction that supports those values.*]

Therapist: What do you see when you look at your life compass?

Client: It doesn't look good. It looks like I am living a life far different from the one I wanted. But I guess that's what happens to everyone. What you want is one thing and how things turn out is something else.

Therapist: Which of those values has changed?

Client: None of them, it's just that some are probably unrealistic and others are just too darn hard.

Therapist: Tell me why they are unrealistic or too hard. What is stopping you from reaching those goals and moving closer to your intentions? Is it okay if I write your reasons under the heading of "stories" or "barriers"?

Go to each area where you see high importance ratings and low activity/consistency ratings, and ask clients to explain the discrepancy. Ask clients to think about what stands in the way of pursuing the valued direction they have identified. Although clients are likely to report a number of barriers that stand in their way, many of them will be directly related to anxiety. Summarize them in succinct one-line statements and write them into the Valued Directions worksheet. The barriers can also be written in brief telegram-style fashion on the Life Compass next to the corresponding arrow. It is helpful to separate the stories into internal and external barriers. Typical examples of internal barriers are thoughts, feelings, and worries. Common examples of external barriers are lack of money, time, space, and availability. At this point, therapists need not discuss how to deal with barriers. This will be a major focus of subsequent sessions.

In our experience, making concrete the major discrepancies between highly valued intentions and low consistency ratings is a powerful emotional experience for clients. It shows clients in their own handwriting what they want to do with their lives and how much they have given up in the service of managing their anxiety and worries. Again, the issue is not whether controlling anxiety or accepting anxiety is the better strategy—the question is what type of behavior works in terms of moving clients closer to their chosen life goals.

We have found that by working on and rewriting intentions and barriers, the Life Compass tends to look rather messy by the end of the session. For this reason, we give clients a clean form to take home and ask them to copy the statements and rating numbers from the form used in session onto the clean form at home. Doing so alone at home will once again let clients experience what they care about and what they have been missing out on.

5. Experiential Life Enhancement Exercises (Home)

■   Practice the Acceptance of Anxiety exercise for at least 20 minutes daily, and complete the practice form after each practice

■   Continue monitoring anxiety and fear-related experiences using the LIFE form

■   Complete the Daily ACT Ratings

■   Rewrite the Life Compass based on in-session discussion

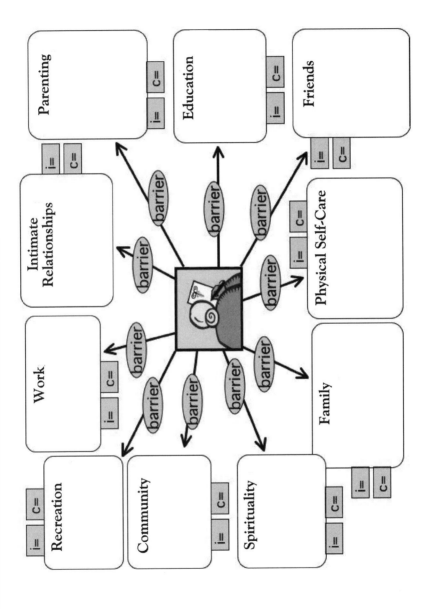

Figure 3. The Life Compass—a behavioral compass of valued life domains, intentions in each area, and potential barriers to reaching those goals (adapted from Dahl et al., 2004; Copyright 2004 by the Association for the Advancement of Behavior Therapy). Reprinted by permission of the publisher.

CHAPTER 10

Creating Flexible Patterns of Behavior Through Value-Guided Exposure

Session 6

It is only by practicing through a continual succession of agreeable and disagreeable situations that we acquire true strengths. To accept that pain is inherent and to live our lives from this understanding is to create the causes and conditions for happiness.

—Suzuki Roshi

GOALS AND THEME

The major goal of Session 6 is to create broader and more flexible patterns of behavior by means of exposure, mindful observation, and defusion. Recall that the main problem with anxiety disorders is not that clients experience extreme or intense levels of anxiety. The problem is that clients approach anxiety management much like they would a full-time job. This managerial position is demanding and requires that clients put their lives on full or partial hold to get the job done right. In the process, living is not getting done. If there were such a thing as a company called Life, many anxious clients would end up being fired for spending too much time with anxiety management decisions. This sharp narrowing of behavioral response patterns focused on dealing with anxiety is the source of a great deal of suffering and a major barrier to living (Wilson & Murrell, 2004).

During in-session exposure-like FEEL exercises, clients learn to let go of the struggle to escape or control anxiety-related thoughts, worries, and bodily sensations by acknowledging their presence and even embracing and leaning into them. The general goal of these exercises is not to reduce or eliminate anxiety. Instead, the goal is to provide clients with more flexible patterns of behavior when experiencing anxiety. By increasing their psychological and experiential flexibility, clients gain space to move in valued directions and freedom to become general contractors of life. In the process, clients may experience fear reduction as a by-product of running toward reality instead of away from it. This is so, in part, because extinction (i.e., anxiety attenuation) processes operate when one is willing to be exposed to reality as it is, regardless of the reasons used to justify exposure.

Session Outline

1. Centering Exercise (5 min.)

2. Review of Daily Practice (5 min.)

3. Emotional Willingness (5–10 min.)
   - Trying Versus Doing: The Pen Exercise
   - Willingness Thermostat Metaphor

4. Dealing with Intense Feelings and Thoughts (15 min.)
   - The Bus Driver Exercise

5. Exposure Within ACT: FEEL Exercises (25 min.)
   - How Does Traditional Exposure Work?
   - The Context and Purpose of Exposure in ACT

- Rationale for FEEL Exercises: To Facilitate Valued Living
- Determining Appropriate FEEL Exercises
- Types of Interoceptive FEEL Exercises
- Implementation of FEEL Exercises
- Dealing with Urges to Escape During Panic Attacks and in OCD

6. FEEL Exercise Practice (Home)

- Daily practice of Acceptance of Anxiety exercise for at least 20 minutes
- Practice of at least one interoceptive and/or imagery exercise chosen by client for at least 30 minutes per day
- Continue monitoring anxiety and fear-related experiences using the LIFE form
- Complete Daily ACT Ratings form

7. Session Materials and Handouts

- Acceptance of Anxiety practice form
- Living in Full Experience (LIFE) form
- Daily ACT Ratings form
- FEEL Sensation Record forms (as needed; one for each day of practice)
- FEEL Imagery Record forms (as needed; one for each day of practice)
- Weekly Valued Life Goal Activities form
- 4 index cards for the bus driver exercise

Agenda

1. *Centering Exercise (5 min.)*

Begin the session with the centering exercise described in Session 1.

2. *Review of Daily Practice (5 min.)*

Review the client's daily practice of the Acceptance of Anxiety exercise and discuss any problems they may have encountered with the exercise. Next, review the Daily

ACT Ratings form followed by the LIFE form, focusing on any instances of clients engaging in behavior to manage thoughts, sensations, and feelings. Help the client see the connection between such actions and short- and long-term costs in terms of how they want to live their lives. For instance, did behavior in the service of managing anxiety get in the way of something that clients value or care about as mentioned in their Life Compass?

3.   Emotional Willingness (5–10 min.)

Now is a good time for a brief discussion of emotional willingness, because it is directly related to internal barriers ("too much anxiety" or "can't stand it") that clients will have mentioned. Discussion of willingness also is important because it represents an essential aspect of the upcoming exposure-like exercises.

Recall that willingness is a concept that can easily be misunderstood. Many clients think that willingness is something they do not feel when it comes to anxiety. That is, they tend to see willingness as a feeling that does not make a whole lot of sense given that they clearly do not like the way they feel about anxiety. When you, as a therapist, use the term "willingness," clients might think that you are asking them to change how they feel about anxiety. This is not the case. According to Webster's dictionary, willingness is "readiness of the mind to do." For an individual with an anxiety disorder, anxiety is already present anyway. Willingness means simply choosing to experience that anxiety. In this sense, willingness is the opposite of control. It means making a choice to experience what there is to be experienced, and then experiencing it without trying to change the experience. In this way, willingness is similar to mindfulness. It means being open and accepting of your experience, whatever it may be.

Recall our discussion in chapter 5 where we pointed out the close relation between acceptance, willingness, and purposeful action. With your clients, you will want to emphasize that acceptance and willingness are not feelings. Instead, they are a stance toward life and about behavior and action. That is, willingness is about doing, not trying to do. We have found that the pen exercise helps clients experience that distinction in a practical and simple way.

Trying Versus Doing: The Pen Exercise

"I will try" is one of the most common answers clients give when an ACT therapist asks them whether they are willing to do an exercise or commit to a certain activity. At this point in therapy, you have probably heard this sort of response from your client already. At other times, clients return to a session saying something like, "I have tried to go to work and face my fear of failure. I have tried *really* hard, but I just couldn't do it. My anxiety was just too high. So I stayed at home." Similarly, right before doing something that could provoke anxiety, a client might say, "I can try to do it—honestly, I will definitely try—but I don't know whether I can go through with it." Rather than explaining the difference between trying and doing, we recommend doing the pen exercise

(Hayes et al., 1990). This brief exercise is a powerful demonstration that willingness is an all-or-nothing action: It is something you do, not something you try to do.

Therapist: What I would like you to do is to *try* to pick up this pen. Try as hard as you can. Go ahead and *try* it. *[Therapist puts a pen on a table or desk in front of the client and then waits. Just when the client is about to touch the pen, the therapist interrupts.]* Wait—you're actually picking up the pen. I only wanted you to *try* to pick it up.

Client: *[probably a bit confused]* Well, I can't do that. Either I pick it up or I don't.

Therapist: So what exactly happens when you only *try* to pick it up?

Client: My hand is hovering over the pen, but I am not actually picking it up.

Therapist: So trying is really "not doing," and that is why I never want you to try anything. You must first make a choice about whether you are willing to have what there is to be had. And if you are willing, if you are *completely* willing rather than just a bit willing, then go ahead and just do it. If you're not willing, I will respect you making that choice. Simply tell me, "I won't do it." There is no gray area here. It's either yes or no.

Spend a bit of time talking about the issue of trying, and that there really is no such thing as trying, there is only doing or not doing. Your clients may equate trying with failures of doing. For instance, they pick up the pen and it slips from their fingers and drops to the floor. They say, "You see, I tried … but it didn't work." Note, however, that nothing would prevent the client from bending over and repeating the act of picking up the pen if that is what they are willing to do. Some activities in life simply require persistence and doing something over and over again. Failure is an evaluation that the mind may dish out, but that need not get in the way of willingly doing what is important, even if that doing takes time. If you deem it useful, you can repeat the pen exercise to drive home the important point that we cannot try to do—we can only do or not do.

Willingness Thermostat Metaphor

Hayes et al. (1990) originally developed the willingness thermostat metaphor for clients with anxiety disorders and later expanded it for use with persons suffering from other disorders (Hayes, Strosahl, & Wilson, 1999). We have shortened and simplified this metaphor for the purpose of this program. One of the implications of this metaphor is that it can lead into a useful discussion on the issue of response-ability versus being a victim of anxiety.

Look at these two thermostats. They are like the ones you use to control the temperature in your house. One thermostat is called "anxiety" and the other is called "willingness." Both thermostats can go from 0 to 10. [Therapist draws two vertical lines on a piece of paper and labels them accordingly.] When you came to this clinic, you were probably thinking, "My anxiety is too high—it's way up here [therapist points to the top of the anxiety thermostat]. I want it to be down here instead." In contrast, your willingness thermostat was set the exact opposite way because you really didn't want to experience any anxiety. So you set it all the way down here [therapist points to the bottom of the willingness thermostat]. Now, for the past few weeks we've been playing with changing the setting on the willingness thermostat to see what happens when you set it higher, as in the mindfulness exercises. I understand that you're more concerned about the anxiety thermostat. So I'd like to share a little secret with you. The willingness thermostat is really the more important of the two, because it is the one that is going to make a difference in your life. When you experience a lot of anxiety and you're trying hard to bring it down, you set your willingness thermostat down here at 0. Yet, when you're not willing to have and feel this anxiety, then your anxiety is something to be anxious about, and it locks into place: When you're not willing to have it, you've got it.

This may even make you feel like you're a victim of anxiety, that you are helpless, because if *you* were in control of it, you would have already brought it down to 0. It's not that you didn't work hard enough or weren't clever enough; it simply doesn't work. Now, what if you stopped trying to set the anxiety thermostat, because you know from experience you cannot control that, and instead turned your attention to willingness? In contrast to the anxiety thermostat, you actually do control where you are on the willingness thermostat. This is a place where you are *response-able*. It is your choice whether you keep it down here or whether you turn the willingness thermostat up all the way. I'm not sure what would happen with your anxiety if you did that. I only know one thing: You really can set the level on that willingness thermostat exactly where you want it to be. And if you make a choice to set that willingness thermostat high, things might start to happen in your life. For instance, you could start doing what you want to do and [insert a client valued direction here].

At the end of this metaphor, it is important to emphasize that this is *not* talk about ignoring anxiety. Clients probably do not know how anxiety will work in the absence of attempts to control it. They may have a prediction. Yet, based on experience, they simply may not know because they may never have approached anxiety with willingness to have it. Clients may ask how exactly they can set their willingness thermostat high. Tell them it is neither a feeling nor a thought. It is a choice they can make that needs to be followed up with committed action. The crucial question is, "Are you willing to go out with your hands and feet and take your anxiety with you? Remember, willingness is simply a choice and a commitment to have what you already have. Like in the pen exercise, you either do it or you don't."

4. Dealing with Intense Feelings and Thoughts (15 min.)

Although clients may be willing to have their anxiety-related thoughts and feelings, avoidance and escape are old habits that have been learned and reinforced in many situations typically over long periods of time. As a result, these old habits are powerful and difficult to break. The exposure-like exercises to be introduced in this and subsequent sessions are meant to elicit feared feelings, images, and thoughts that previously prompted clients to engage in escape and avoidance behavior. Before we start with these exercises is therefore an opportune time to introduce the bus driver metaphor as guidance on what to do, and what not to do, when intense and highly aversive thoughts and feelings seemingly threaten to take over the clients and "make" them do things, such as leaving the room.

The Bus Driver Exercise

The bus driver metaphor was originally described by Hayes, Strosahl, and Wilson (1999). This metaphor is useful because it can teach clients what to do with thoughts and feelings that seem to bully them around. It also illustrates the costs of allowing thoughts and feelings to be bullies. The client is pictured as the driver of a bus called "My Life." Along the road, the client picks up a number of unruly bully passengers (anxiety-related thoughts and feelings) that yell at the client to change course and go where they want to go instead of where the client wants to go. Joanne Dahl (in press) has converted the metaphor into a powerful experiential exercise that we have adopted for the purposes of this treatment program. The basic idea is that clients can drive and act in a valued direction no matter what the anxious passengers throw at them and tell them to do. It encourages clients to let values, not their anxious thoughts and feelings, guide them through life.

Therapist: Imagine yourself as the driver of a bus called "My Life." Along your route, you pick up some unruly passengers, which are unwanted anxiety-related thoughts that your mind serves up for you. These passengers intimidate you as you drive along your chosen route. Perhaps you can think of a recent experience where you experienced anxiety. What are some of those statements that seem to be very intense and steer you off course? Is it okay if I write them down on these index cards?

[Therapist takes out four index cards and writes down four passenger statements, such as, "This anxiety (or panic) is too much to handle," "This is really dangerous and is going to take me down," "Everyone is going to think I'm stupid," and "I can't stand all these germs on me." After writing each statement on a separate index card, the therapist puts the index cards on the floor in a semicircle resembling a clock, putting one card at 12 o'clock, the next at 2 o'clock, the third at 4 o'clock, and the last card at 6 o'clock (see illustration below). Then therapist and client both get up and face one another. The therapist reads the statement on the card

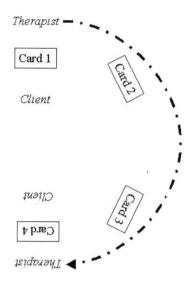

at 12 o'clock and asks the client to respond to it by disputing it or coming up with some other statement or strategy to silence the passenger. Then the therapist asks the client to move to the next passenger statement. While facing the therapist at the second card, the client attempts to cope with that statement. This move will require the client to "change course" and move side-ways toward the 2 o'clock position. Following the same procedure and moves, the client will stay facing the therapist but will eventually end up turned the opposite direction from where they were going at the start. The procedure is illustrated above.]

Therapist:	What has happened? Where are you headed?
Client:	Not where I was going! I can't even see the road ahead anymore.
Therapist:	Isn't that a high price to pay for attempting to silence the passengers? Every time you responded to, and got tangled up with, your thoughts and feelings, you ended up no longer moving in the direction you wanted to go and got further off course.
Client:	I feel I just had to respond. These thoughts seem to be so forceful and have such power over me.
Therapist:	Well, there is another way of responding. You don't have to struggle with those thoughts and let those passengers steer you in a direction that is not yours but theirs.
Client:	How do I do that?
Therapist:	I will read the same passenger statements to you one more time. However, this time, why don't you just listen to the statements—they're just thoughts anyway. You won't be able to avoid hearing them, because I will

be very loud. You can choose to focus on going forward and *not* doing what the thought says. You can choose to continue to drive the bus in your direction rather than where the thoughts are trying to get you to go. Remember that this is *your* life bus and *you* are the driver. Your hands, not the words of the passengers, steer that bus. Words and thoughts alone cannot take you off course, no matter what they say. They will probably be right in your face and even get louder when you don't do as they say. You can make a choice to be willing to have the thoughts *and* stay on the valued route no matter what the passengers say to you. You can simply let them yell while you stay committed. Are you willing to do that?

Client: Okay. It will be hard and I won't *try* [*laughing*]—I'll *do* it.

[*After the client commits, therapist moves the client to the starting position and repeats the exercise. This time the therapist moves around from card to card reading the passenger statements as before, while the client stays put facing forward, not disputing or otherwise responding to the statements. Afterward, therapist and client should briefly discuss the experience, focusing on the different outcome this time around.*]

Therapist: There may be times both here in session and at home when you carry passengers on your bus that try to convince you that you don't feel like doing this anymore or that it's all too much and too difficult. Even if you start to think about giving up on a valued direction, continue moving. You have already experienced in the mindfulness exercises that thoughts and feelings come and go, but the progress you make toward your goals will be for real and won't just go away. This is what really matters. Ultimately, you are in control of the direction of your life bus—you control it with your hands and feet. Although you can't control what kind of anxiety-related passenger feelings, thoughts, or worries will ride along with you, you do control the steering wheel of your life bus with your hands and the accelerator with your feet. You will go where you let your hands and feet take you. *That* is what you truly can control.

---

5. Exposure Within ACT: FEEL (Feeling Experiences Enriches Living) Exercises (25 min.)

How Does Traditional Exposure Work?

We pointed out in chapter 3 that exposure therapy is founded on two interrelated learning processes. The first of these is based on extensive laboratory research showing that stimuli can acquire fear-evoking functions via Pavlovian or respondent learning processes. The controlled and systematic presentation of such fear-evoking cues without the anticipated aversive consequences can attenuate the capacity of such stimuli to evoke fearful responding. This reduction in fearful responding over repeated nonreinforced exposure trials is based on the principle of extinction. Accordingly, the exposure-like exercises in this and subsequent sessions will likely result in some extinction of conditioned emotional responses to bodily sensations (most relevant to panic disorder and specific phobias) and to thoughts or images (most relevant to PTSD, social phobia, OCD, and GAD). If clients show only minimal responses to any of the internal fear cues—thoughts, sensations, images—therapists would normally move on to exposure to external cues.

ACT therapists use these principles and techniques too, but as you will see, exposure exercises are framed quite differently within ACT compared to traditional CBT. Exposure within ACT targets conditioned emotional responses that may occur in situations and contexts that have particular meaning and personal value for clients. Initial behavioral testing, described below, should enable therapists to make an informed choice about what type of exposure-like exercises are most appropriate (e.g., internal bodily sensations or images).

The second learning process is not as well understood. It refers to factors that account for clients' tendency to respond fearfully to conditioned processes associated with otherwise normal bodily cues, and specifically what type of exposure can change this tendency. This issue is critical when considering that there is nothing inherently abnormal about conditioned fearful responses. As we discussed in chapters 3 and 4, the responses themselves are quite adaptive and become problematic only when clients (a) respond to them in narrow, inflexible ways in an effort to reduce their frequency, intensity, duration, and (b) when such behaviors interfere with and restrict a client's capacity to live a full and valued life. In other words, both (a) and (b) are *the* problems, and barriers to living. This view is where an ACT approach departs from traditional exposure-based therapies.

The Context and Purpose of Exposure in ACT

Exposure within ACT is always done in the service of a client's valued life goals. We think of exposure as a logical extension of the mindfulness exercises begun earlier. Recall that these exercises were designed to promote an observer perspective, whereby thoughts, feelings, and physical sensations are noticed and experienced as they are, with a nonjudgmental and compassionate posture. This posture works to undermine cognitive fusion, which lets evaluative forms of verbal-cognitive activity get in the way of action. Mindfulness also makes experiential avoidance and escape nonsensical, because such actions run counter to what is needed to be accepting of experience in all its forms.

What we are doing in this section is encouraging clients to set the willingness thermostat quite a bit higher by using experiential life enhancement exercises designed to help clients make full contact with thoughts, feelings, and sensations that normally accompany anxiety. We are also going to help clients make contact with the disruptive consequences of experiential avoidance in their lives. We call these FEEL (Feeling

Experiences Enriches Living) exercises to avoid the somewhat perjorative connotations of the term "exposure." We encourage clients to use the mindfulness skills they have been practicing at home to embrace reality as it is. In fact, with FEEL exercises, the targeted processes are the same as in those exercises. The main change is that the therapeutic focus and context are now much broader.

The context for FEEL exercises must be framed in the service of client values and goals. This alone is quite different from traditional exposure therapies, wherein the goal typically is to master anxiety and test the accuracy of catastrophic predictions. This, we believe, is one reason why many anxious persons look upon traditional exposure with dread. Symptom reduction for its own sake seems quite limiting, particularly when considering the amount of pain clients must experience in the hope of feeling better. Recall that living better does not necessarily follow feeling better. Within ACT, therefore, FEEL exercises are presented and conducted with an eye on the real prize—living fully, richly, and meaningfully. They foster growth and movement in valued directions by encouraging clients to be with, and not act upon, the urge to avoid and escape anxiety, while doing what is important to them.

We have included a fair number of exposure-like exercises in the sections that follow. The mindfulness and other exercises conducted in previous sessions, along with the rationale provided below, should provide the motivation, willingness, and commitment to feel anxiety-related experiences as they are, and for what they are, rather than letting these experiences deter clients from their path toward living the life they have chosen.

Rationale for FEEL Exercises: To Facilitate Valued Living

Providing clients with a thorough rationale for the FEEL exercises presents an opportunity for the therapist and client to develop a collaborative effort, set expectations, and prepare the client for exercises that are probably difficult to do initially. The basic goal is to provide clients with an easy-to-understand explanation of the procedure, the rationale underlying it, and the anticipated costs and benefits. Therapists should refer to the earlier experiential exercises and metaphors when explaining the rationale.

Emphasize to clients that the ultimate purpose of these in-session exercises is to help them deal with the anxiety-related barriers listed on the Valued Directions and Life Compass worksheets in real-life situations. Using examples from these worksheets, review with clients how subtle and overt forms of avoidance and escape behavior have served to maintain their difficulties and how efforts to run away from or avoid anxiety have not worked and have ended up constricting and debilitating their lives. Describe FEEL exercises as focused opportunities for clients to practice running into, rather than away from, their anxiety. It's about making space for all those unwanted experiences that clients have avoided for so long.

You can guarantee clients that as long as they respond the way they have been responding (i.e., attempts to avoid or escape from their own psychological and emotional experiences), they will continue to have the problems they are having. At some level, most clients suffering from anxiety know this already. So the purpose is to learn to do something different from what they have been doing, a process that should be well underway by this point in therapy. Instead of struggling with what their mind and body are doing during fear and anxiety, they can drop the rope and face these experiences. This is a new way of responding to their own responses in order to get back onto their chosen path and do all the things they care about and want to do.

For this process to come about, clients must be willing to experience their fear, worries, and anxiety, because change and new learning occur through experience and doing, not by talking or thinking about doing. Sensations that will be induced during FEEL exercises (e.g., bodily sensations during interoceptive FEEL exercises) are precisely those that the client wishes not to experience. As with traditional exposure, there is some truth to the trite phrase "no pain, no gain." Yet, exposure is more than this. In our view, exposure transforms suffering about pain (i.e., nonacceptance plus pain), into the very real human experience of pain and pain alone. Therapists can revisit the example we outlined earlier about the process of learning how to ride a bike. FEEL exercises, like riding a bicycle for the first time, are difficult. This is to be expected, particularly given that clients are unfamiliar with how to ride feelings on the path to living. The good news is that these exercises will get easier over time and with practice. They are designed to help clients to move in valued directions. Ask clients, "Are you willing to have what you have in the service of moving closer to your stated intentions (values)?"

Therapists can describe FEEL exercises as experiential strategies that are designed to assist clients in mastering their ability to experience a full range of emotional responses, fully and without defense, for what they are and not for what their mind tells them they are (i.e., something dangerous and harmful). Remind clients of the tug-of-war exercise showing that when one side pulls, the other side simply pulls back harder. Likewise, when anxiety and fear are met with resistance, there is only one natural outcome: more resistance and suffering. Wars rarely emerge in the context of acceptance, joy, compassion, and genuineness toward the self and others.

The same is true with anxiety. Defending themselves from their own experiences tends to foster more negative experiences and prolongs the struggle. This context breeds suffering. Tell clients they cannot be at peace with themselves if they remain in a fight with their own experience. FEEL exercises are designed to assist them in approaching their anxiety and fear from a nonjudgmental, loving, and compassionate perspective—to be the chessboard instead of one of the struggling teams. Dropping the rope liberates them from the losing battle with their own thoughts, memories, physical sensations, and histories. Just like in the finger trap exercise, clients can choose to lean into their experiences and treat themselves with the same compassion, openness, love, and caring that they would extend to other human beings. Over time, the result is that they learn to respond to their responses differently and without defense. This nonavoidance posture, in turn, frees them to live differently. Therapists can accelerate this process initially by repeating exposure exercises in a controlled, systematic fashion with minimal variability.

Determining Appropriate FEEL Exercises

Before starting the first exercise, it is useful to reiterate to clients that the processes and principles that have contributed to their anxiety are quite normal and adaptive. Perhaps you can remind clients of an example from their lives where fear or anxiety was originally adaptive. Somewhere along the path of life, your clients began treating anxiety as if it were the enemy, and began to make strong efforts to reduce, eliminate, and avoid experiencing any fear-related sensations, images, and thoughts. This is when the situation gets tricky—remember President Franklin Roosevelt's famous statement, "The only thing we have to fear is fear itself"? Fear takes its toll on the lives of anxious persons when they do not want to experience it and start running away from it. When that happens, their lives become constrained and limited because clients will act to avoid any activity or experience where the probability of experiencing unwanted sensations, images, and thoughts is high.

For someone with panic disorder, such experiences include, but are not limited to, anger, surprise, excitement, stress, medications, drinking caffeinated beverages, exercise, driving, and interpersonal situations where anxiety and other unpleasant feelings are likely. Attempts to avoid changes in physical state or activities that induce shifts in bodily state prevent corrective learning that the physical sensations are not harmful, need not be avoided, and can be tolerated. This sets up a trap for anxiety to become disordered. Let clients know that the goal of these exercises is to help them get out of that trap. Explaining this sequence as part of the rationale for conducting FEEL exercises is appropriate for most persons suffering from anxiety problems, and particularly for clients who suffer from panic disorder, PTSD, specific phobias, and social phobia.

Similar principles and processes apply to images and thoughts. Examples of such images for each anxiety disorder are as follows:

- Panic disorder—suffocating and writhing on the floor

- Social phobia—being jeered at or criticized by a group of people

- PTSD—being abused or reliving the trauma

- GAD—being found out as a sham or incompetent

- OCD—doing something violent, obscene, or blasphemous

In previous sessions, the goal has been to mindfully observe unwanted thoughts and feelings when they arise naturally. Now, the goal is to deliberately bring about the physical sensations and images that normally would elicit distress so as to place such sensations in a context where the tendency to avoid or escape from them is unworkable and unnecessary. That is, one cannot be mindful of anxiety while avoiding anxiety. The goal is to increase client response-ability by helping them to accept their anxiety-related experience for what it is.

Types of Interoceptive FEEL Exercises

In this section, we describe a number of commonly used interoceptive exposure activities. In ACT, the choice of interoceptive and imagery FEEL exercises should be largely determined by whether the client's reactions to the images or sensations brought on by these exercises have functioned as a barrier on the path to some valued life domain.

The next step is to establish relevant bodily cues and images for each client. Here the universe of possible FEEL exercises is limited only by a therapist's creativity and available resources. The following is a partial list of commonly used in-session exposure exercises, including information about their implementation and typical effects. All can be completed in session and practiced outside of session.

Therapists should be mindful that contextual effects may modulate reactivity to interoceptive cues. Context may even move the tendency toward experiential avoidance up or down. Thus, some individuals will show a generalized tendency to respond to bodily sensations with fear in all contexts. That is, no matter where they are, these individuals are anxious about physical sensations and act to avoid them. In other clients the tendency to avoid experiencing bodily sensations becomes acute only in some contexts and not in others (e.g., only when clients are alone or in unfamiliar places, or only when they have no good explanation for the physical symptoms).

Spinning

This FEEL exercise can take several forms, and is designed to defuse fearful reactions evoked by sensations of dizziness and vertigo. Such exercises may include spinning in an office chair, spinning while standing, or having a client place their head between their knees, then suddenly move to an upright sitting position.

Hyperventilating

This procedure involves voluntary paced overbreathing and is capable of inducing panic attacks, including dissociative symptoms, in susceptible individuals. This occurs, in part, because oxygen is inhaled at a rate greater than metabolic demand, leaving too much oxygen and too little carbon dioxide in the blood. After first demonstrating a few full exhalations and inhalations through the mouth at a pace of about one breath for every 2 seconds, the therapist asks the client to join in and continue with this procedure for up to 3 minutes.

Breathing Through a Small Straw

Several inexpensive small- and large-bore straws can be used for this FEEL exercise. The nose should be occluded while the client breathes through a straw for 30 seconds or more. This exercise evokes breathlessness and sensations of smothering, and can be combined with other FEEL exercises, for example, breathing through a straw while climbing stairs.

Breath Holding

Breath holding involves asking the client to hold their breath for a period of time. The duration of breath holding can be increased in a graduated fashion over repetitions of FEEL exercises. This procedure typically evokes broadband cardiorespiratory sensations, and specifically the feeling of suffocation or air hunger.

Climbing Steps or Step-Ups

These exercises and their variants (e.g., fast walking, jogging in place) evoke cardiorespiratory sensations and more widespread sensations of autonomic arousal associated with physical exertion. Modifications to this procedure can range from climbing up and down one or two steps to climbing several flights of stairs. As appropriate, the pace of climbing or step-ups can be graduated within different levels (e.g., two steps, five steps, ten steps, and for varied durations within each level).

Staring at Self in the Mirror

This exercise involves simply looking at oneself for 2 minutes. The procedure typically elicits feelings of derealization and is particularly suitable for clients who report such feelings as part of their anxiety experience.

Other Interoceptive FEEL Exercises

Other exercises can be designed to suit particular client fears. For example, if your client is frightened by visual symptoms, you could ask them to stare at a light for 30 seconds and then look at a blank wall to see the afterimage. Alternatively, you may have them stare at a disorienting visual stimulus. For persons afraid of throat sensations or choking, suggest they press down on the back of their tongue with a tongue depressor or toothbrush. Alternatively, spend 1 minute just focusing on swallowing. Other means to produce interoceptive FEEL experiences include wearing nose plugs (used for swimming) to generate the sense of suffocation; strong smells (e.g., Worcestershire sauce) to induce nausea; tight collars, ties, or scarves to induce a sense of tightness around the throat; looking at venetian blinds with the sun shining in from behind the blinds to induce visual symptoms; and somersaults to induce a sense of being off balance or falling.

Implementation of FEEL Exercises

The general format and procedure for FEEL exercises is summarized below. It is important to let clients know what they should do during these exercises. Remind them to apply the same behaviors of acceptance and mindfulness during FEEL exercises as they have in previous exercises in session and at home. Their general task is to practice mindful observation in the presence of feared bodily sensations, thoughts, or imagery. This posture creates a dialectic between approach and avoidance tendencies, while undermining various forms of cognitive fusion. The basic idea is to observe, accept, and make space for anxiety-related experiences rather than suppress or struggle with them.

General Format and Procedure of FEEL Exercises

1. Provide the rationale for the exercise and ask clients to apply a mindfulness posture during exercise.

2. Conduct FEEL exercises, continuing for 30 to 60 seconds beyond the point at which the sensations are first noticed, and 5 minutes beyond the point at which the imagery is vivid.

3. Obtain FEEL Record ratings.

4. Ask clients to return to mindfulness practice for approximately 1 to 2 minutes, and provide occasional prompts for clients to observe and make space for what they are experiencing.

5. Ask what clients did during the FEEL exercise and briefly discuss their experience; also provide feedback and, if necessary, make suggestions for mindful acceptance.

6. If clients report or show high levels of unwillingness, struggle, or avoidance, therapists should conduct a more closely guided FEEL exercise (see section below). Therapists can also use these exercises to defuse any evaluative thoughts clients report ("This is not working," "I can't stand this anxiety anymore"). Ask clients to approach the exercise from an observer perspective the next time ("*I am having the thought* that this is not working," "*I am having the thought* that I can't stand this anxiety anymore").

7. Repeat FEEL exercises in this session and, if necessary, in subsequent sessions until client willingness levels are 7 or higher and struggle and avoidance levels are 3 or lower.

8. Include at least one full repetition of a particular FEEL exercise in subsequent sessions.

Implementation of Interoceptive FEEL Exercises

Prior to having the client engage in an exercise, you should explain and model it from the same posture that you want clients to adopt: mindful, nonjudgmental, and open. After you model the FEEL exercise, you should then carefully observe the client doing it to ensure it is completed correctly. During the exercises, therapists need to be particularly watchful for subtle and overt forms of escape or avoidance (e.g., distraction, taking fewer and more shallow breaths during hyperventilation), because such avoidance indicates low levels of acceptance of the client's experience, which can retard the process of thought-emotion-action defusion. Therapists should introduce and practice exercises in a graduated fashion. Before each exercise, ask clients' permission to proceed and whether they are willing to go ahead with the exercise. If they report being willing, ask clients to approach these exercises very much like they have practiced experiencing bodily sensations, thoughts, and images in the mindfulness and acceptance exercises at home.

Ask clients to focus on the experience without trying to change what they experience. When they notice bodily sensations or unwanted thoughts or images, encourage them to acknowledge their presence, stay with them, and see whether they can make some room to have them instead of attempting to make them go away. Ask clients to simply allow them to be and to give themselves space to have whatever they have while bringing a quality of kindness and compassion to the experience. You can use similar language as in the Acceptance of Anxiety exercise.

Then the therapist induces bodily sensations, continuing for 30 seconds to 1 minute beyond the point at which the sensations are first noticed. Following the induction, use the FEEL Sensation Record and ask clients to rate the intensity of the sensations, level of anxiety, how willing they were to experience what they experienced, how much they struggled with their experience, and how much they tried to avoid it. All ratings are made on a 0 to 10 scale with 10 being the maximum rating. After obtaining the ratings, the therapist redirects the client to return to mindfulness practice for approximately 1 to 2 minutes, occasionally prompting them to observe and make space for what they are experiencing. Then, the therapist asks clients what they did during the FEEL exercise and briefly discusses the client's experience, providing feedback and, if necessary, making suggestions for mindful acceptance using similar language as in the Acceptance of Anxiety exercise. For instance, therapists can encourage clients to notice any thoughts and feelings, acknowledge their presence, and stay with them rather than attempt to push them away. Ask clients to see if the bodily sensations need to be their enemy or whether they can open up to them and make space for them, accepting and allowing them to be, always noticing them for what they are (just normal bodily sensations) rather than what their mind tells them they are.

If clients report only low to moderate sensation intensity (less than 4), reassess the appropriateness of the exercise, the way a client might be doing it, and/or subtle forms of avoidance behavior. For instance, a client may only hyperventilate very mildly. If a FEEL exercise fails to elicit any anxiety, then ask clients if they would be distressed by the exercise if it was done alone or without the presence of the therapist. If so, it can still be practiced as an experiential home exercise.

FEEL SENSATION RECORD
(FEELING EXPERIENCES ENRICHES LIVING)

Date: _____   Time: _____ A.M./P.M.

0	1	2	3	4	5	6	7	8	9	10
Low					Moderate					Extreme

Exercise	Sensations Intensity (0–10)	Anxiety Level (0–10)	Willingness to Experience (0–10)	Struggle with Experience (0–10)	Avoidance of Experience (0–10)
Spinning	_____	_____	_____	_____	_____
Hyperventilating	_____	_____	_____	_____	_____
Breathing through straw	_____	_____	_____	_____	_____
Breath holding	_____	_____	_____	_____	_____
Step-ups	_____	_____	_____	_____	_____
Climbing steps	_____	_____	_____	_____	_____
Staring at self in mirror	_____	_____	_____	_____	_____
Other	_____	_____	_____	_____	_____
Other	_____	_____	_____	_____	_____

Implementation of Guided FEEL Exercise

If clients report or show high levels of unwillingness, struggle, or avoidance, thera-pists should conduct a guided FEEL exercise. During a guided FEEL exercise, the thera-pist again elicits the bodily sensations and guides the client's attention to two to three bodily sensations, one at a time. Therapists ask clients to acknowledge the presence of this discomfort, stay with it, breathe with it, accept the discomfort, and open up to it. Just like in the Chinese finger trap exercise, this is the perfect time to lean into anxiety and invite it in rather than struggling with it. If the clients report evaluative thoughts and labels ("dangerous," "getting worse," "out of control"), ask clients to thank their mind for such labels and continue to observe what they experience with gentle curios-ity, openness, and compassion. In addition, therapists can help clients reframe such statements by means of defusion techniques. For instance, a client statement such as "I'm losing control" can be defused and recontexualized as "*I'm having the thought/feeling that I'm losing control.*" Similarly, a statement such as "I'm too weak for this" might become "*I'm having the thought* that I'm too weak for this," whereas the thought "I want to do this *but* it is so hard" becomes "I want to get better *and* it is too hard." A sample dialogue below illustrates the guided FEEL procedure.

Therapist: *[after spinning the client around in a chair]* What sensations are you experiencing?

Client: I feel dizzy and my heart is racing. I've been trying to calm myself down.

Therapist: *[asks for all five FEEL ratings]*

Client: Sensations are 7, anxiety is 8, willingness is 4, struggle is 7, and avoidance is 6.

Therapist: Okay, I want you to close your eyes for a moment. See if you can allow this dizziness to be what it is, a feeling in your head, nothing more and nothing less. Is this something you need to push away from, or can you acknowledge its presence and make room for it? *[pause 5 seconds]* Can you make space for it? *[pause 5 seconds]* What does this dizziness really feel like? Where does it start and where does it end? *[pause 5 seconds]* Must this particular feeling be your enemy? *[pause 5 seconds]* Is this dizziness and the anxiety something you *must* not have, something you *cannot* have? *[pause 5 seconds]* Even if your mind tells you that you can't have it, are you willing to open up a space for it in your heart? *[pause 5 seconds]* Is this something you absolutely need to struggle with, or is there room inside you to feel all that and stay with it? *[pause 5 seconds]*

Client: I don't like it, and no matter what I do, I am having it anyway.

Therapist: I understand you don't like it. And can you be willing to have it? As you said, you are having it anyway. Can you not like it *and* be willing *and* have it? Is that possible? *[pause 5 seconds]* So are you willing to do this again? *[If client is willing, repeat exercise, obtain ratings, and focus attention on another core sensation such as the racing heart.]*

The therapist can use the same procedure with all major bodily sensations and with evaluative thoughts. To maximize the process of corrective emotional learning and teaching the client new ways of responding to their own responses, clients should practice each exercise for several minutes and repeat it two or three times during the therapy session. A client should make willingness ratings of 7 or higher and struggle and avoidance ratings of 3 or lower within the same exercise before moving on to the next exercise.

FEEL exercises may require several in-session practices before any clinically meaningful increases in willingness and reductions in struggle and avoidance are observed. This is fine and to be expected. After clients complete exercises successfully in session, ask them whether they are willing to complete the exercises at home during the following week and keep track of their daily practice using the FEEL Sensations Record form.

The Mirror Exercise

Many of the FEEL exercises are not simply about evoking and being with unwanted bodily sensations. They are also about developing acceptance for the self when being anxious and in the eyes of others. Thus, we suggest that for people with social phobia, and others who are concerned about experiencing anxiety in public, interoceptive FEEL exercises be done, to the extent possible, in front of a mirror. The purpose of having the mirror always present is to help the client develop acceptance and compassion for how they appear in front of themselves and others when being anxious. Many clients tend to feel self-conscious when anxious. Using a mirror provides opportunities for clients to practice acceptance and defusion about how they appear when anxious. The goal here is to help clients develop compassion for themselves and how they look when they are anxious or afraid. In the process, they may become more comfortable with the way they appear in the public eye, and also less anxious about how they appear to others—a welcome by-product, although not an explicit target. Ask clients if they are willing to practice interoceptive FEEL exercises at home in front of a full-length mirror. If so, they are to follow the steps outlined below.

1. Practice interoceptive FEEL exercises in front of a full-length mirror.

2. After completing an exercise in front of the mirror, clients should make their ratings using the FEEL Sensation Record.

3. After making their ratings, they are to take a good hard look at themselves in the mirror. Here clients should observe and describe their bodies from head to toe. What do they see? How do they look?

4. Ask clients to come up with descriptions, not judgments, about how they look in the mirror. When experiencing judgmental thoughts, such as those listed below, clients should simply notice the thoughts and feelings that arise as they are. Just listen to them, be with them, notice them from a compassionate observer perspective.

    Judgments:

    "I look terrible, blotchy, all red in the face. People will notice how anxious I am."

    "I look bad."

    "The way I look is embarrassing."

Descriptions:

"I can see that my face is flushed."

"I notice that I am sweaty and out of breath."

"I experience some shakiness in my hands and legs."

5. Ask clients to allow themselves to experience those thoughts and feelings as they are. Can they develop room for being with their anxious self in the mirror? Can they bring compassion and acceptance to this experience? It is important that clients stay committed to the exercise. Ask them to watch themselves in the mirror after each interoceptive FEEL exercise for at least 1 to 2 minutes. It is important for clients to stay the course, meaning that we do not want them to give in to their discomfort by terminating the exercise prematurely.

Imagery FEEL Exercises*

For clients with recurrent fear-producing images (particularly relevant to clients with PTSD, OCD, or GAD), generate a list of fear-provoking images based on their "worst-case scenario." Ask clients to generate a few sentences to describe each image, particularly in terms of their responses, the stimuli associated with it, and their meaning. Here are some examples: "My children drowned in the bathtub, and it was my fault; I feel sick to my stomach and my heart is pounding"; "I am living on the streets, without food or help, because I am incompetent, weak, and unable to think"; "I am in a psychiatric ward because I am crazy; my hands are shaking, I am disoriented, and nobody can understand me"; "I am being attacked and I'm frozen in fear; I can't lift my hands to protect myself, I am helpless"; "If my husband's health gets worse, he might die and we will lose our home."

Generate a series of images and ask clients to rate their willingness to have that image. Next, establish a graded hierarchy of images based on your clients' willingness ratings. Gradation is particularly important for PTSD, where images of past traumas are very provocative. Throughout the imagery scene construction and later during FEEL imagery exercises, there may be occasions of numbing, dissociation, or a full flashback in cases of severe PTSD. If you suspect this is going to happen, talk with the client in advance about ways of dealing with such experiences, such as methods of reality checking, touch, and approaching the experience from an observer rather than a participant or player perspective. Note that such experiences are consequences of the fusion of verbal evaluations with reality. They are within the range of human experience. If they happen in session, then they are likely a part of the client's experience outside of session. When the client responds to the flashback in ways so as not to have it or to make it go away, these responses are likely barriers to living. In such cases, you may focus attention on the psychological and experiential consequences of the imagery for the client, rather than on the imagery itself. The task is to develop a mindful and accepting posture

---

*   We are grateful to Dr. Michelle Craske for allowing us to use and adapt the scenarios and suggestions contained in her 2005 treatment manual *Cognitive-Behavioral Treatment of Anxiety Disorders*.

toward those consequences. After all, the problem is the client's reactions to the consequences of FEEL exercises, not the consequences themselves.

In the case of generalized anxiety disorder, the catastrophic images that usually underlie excessive worry may not be immediately apparent to clients. Such images can be identified by asking the client to find the "picture" of the worst-case scenario at the end of the worry chain. For example, if the client worries excessively about their children's safety on the public transport from school to home, an underlying catastrophic image may be of the children lying on the road in an automobile accident. The meaning of the catastrophic image typically pertains to the client's sense of self-competency. In the example just given, the image is not restricted to the children's injury. It extends also to the meaning that the client was a bad parent for letting that happen to the children. The latter image in this chain likely cuts to the core of a client's sense of self and value. The client is then asked to imagine this scene using the same general procedure described on the next page.

Clients with obsessive-compulsive disorder mostly find their images to be abhorrent and unacceptable, and their sense of shame and guilt may lead to resistance in verbalizing the content of the images. Similarly, fears that putting the content of the images into words might make them "come true" may also contribute to resistance. This type of internal barrier (resistance) is just another form of experiential avoidance. In therapy it means that the client is not showing up with willingness. Therapists need to address such barriers whenever they come up. For instance, a therapist might say,

> You seem to not want to tell me what you are thinking right now, and I
> understand that you think the thought may come true. I'd like you to think for a
> moment about how this "not telling" is working for you, right here, right now.
> We are both here together in this room to help you live life more fully, richly, and
> deeply. Is not speaking out your thoughts getting in the way of your commitment
> to treatment and improving your life? Is it getting you closer to or further away
> from your valued directions? Is it taking your life bus north or south? What does
> your experience tell you? Where do you want to go? Can you be willing to set
> your willingness thermostat high?

In addition, therapists can do more defusion work by asking clients to hold the thoughts or images gently in awareness and recognize and label the images as images rather than as facts or actual occurrences. Such mindful, compassionate, and kind observation is a new way of dealing with unwanted cognitive material and is different from past attempts to get rid of them or resolve them somehow. Referring back to the bus driver exercise, therapists can help clients identify these thoughts as bullies that will not steer them off course as long as clients choose to stay in the driver's seat of their life bus and continue on their chosen path. In the case of this exercise, it means continuing with the exercise, observing the experience, and noticing bully thoughts and feelings for what they are (just thoughts and feelings). In the next chapter, we provide additional suggestions to help clients relate to unwanted cognitive and emotional material both in session and in situations of everyday life.

Before each exercise, ask the client's permission to proceed and whether they are willing to go ahead with the exercise ("Have you set your willingness thermostat high?"). The general format for FEEL imagery exercises is similar to the interoceptive exercises. Imagery exercises, however, tend to be longer and should be continued 5 minutes beyond the point at which the imagery is vivid. If the imagery is insufficiently vivid, consider incorporating newspaper stories about tragedies, illnesses, or accidents to elicit imagery. Also, movies or photographs of places or people can be helpful. After obtaining ratings using the FEEL Imagery Record below, ask what clients are experiencing. Encourage them to notice any thoughts and feelings, acknowledge their presence, and stay with them rather than attempting to get rid of or push them away. Ask them to see if the thoughts, feelings, and worries need to be seen as enemies or whether they can open up to them and make space for them, accepting and allowing them to be, always noticing them for what they are (just thoughts and feelings) rather than what their mind tells them they are.

Again, if clients report or show high levels of unwillingness, struggle, or avoidance, then therapists should conduct guided FEEL exercises. These exercises help clients to create space for their discomfort, encourage them to accept rather than struggle, and defuse any evaluative thoughts clients report, as described in the interoceptive exercise section.

FEEL IMAGERY RECORD
(FEELING EXPERIENCES ENRICHES LIVING)

Date: _____   Time: _____ A.M./P.M.

0	1	2	3	4	5	6	7	8	9	10
Low					Moderate					Extreme

Exercise	Sensations Intensity (0–10)	Anxiety Level (0–10)	Willingness to Experience (0–10)	Struggle with Experience (0–10)	Avoidance of Experience (0–10)
_____	_____	_____	_____	_____	_____
_____	_____	_____	_____	_____	_____
_____	_____	_____	_____	_____	_____
_____	_____	_____	_____	_____	_____
_____	_____	_____	_____	_____	_____
_____	_____	_____	_____	_____	_____

Some clients may continue to report low willingness and high levels of struggle and avoidance over either the physical symptom induction or imagery induction. In those cases, continue with repeated FEEL exercises in this and subsequent sessions until client willingness levels are 7 or higher and struggle and avoidance levels are 3 or lower before moving on to the next exercise. Also be sure to frame these exercises in the context of barriers to valued living. Remember that these exercises are all about movement north. They are not about being with anxiety and fear for the sake of being with anxiety and fear. Values help contextualize the FEEL exercises and give them meaning and real purpose.

Dealing with Urges to Escape During Panic Attacks and in OCD

Virtually all cognitive behavioral programs for anxiety disorders emphasize that it is important to prevent escape behavior in the presence of high anxiety, such as during panic attacks. For instance, cognitive behavioral programs for OCD emphasize how essential it is for clients not to undo the exposure imagery exercises by carrying out rituals or other forms of neutralizing. These compulsions are functionally forms of experiential avoidance and precisely what these exercises are designed to undermine. The typical strategy used within standard CBT is first to find out what a client normally does in response to their intrusive images (e.g., compulsions, neutralizing behaviors, checking on the safety of others, seeking reassurances), and second to instruct the client *not* to carry out those reactions during or after the imagery exposure. The reason is that such actions undermine any corrective learning that may come about via imagery exposure and serve to reinforce old, problematic patterns of behavior.

Preventing Escape Behavior

From an ACT approach, it is also desirable to prevent escape behavior in clients with OCD or during panic attacks. However, simply instructing the client not to engage in the ritual or other escape behavior is not congruent with an ACT approach. The reason is that the compulsion is already in a tight functional relation with various obsessions and related negative consequences. Suppressing or avoiding the elements may, therefore, bring about the other undesired elements that are part of a network of relations. Ask clients to recall what happens when they try not to think of pink elephants. They actually get more thoughts of pink elephants. The most important aspect of FEEL exercises in clients presenting with OCD is this: to let them experience intrusive recurrent thoughts, along with the urge to act on them, for what they are—thoughts and feelings. Efforts to suppress or neutralize thoughts and urges should be examined for their workability and defused. Ask the client to recall what happens when they do engage in rituals in terms of both their obsessive thoughts and their urges (anxiety goes down for a while, but tension and urge always come back). So compulsions do not work because the obsessive thoughts always come back and, more importantly, because these actions get in the way of living a valued life.

Then, move on to helping clients relate to urges from a mindful, accepting stance. Rather than instructing clients not to engage in a compulsive ritual, therapists can explore such urges and employ defusion methods during FEEL imagery. This strategy is also relevant for clients with other anxiety disorders, particularly when they report a strong urge to escape from a situation (e.g., while experiencing a panic attack). If clients report urges to wash their hands (OCD) or leave a situation where they experience anxiety, Hayes and colleagues (1990) recommend taking clients into these thoughts and helping them defuse from their thoughts. This is also a good opportunity to reintroduce the Anxiety News Radio metaphor from Session 5 (see chapter 9). Therapists can ask clients to read the text in the voice of a news anchor to help them defuse the thought-action relation while not buying into the content of their thoughts. If the person is *actually* about to run away or wash their hands, do not physically prevent it. Instead, therapists may be able to delay such escape by saying something like this:

> *That's fine. You could do that. Now, I'd like you to stay for just a couple of minutes. And right here and now, we have the opportunity to work on this—the thoughts and feelings associated with wanting to run out of the room [or wash your hands]. If you choose to go, you can go, although right now you have the opportunity, rather than the problem, of experiencing what it's like to have these thoughts and feelings in the context of being willing to have them. What is it like to have them when you set the willingness thermostat on high?*

Putting Thoughts and Urges on Cards Exercise

Hayes, Strosahl, and Wilson (1999) devised another simple defusion exercise that helps clients make contact with the effort involved in fighting off urges and unwanted thoughts as opposed to observing them with mindful acceptance. In this exercise, the therapist writes the client's urge, worry, or other unwanted thought on an index card. Then the therapist puts the card in the palm of their hand and asks the client to push against the card. As clients push, the therapist can adjust the strength of their pushing to let clients experience that when they push harder to make the urge or thought go away, the urge or thought pushes back harder too. After taking down the card, the therapist asks the client to simply sit there and do nothing. Then the therapist puts the card in the client's lap and asks them to look at the card and the text on it, and notice the difference in effort between pushing the urge away compared to simply letting it be and looking at it.

These strategies may be enough for clients to stay and not engage in escape behavior. The goal is to hold them as long as possible without making it look like the therapist is doing the holding, and to help the client engage in the experience fully and without defense. Therapists should obtain FEEL ratings and continue engaging the client in this exercise and dialogue until willingness ratings are high and struggle and avoidance ratings come down. The main purpose of this dialogue is to remind clients of the skills they have learned and assist them in whatever way is appropriate to apply these skills in this difficult situation.

6. FEEL Exercise Practice (Home)

- Practice the Acceptance of Anxiety exercises for at least 20 minutes daily and complete the practice sheet after each practice.

- Practice of at least one interoceptive and/or imagery exercise chosen by the client for 30 minutes per day. The sensations and/or imagery induced by the exercise should be barriers to valued activities in the client's life.

- Continue monitoring anxiety and fear-related experiences using the LIFE form.

- Complete the Daily ACT Ratings form.

Take a moment to explain to clients that their practice of FEEL exercises outside of therapy is an integral component of the treatment and ultimately more important than in-session work. Emphasize that the real purpose of these in-session exercises is to help clients move with and eventually let go of their anxiety-related barriers in real-life situations. The exercises are about making space for all of the unwanted experiences that clients have avoided for so long. This space will then allow them not to be steered off course by the anxiety bullies on their bus and to get on with the task of creating their life and living it. The purpose is to learn to do something different from what they have been doing. Instead of struggling with their mind and body during fear and anxiety, they can face these experiences for what they are and as they are, while staying on their chosen path and doing all the things they care about and want to do.

A similar process is at work with FEEL practice outside of therapy. Initially, such exercises may simply include practice with the FEEL exercises covered in session (e.g., practicing breath holding at home). Doing FEEL exercises in a structured format at regular, clustered intervals (i.e., several times a day) and in a comfortable environment (e.g., at home) will help clients learn the skill of experiencing anxiety for what it is. Ask clients to follow the same general procedure that was used in session. Remind them that their task is to practice mindful observation in the presence of feared bodily sensations, thoughts, or imagery during FEEL exercises. In the coming weeks, they are to use the same skills in session that they have been practicing at home during mindfulness exercises. The basic idea is to observe, accept, and make space for anxiety-related experiences rather than suppressing or struggling with them.

Returning to the simple metaphor of learning to ride a bicycle for the first time can be helpful to convey to clients the importance of practice. Nobody learns to ride a bike the first time they try, and often the process can be painful. To make learning a bit easier, we add training wheels. Home practice is analogous to using training wheels when learning to ride a bike. The goal is to learn the basic skills first before applying them in other situations and settings that are more challenging and more important to them. With repeated practice, clients can expect to get to the point of being able to remove the training wheels and ride without them. At that point, there may be a few more bumps and bruises along the way. Recall that even seasoned bicyclists fall once in a while, but they spend more time on the bike riding than they do falling on the ground.

Ask clients whether they are willing to practice FEEL exercises at home regardless of whether they feel anxious or distressed about exercises or other matters. If clients indicate they are willing to do so, ask them whether they are willing to keep a daily record of their practice and activities using the Valued Life Goal Activities form provided at the end of this chapter and on the book CD. If they agree, give them a copy of the form and ask them to write down their commitment to practice on the form for every day they intend to practice. The client takes this form home and records whether they engaged in the activity and how much time they spent on each activity. They also rate how much anxiety they experienced, how willing they were to have what they experienced, and how much they struggled with their experience at the beginning and at the end of each activity using the same 0 (low) to 10 (high) scale as on the FEEL forms. During the week, they can record whether and for how long they practiced every day. Give clients seven copies of the FEEL record form (one copy for each day of the week). This form provides more detailed information about their experiences during those exercises.

Both forms are designed to help clients keep track of their daily practice. It is essential that therapists convey to clients the importance of keeping commitments and daily practice of the FEEL exercises as part of that commitment. Therapists should routinely collect and review practice records at the beginning of each session. Practice reviews, along with verbal statements acknowledging the client's work, serve to reinforce client commitment to treatment and effort to make meaningful life changes. Therapists who do not review or discuss home practice activities send their clients the message that such work between sessions is not important—so clients may wonder, why bother doing them?

Lastly, and perhaps most importantly, we must stress the importance of maintaining a value-focused context for FEEL exercises. These and many of the exercises to come are designed to help clients use their hands and feet to move in the direction of valued life pursuits rather than to spend their time trying to get rid of anxious thoughts and feelings. If therapists do not relate such exercises to client values and goals (short- and long-term), then the FEEL exercises will look, feel, and sound like exposure in disguise. Clients, in turn, may rightly ask, "Why should I go through more pain and suffering? I have enough of this in my life already." Thus, we suggest that therapists clearly link FEEL exercises to client values and goals and encourage the client to do the same with home practice. Keeping the focus on values serves to dignify the treatment. For instance, a client may notice how her responses to dizziness and shortness of breath get in the way of leaving her house and doing what she cares about. During FEEL exercises, this client may focus from a compassionate perspective on the thoughts and sensations brought on by voluntary hyperventilation, while keeping a mindful eye on what she would like to do with her hands and feet when such sensations arise again. The real prize here is moving openly, willingly, and with feeling and purpose in the direction of what matters most in a client's life. This is precisely what the FEEL exercises and this treatment program are about.

WEEKLY VALUED LIFE GOAL ACTIVITIES

Life Enhancement Exercise Record Form

Record your FEEL exercises and other goal-related activities for each day of the week, based on your commitments made in session. Record whether you engaged in the activity and how much time you spent on each activity. Then rate how much anxiety you experienced, how willing you were to have what you experienced, and how much you struggled with your experience at the beginning and at the end of each activity using the same 0 (low) to 10 (high) scale as on the FEEL forms.

Day	Activity Commitment	Yes/No	Duration (minutes)	Anxiety Beg/End	Willingness Beg/End	Struggle Beg/End
Mon	_____ _____ _____	Y / N	_____	/	/	/
Tues	_____ _____ _____	Y / N	_____	/	/	/
Wed	_____ _____ _____	Y / N	_____	/	/	/
Thurs	_____ _____ _____	Y / N	_____	/	/	/
Fri	_____ _____ _____	Y / N	_____	/	/	/
Sat	_____ _____ _____	Y / N	_____	/	/	/
Sun	_____ _____ _____	Y / N	_____	/	/	/

CHAPTER 11

Staying Committed to Valued Directions and Action

Sessions 7–12

We can try to control the uncontrollable by looking for security and predictability, always hoping to be comfortable and safe. But the truth is that we can never avoid uncertainty and fear. So the central question is not how we avoid uncertainty and fear but how we relate to discomfort.

How do we practice with difficulty, with our emotions, with the unpredictable encounters of an ordinary day? When we doubt that we're up to it, we can ask ourselves this question: "Do I prefer to grow up and relate to life directly, or do I choose to live and die in fear?"

—Pema Chödrön

GOALS AND THEME

The major purpose of Sessions 7 through 12 is to continue to create broader and more flexible patterns of relating with the stimuli, events, and situations that elicit fear or anxiety in clients. This goal will be achieved by continuing to conduct in-session and between-session FEEL exercises, as well as value-related activities in the real world. It is fine if anxiety goes down as a result of these activities, but that is not our main concern. The crucial point is for clients to learn that anxiety does not have to go down first in order to do what is important to them. Continue to emphasize that the purpose of FEEL exercises and value-related activities is to let clients experience that they can do things that matter to them *and* be anxious at the same time.

The general goal is to put valuing into action and to learn to be in and with the situations, feelings, thoughts, and other barriers to valued living through continued exposure, mindful observation, and defusion. The therapist's task is to help clients implement meaningful activities that will move them toward reaching selected goals by helping clients develop a specific plan of action for each week and identifying sequences of actions that need to be taken to achieve goals (preferably involving previously avoided situations or events). Therapists can give feedback and help clients set realistic goals and criteria, monitor progress, and brainstorm solutions for overcoming barriers. Such assistance is to be framed in the context of what clients want out of a life lived well.

Session Outline

1. Centering Exercise

2. Review of Daily Practice

3. Repeated FEEL Exercises
   - In-Session Exercises
   - Consolidating Progress Through Home Exercises

4. Naturalistic Value-Guided Behavioral Activation
   - Behavioral Activation Treatment: The Core of Value-Guided Action
   - Selecting Activities Based on Life Compass
   - Creating an Activity Hierarchy and Commitment for Action
   - Monitoring Progress and Giving Feedback

5. Dealing with Barriers and Avoidance

    ■ The Basic ACT Value Question: Are You Heading North or South?

    ■ Defusion and Mindfulness Techniques

    ■ Recognizing Mind and Language Traps

    ■ Eliminating Safety Signals and Behaviors

    ■ Problems with Values

    ■ Traveling with Your Fears

6. Dealing with Setbacks Through Mindful Acceptance and Compassion

7. Experiential Life Enhancement Exercises (Home)

    ■ Practice Acceptance of Anxiety exercise once a day for at least 20 minutes and complete practice sheet after each practice

    ■ Daily practice of FEEL exercises (interoceptive and/or imagery exercises) and/or Valued Life Goal Activities

    ■ Keep track of FEEL practice and value-related activities by completing the Weekly Valued Life Goal Activities record form each week and the Goal Achievement Record

    ■ Continue monitoring anxiety and fear-related experiences using the LIFE form

    ■ Complete Daily ACT Ratings form

8. Preparing Clients for End of Treatment (Session 12)

    ■ Provide Treatment Summary

    ■ Prepare for Relapse and Setbacks

    ■ Identify High-Risk Situations

9. Session Materials and Handouts

    ■ Acceptance of Anxiety practice form (1 form for each week)

    ■ Living in Full Experience (LIFE) form (1 form for each week)

    ■ Daily ACT Ratings form (1 form for each week)

    ■ Weekly Valued Life Goal Activities form (1 form for each week)

    ■ Goal Achievement Record form

- FEEL Sensation Record forms (as needed)
- FEEL Imagery Record forms (as needed)

Agenda for Sessions 7–12

1. Centering Exercise

Begin all sessions with the centering exercise described in Session 1.

2. Review of Daily Practice

Review the client's daily practice of the Acceptance of Anxiety exercise and briefly discuss their experiences with it. After reviewing the Daily ACT Ratings, briefly discuss the LIFE form and any instance of clients engaging in behavior to manage thoughts, sensations, and feelings. Again, help the client see the connection between such actions and short- and long-term costs, particularly in the context of how they want to live their lives. For instance, did behavior in the service of managing anxiety get in the way of something that a client values or cares about, as described in the client's Life Compass? Next, review practice of FEEL exercises and other goal-related activities. Praise clients for their practice and progress and discuss any difficulties they may have had. Any obstacles and barriers should be dealt with as outlined in this chapter.

3. Repeated FEEL Exercises

In-Session Exercises

Due to time constraints, only a few FEEL exercises were probably conducted in Session 6. In Sessions 7 and 8, therapists should set aside 25 to 30 minutes to conduct several more of the interoceptive or imagery exercises outlined in chapter 10. As indicated, the choice of exercises needs to be individualized and ought to produce sensations and/or images that are related to barriers that have gotten in the way of valued activities in the client's life. For guidance here, look to responses that came up as barriers when discussing the Life Compass and home exercises. It is critical that FEEL exercises continue to be framed in the service of client values and goals. These exercises are nothing more than focused opportunities to practice running into, rather than away from, anxiety in order to foster personal growth and movement in valued directions. Therapists should emphasize that the ultimate purpose of in-session exercises is to help clients move with rather than around anxiety-related barriers that come up when engaging in out-of-session goal-related life activities that matter to the client. The general format and procedure for conducting these exercises is the same as described in Session 6 (chapter 10).

Consolidating Progress Through Home Exercises

Once clients begin to show clinically meaningful and stable increases in willingness and reductions in struggle and avoidance during the FEEL exercises conducted in session and at home, therapists can move to the next step, which involves clients engaging in the same acceptance posture while going about their usual daily activities and when they experience anxiety. The purpose here is to remove the training wheels and to start allowing clients to practice experiencing the totality of their feared experiences while performing routine activities. For instance, practice with interoceptive FEEL exercises should continue several times during the day and should occur in those situations where the anxious thoughts, feelings, or sensations are particularly disruptive—that is, when they are normally allowed to get in the way of the client doing what they care about doing (e.g., school, work, driving, walking, attending a meeting). For example, interoceptive FEEL exercises such as applying pressure to the throat or standing up suddenly can be performed at a desk while at work (Zuercher-White, 1997). To derive the maximum benefit, clients should perform FEEL exercises in as many different contexts and situations as possible. This will serve to broaden the client's range of functioning while counteracting the disruptive and life-limiting tendency to engage in avoidance of anxiety. Recall that the clinical goal here is to foster greater psychological, experiential, and behavioral flexibility.

Before the end of the session, obtain a commitment from the client to perform at home the FEEL exercises practiced during session and ask them whether they are willing to engage in any other goal-related activities. If clients indicate they are willing to engage in exercises and activities, ask them whether they are willing to keep a daily record of their practice and activities using the Valued Life Goal Activities form they're already familiar with. Again, ask clients to write down commitments to activities for each day of the week on the form.

Also explain to clients that there are several ways to maintain and consolidate the progress they have made so far. First, hesitation to engage in a valued activity because of fear is a clear signal for clients that they should go ahead and do it, particularly when they have committed themselves to the activity already. These are opportunities for practicing leaning into and creating space for anxiety analogous to pushing into, rather than pulling out of, the Chinese finger trap. At those turning points, clients need to ask themselves whether they can make space for their discomfort *and* be willing to go ahead and do what they committed to doing. For instance, hesitation about driving for fear of having a panic attack is a signal to make space for and accept that discomfort *and* deliberately drive anyway. Similarly, starting to avoid hot places or certain foods for fear of a panic attack is a signal to make space for and accept that discomfort *and* deliberately enter hot places and eat those foods. If clients are not willing to have these thoughts *and* act effectively in their lives, keeping value-driven commitments will be impossible (Wilson & Murrell, 2004). Obstacles that emerge, such as "This is too painful" or "I just can't do it" ought to be addressed with experiential exposure and defusion exercises as discussed later in this chapter.

4. Naturalistic Value-Guided Behavioral Activation

Traditional CBT typically follows in-session exposure exercises with naturalistic exposure exercises in a wide range of situations and under diverse circumstances. The aim of naturalistic exposure exercises is to promote generalization of extinction (Taylor, 2000). These exercises may involve clients performing common daily activities (e.g., drinking coffee, having sex, watching scary TV programs) or entering situations that produce feared somatic sensations in increasingly more dreaded and less "safe" situations (Otto & Deckersbach, 1998). For example, the client may begin by performing a particular exercise at home, first with their spouse present and then without a safe person present, then in a shopping mall with a safe person present, and ultimately in the mall alone.

Other common examples of naturalistic interoceptive exposure include going to an amusement park and going on scary rides, or engaging in a workout program such as running, cycling, or aerobics. Though naturalistic interoceptive exposure and situational exposure have common elements, they differ in that the goal of naturalistic interoceptive exposure is to induce symptoms of autonomic arousal, whereas the goal of situational exposure is to expose the client to the feared situations themselves, without regard for the somatic sensations they produce (Taylor, 2000). Nonetheless, both interoceptive and situational exposure are designed to promote anxiety reduction through extinction processes.

The purpose of naturalistic activities in ACT is to promote valued living. The Life Compass and Valued Directions worksheets serve as the basis for activity selection because many of the tasks we ask clients to do are highly aversive, particularly early in the process. In terms of treatment compliance, evidence suggests that we ought to make the client's choice to engage in painful therapeutic work as salient as possible (Wilson & Murrell, 2004). Apart from helping clients get moving on the road toward establishing meaning in their lives, it also gives them a sense of control. Lab studies show that people and animals clearly prefer controllable painful events and tend to show less fear under such circumstances compared to uncontrollable pain-inducing events (e.g., Lejuez, Eifert, Zvolensky, & Richards, 2000; Zvolensky, Lejuez, & Eifert, 1998).

Behavioral Activation Treatment: The Core of Value-Guided Action

The greatest challenge for therapists is to keep clients on track as they move to re-create the life they have given up on in the service of managing anxiety. The problems that therapists encounter here are twofold: one has to do with helping clients engage and stay committed to a program of life goal–related activities, and the other has to do with barriers that clients encounter along the way. Both issues concern motivation and keeping commitments. Unfortunately, neither existing CBT manuals nor the ACT literature provide much guidance here. This section, therefore, is designed to provide therapists with some guidelines for keeping clients on track on their path to reclaiming their lives. We have adapted these guidelines from behavioral activation programs that have been used successfully in the treatment of clients with depression (Hopko, Lejuez, Ruggiero, & Eifert, 2003) and with concurrent anxiety and depression (Hopko, Hopko, & Lejuez, 2004).

Behavioral activation treatment (BAT) is based on two major premises (Lejuez, Hopko, & Hopko, 2001, 2002). The first is consistent with ideas presented throughout this book, namely, that it is difficult to control or directly change negative emotional states and that the best strategy to improve negative affect is to directly target what is controllable. The second premise involves a behavioral principle called the "matching law" (McDowell, 1982). Applied to anxiety, this principle states that the relative value of anxiety-related behavior, compared to life goal–related behavior, is proportional to the relative value of reinforcement obtained for anxiety-related behavior compared with life goal–related behavior. One critical therapeutic implication of this principle is that we can reduce the relative value of anxiety-related avoidance behavior by increasing client contact with positive consequences resulting from engaging in more life goal–related behavior (e.g., driving to visit friends; going to a job interview to get a job). This is why we have stressed values from the beginning. Values matter. Activities that get in the way of valued living result in suffering. Behavioral activation should help promote increases in the frequency of life goal–related behavior, while decreasing anxiety-related avoidance and escape behavior. Acceptance, mindfulness, and defusion exercises can help accelerate this process by weakening forms of evaluative struggle focused on anxious thoughts and feelings, thereby promoting willingness and full contact with experiences that matter to the client.

BAT involves a number of steps that we outline in the next sections. These steps are (a) selecting activities based on chosen life goals, (b) creating an activity hierarchy and commitment to action as well as setting criteria for action, and (c) monitoring progress and giving feedback. BAT as used within ACT is, at the core, about fostering commitment to engage in value-guided action.

Selecting Activities Based on Life Compass

The first part of this process is for you and your client to revisit the importance of various valued life domains and goals consistent with those domains. The next step is to identify actual activities that move clients in the direction of living according to their values. Although activity selection in BAT is guided by life goals, the ultimate choice of an activity is determined largely by how pleasant the activity, or the outcome of the activity, is for the client. Making pleasantness the criterion for activity selection could perpetuate the seek-pleasure-and-avoid-pain approach to life that underlies a good deal of human suffering (see chapter 4). In ACT, we suggest using importance of the value as the criterion for activity selection, particularly when the client's anxiety is linked to a low frequency of activity in an area. Thus, both values and high avoidance of value-related activities provide us with the targets for exposure. They also guide the choice of what activities to pursue in behavioral activation.

To start, refer back to the Life Compass and Valued Directions worksheets. Ask the client to identify one or two value areas and some activities that are part of those areas that could serve as goals they want to work toward. The activities should be those that the client has put on hold or avoided in the past because of their anxiety problem. The next step is to identify clusters of actual activities related to living in the direction of the valued domain (Lejuez et al., 2001, 2002). For monitoring purposes, it is best to select activities that are both observable and measurable. For example, one value area may be education. Education, in turn, may include a long-term goal of attending college. This goal, in turn, includes smaller specific actions such as making a phone inquiry about programs, driving to campus to make more specific inquiries or speak to an admission officer, enrolling in classes, and buying textbooks. Another example of a broad valued direction may include developing closer relationships with a family member. This direction, in turn, may include several activities such as spending more time with a family member in places that a client has previously avoided (e.g., going to a movie or theater show, dining out, traveling out of town, or riding a bike). Recall, however, that value-guided action is not simply about the achievement of goals. It is an ongoing process with several intermediary steps (i.e., small goals or tasks). The steps are the goals that move clients in a direction that is part of a much larger process. Recall also that valued living takes commitment and has no clear end point. Goals, on the other hand, are steps in the direction of values that can be ticked off as one moves in that direction.

Creating an Activity Hierarchy and Commitment for Action

First, discuss with clients the perceived difficulty of value-guided activities as you and your client create an activity hierarchy. This hierarchy will help clients break down complex goals into smaller and more manageable tasks and give them a concrete plan of action and a clear sense of what lies ahead of them. For each activity, the therapist and client collaboratively determine clear criteria for doing the activities in terms of when and where to do them as well as how to do them and for how long. Next, when asking clients whether they commit to engage in one or more activities for the next week, make sure they have a clear understanding of what commitment means and what it does not mean.

Therapist: Doing this activity at home is probably not going to be easy for you. In fact, I am pretty sure that the passengers on the bus will be yelling at you with full force, "Don't do this," "You'll never make it," "You will just make a fool of yourself," or "You're going to get hurt." Anticipating all that, are you willing to commit to this activity 100 percent and go through with it? Remember, willingness is not something you can try or have a bit of.

Client: It seems tough. I'm not sure whether it will work.

Therapist: I am not asking you to commit to a particular result or outcome. What I am asking is whether you are willing to commit to doing something that will work for you *and* to taking all those passengers with you on your life bus. Will you do that and mean it?

Client: Yes, I do mean it, but what if I can't keep it?

Therapist: The commitment is to do it and mean it. The commitment is not that you will never break it. In fact, I predict you will break it at some point. Your commitment is that if and when you do break a commitment, then you will recommit, mean it, and get back on track and do whatever you can to keep your commitment as best as you can.

Client: Okay, I will do it. I don't know how well it will go but ... I mean *and* I will do it.

After the client has committed to doing particular exercises and/or activities for the upcoming week, ask the client to enter them on the Weekly Valued Life Goal Activities form provided at the end of the previous chapter (see also the book CD). FEEL exercises and other goal-related activities are also entered on the Goal Achievement Record. This form provides more of a summary of exercises and activities. At the top of the form, clients state the name of the goal and record the date on which they set the goal and committed to it. Then they record the activities (mini-goals) necessary to achieve the larger goal and record the session date they committed to doing an activity. Later at home clients can record the date when they completed the activity. For instance, if the client's goal is to attend a school concert, guided by her value of having a supportive relationship with her son, during the first week of conducting FEEL exercises at home, an activity entry could be "Do FEEL exercises on 6 out of 7 days to prepare me for driving to Paul's school concert." Apart from linking activities and values, this form also becomes an important record of achievement for the client on their path to valued living

Monitoring Progress and Giving Feedback

At the start of each session, the Weekly Valued Life Goal Activities form needs to be examined and discussed. Praise clients for their practice and progress and discuss any difficulties they may have had. Any obstacles and barriers should be dealt with as outlined in section 5 of this chapter. Based on the client's entries from the previous week, clients can then record on the Goal Achievement Record the next set of activities. If it is possible to convert records of activities into some type of visual graph, therapists should do so because such graphs are an easy-to-understand and compelling record of progress. The treatment manuals provided by Lejuez and colleagues (2001, 2002) provide more detailed suggestions on how to chart progress and also contain a number of additional record forms (e.g., daily activity logs, activity hierarchy sheets) that therapists might find useful during this part of treatment. The Goal Achievement Record should be kept and reviewed by clients periodically. Doing so provides clients with valuable feedback on how they are progressing and is a great method of self-reinforcement.

5. Dealing with Barriers and Avoidance

During both in-session and home exercises, clients will invariably experience barriers that have the potential of keeping them stuck where they are. A common example is a client telling the therapist that, despite committing to an out-of-session activity, they simply could not do it because they were too anxious. Therapists need to examine what got in the way of task completion and deal with obstacles to valued action using some of the strategies described earlier and in the next section. It is really important that we do not approach such barriers with a stance of wanting to overcome them. Overcoming and coping imply struggle. As Hayes, Strosahl, and Wilson (1999) point out, "commitment involves getting in contact with these barriers and moving ahead, not by getting over [or] around them, but rather by embracing and moving through or with them" (p. 271).

Some barriers are external, such as lack of money, time, opportunity, physical space, geographical constraints, or even weather. Therapists can often help clients work through some of these barriers by brainstorming alternatives and making appropriate suggestions that clients may not have thought of. Yet by far the most frequent and difficult barriers that clients with anxiety disorders face are those nagging internal barriers in the form of anxiety-related thoughts, feelings, worries, and bodily sensations.

Regardless of their specific content, all these thoughts and reasons send the same old loud message as broadcast 24/7 on Anxiety News Radio: *Do not do what you have decided and committed to do (although it might change your life for the better)—instead, do what you've always done and what is safe (although it hasn't worked for you and will keep you stuck). Commit to struggling to manage your thoughts and feelings!* Below we suggest a number of specific defusion, mindfulness, and value-related techniques therapists can use to deal with these internal barriers. In addition, there is one question that therapists can almost always ask clients when these barriers come up. This question refers back to the workability of past solutions and the direction clients want their lives to take.

The Basic ACT Value Question: Are You Heading North or South?

Whenever clients come up with internal barriers, take out a copy of the Life Compass and ask them this crucial question: "Is your response to this thought, feeling, worry, or bodily sensation moving you closer to or further away from where you want to go with your life?"

Below are some variations of this critical question that make specific reference to the life compass "heading north" analogy:

- If that thought (emotion, bodily state, memory) could give advice, would the advice point you north?

- In what valued direction have your feet taken you when you listened to this advice?

- What does your experience tell you about this solution? And what do you trust more, your mind and your feelings or your experience?

- If your intention is true north, does a particular action (e.g., an avoidance or escape-type behavior) head true north?

- What advice would the value [insert a pertinent client value here] give you right now?

- What would you advise someone else or your child to do?

It is important not to get involved in a discussion of the content or correctness of a concern or reason clients come up with. Instead, therapists should acknowledge the presence of these concerns ("Thank your mind for this") and consistently go back to variants of the above questions to model for clients what they need to ask themselves in the face of adversity. All of these questions and their answers may also bring creative hopelessness back into the room by again highlighting the unworkability of past solutions and the current opportunity to do something radically different.

Defusion and Mindfulness Techniques

Apart from referring back to variants of the basic ACT question, therapists can use a number of defusion techniques to help clients deal with their numerous mind and language traps. These techniques are designed to disentangle client evaluations of their experience from their actual experience and help them observe their experience with compassion.

Recognizing Mind and Language Traps

There are a number of language conventions that tend to keep people stuck. "Yes-butting" and "buying their thoughts" are two pervasive problems that can trap clients into corners, keep them stuck where they are, and seemingly prevent them from moving forward. Clients often mention both of them as reasons for not changing what they have been doing and to justify avoidance and escape behavior. For this reason, making some simple and subtle changes in verbal behavior can make a big difference. Such changes can help clients get unstuck by buying less into their thoughts so that they may move on with actions that are consistent with the life they want to live.

Getting Off Your But(s)

You may remember from early sections that one of the most common barriers clients get caught up in is the "yes-but" trap. Almost invariably, clients will say something like "I like to go out, *but* I am afraid of having a panic attack." What a client is saying here is that going out cannot occur along with being afraid. By saying "but" after the first part of the sentence, we undo what we said in that part, that is, we make it go away. This is actually what the word "but" literally means. "But" derives from the words "be out" and undoes or discounts everything that precedes it (Hayes, Strosahl, & Wilson, 1999). So when a client says, "I like to go out, *but* I am afraid of having a panic attack," they will not go out. They stay home because that "but" takes the "like to go out" away. It seemingly makes going impossible. Unfortunately, clients are likely to use the word "but" many times every day as a reason for not acting. This unnecessarily restricts their lives and reduces their options.

Ask clients to imagine what would happen if they simply replaced the word "but" with "and." "I would like to go out, *and* I am afraid of having a panic attack." This little change can have a dramatic impact on what might happen next. If clients put it that way, they could actually go out *and* be anxious and worried all at the same time. It would allow them to go out. It would also be a more correct and honest statement. A client may indeed feel afraid about having a panic attack in the context of going out. Ask clients to imagine what would happen if they started to say "and" instead of "but" every time a "but" keeps them on their butts. Imagine how much more space they would have in their lives. How many more opportunities would they gain to do things? How much space would open up for them? Getting off their but(t)s could be one of the most empowering things they have ever done.

As with other exercises, it is important for therapists to model the use of "and" instead of "but" throughout treatment. These language habits are firmly ingrained in our verbal repertoire and will only change gradually. So repeated modeling by the therapist and exposure to using "and" is essential.

Don't Buy into Your Thoughts

Most of the previously introduced exercises aim to teach clients that they are not their thoughts, and they need not buy into what their mind tells them. Although it often seems to clients that thoughts are factual entities, they are, in fact, still just thoughts, even when those thoughts appear highly believable. Most of us have heard a variant of this truism during our childhood years in the form of "Sticks and stones may break my bones, but words will never hurt me." Still, thoughts, evaluations, memories, and the like can hurt when we take them literally, in the sense of treating them as if they were the same as sticks and stones in the real world. Clients will likely buy into their thoughts from time to time. It means that clients buy into verbal representations of their experience and the world to such an extent that the content of thinking hides the process of thinking (Hayes & Wilson, 2003).

A simple technique to help clients not to buy into their thoughts is to ask them to preface evaluative statements with *I am having the thought that ...* For example, when clients say, "I will have a panic attack if I go out," ask them to say out loud, "*I am having the thought that* I will have a panic attack if I go out." Likewise, if a client says, "If I don't learn to control my anxiety and worries, things are going to go downhill for me," ask them to say out loud, "*I am having the evaluation that* if I don't learn to control my anxiety and worries, things are going to go downhill for me." Tell clients that you realize this sounds awkward. Yet, if they start describing their thoughts in this cumbersome way, it will help them see a thought for what it is (just a thought). Even the most scary and intense thought is still just a thought. This technique helps clients create an important distance between themselves and their evaluations of themselves and their experience.

Anxiety and Panic Are Also Just Words

Recall that anxiety, fear, and panic are generally unpleasant emotional events and well within the range of normal human experience. It is how clients with anxiety disorders evaluate those emotional experiences that gets them into trouble. Such evaluations are heavily tangled up with language. This is how panic, fear, and anxiety can turn into "bad" events—not simply events—that need to be dealt with like other real-world experiences that can truly cause injury or pain (e.g., the sticks and stones). Ultimately, however, these evaluations are just words that, because of unique learning experiences, become fused with a variety of negative consequences and meaning. This sort of fusion tends to get clients with anxiety problems into trouble because it diminishes contact with the world as it is (not as we say it is) and is responded to needlessly when time and effort could be put to better use for events that are truly important and controllable. To undermine and weaken fusion, while illustrating that panic and anxiety are nothing more than words, Hayes, Strosahl, and Wilson (1999) suggest a very simple exercise called "milk, milk, milk." We illustrate an adaptation of this exercise for panic and anxiety below.

Therapist: Can we do another simple exercise? Are you willing to do this?

Client: Sure, I'll give it a shot.

Therapist: Okay. I'd like you to think of the word "milk." Go ahead. Now, tell me what comes to mind.

Client: Well, I picture a drink that is white, cool, satisfying, even creamy.

Therapist: Good. That's right. Anything else?

Client: Hmm. I also see it going well with peanut butter and jelly sandwiches, chocolate chip cookies, cereal … but not with, say, orange juice.

Therapist: Okay. So there is a lot more to milk than just the word. Thinking the word seems to bring about a variety of experiences for you, some of which have little to do with milk itself.

Client: Actually, that happens a lot. I start thinking of something and then something else pops us.

Therapist: Well, let's do a little exercise about that. I'd like you to say aloud "milk *[pause 1 second]*, milk *[pause 1 second]*, milk *[pause 1 second]*" and I will do it with you. Ready? [*Now, both therapist and client say "milk, milk, milk, milk," pausing about 1 second between each word for twenty to thirty repetitions. Then, the therapist speeds up the repetitions faster and faster for another twenty or so repetitions until it is somewhat difficult for the therapist and client to say the word properly. Now ask the client to say "milk" again to see if anything has changed regarding the experience. Ask the client, "What happened to your experience of milk?"*]

Client: The other thoughts and sensations I had before when first thinking about milk are gone. I'd have to work a bit to get them back.

Therapist: What has happened here? The word "milk" once brought about lots of other related experiences for you. You could almost taste it. Now, it is just a word. It has sort of lost its punch. Are you willing to repeat this exercise with a thought or emotion that is bothersome to you? [*After the client agrees and has come up with a word related to a barrier—for instance, panic, anxiety, worry, health, an obsession, or an aspect of pain or emotional trauma—repeat the exercise as before, substituting that word for the word "milk."*]

The milk exercise is a simple way to illustrate how evaluative forms of activity can become diminished as we disrupt the natural tendency to hold onto the evaluations, meaning, and other relations that may be fused with language and problematic content, including emotions, thoughts, imagery, and the like. This exercise strips away those normal functions associated with language, leaving only a word as it is, not as we say it is.

Watching Thoughts Drift By

When clients have a lot of difficulty taking an observer perspective in regard to their anxiety-related thoughts and worries, therapists can introduce two other mindfulness and defusion exercises that can help clients see their thoughts as thoughts, which they can observe without having to change or struggle with their content. The exercise is about watching thoughts on leaves drifting downstream (Davis et al., 2000; Hayes, Strosahl, et al., 1999). If clients find themselves becoming distracted by thoughts and feelings, the basic task is to simply notice and acknowledge the presence of their thoughts and feelings with compassion and gentle curiosity and without trying to force them to go away. Below is a sample script.

---

1.   First, I would like to ask your permission to do another mindfulness exercise. Are you willing to go ahead with that? [Get clients' permission and then move on.]

2. Just get in a comfortable position in your chair. Sit upright with your feet flat on the floor, your arms and legs uncrossed, and your hands resting in your lap, palms up or down, whichever is more comfortable. Allow your eyes to close gently [pause 10 seconds].

3. Take a few moments to get in touch with the physical sensations in your body, especially the sensations of touch or pressure where your body makes contact with the chair or floor [pause 10 seconds].

4. It is okay for your mind to wander away to thoughts, worries, images, bodily sensations, or feelings. Notice these thoughts and feelings and acknowledge their presence. Just observe passively the flow of your thoughts, one after another, without trying to figure out their meaning or their relationship to one another. As best you can, bring an attitude of allowing and gentle acceptance to your experience. There is nothing to be fixed. Simply allow your experience to be your experience, without needing it to be other than what it is [pause 15 seconds].

5. Now, please imagine sitting next to a stream [pause 10 seconds]. As you gaze at the stream, you notice a number of leaves on the surface of the water. Keep looking at the leaves and watch them slowly drift downstream from left to right [pause 15 seconds].

6. Now, when thoughts come along into your mind, put each one on a leaf, and observe as each leaf comes closer to you. Then watch it slowly moving away from you, eventually drifting out of sight. Return to gazing at the stream, waiting for the next leaf to float by with a new thought [pause 10 seconds]. If one comes along, again, watch it come closer to you and then let it drift out of sight. Think whatever thoughts you think and allow them to flow freely on each leaf, one by one. Imagine your thoughts floating by like leaves down a stream [pause 15 seconds].

7. You can also allow yourself to take the perspective of the stream, just like in the chessboard exercise. Being the stream, you hold each of the leaves and notice the thought that each leaf carries as it sails by. You need not interfere with them—just let them flow and do what they do [pause 15 seconds].

8. Then, when you are ready, let go of those thoughts and gradually widen your attention to take in the sounds around you in this room [pause 10 seconds]. Take a moment to make the intention to bring this sense of gentle allowing and self-acceptance into the present moment ... and when you are ready, slowly open your eyes.

Eliminating Safety Signals and Behaviors

Safety signals and behaviors are important obstacles that keep clients off track, away from their goals, because they get in the way of processes that underlie corrective emotional learning (e.g., the extinction process, defusion). The function of safety behaviors such as seeking and giving reassurance, repeated checking, or being with a significant other is to ward off feared events.

Common safety signals include specific people or objects that have come to acquire the property of making clients feel safe from anxiety, physical injury, or embarrassment. Other examples include the presence of other people, water, money (to call for help), carrying a cell phone, empty or full medication bottles, a weapon, scanning for exit signs, looking for familiar landmarks when traveling, going out to run errands when the likelihood of finding many people is low (e.g., early morning or very late at night), or driving during the day and not at night.

These behaviors are problematic because they are part of, and perpetuate, the old unworkable control agenda. They are, in a sense, part of the system that clients have used in varied, and often quite subtle forms, to keep their anxious thoughts and feelings at bay. For this reason, it is essential that therapists watch out for safety signals and behaviors during any of the in-session or home exercises. Specific examples of safety behavior and signals in the various anxiety disorders include:

- *Social phobia:* averting eye gaze; not saying anything controversial or confrontational; being submissive; not appearing in any way out of the norm; never holding small objects for fear of shaking; using aids that prevent shaking, sweating, or blushing, such as wearing light clothing or braces; speaking quietly; diverting attention to others in the group; filling conversation gaps; overpreparing for what to say; using extra makeup; being accompanied by someone else who can carry a conversation.

- *Panic disorder:* getting through situations as quickly as possible; keeping the mind preoccupied throughout activities; reassurance seeking; driving in the far right lane only; driving very fast or very slow; driving only with a significant other present; preparing in advance to know exits, hospitals, or landmarks; staying near exits; carrying a cell phone, emergency phone numbers, paper bags to hyperventilate, or food (hypoglycemia); relying on other people, medications, or distractions.

- GAD: obtaining as much information as possible before decision making; seeking reassurance; diverting decisions to others; avoiding demands and challenges; being overly early; preparing for every potentially negative event or outcome.

- OCD: seeking reassurance from others; checking on safety of others; being overly clean; having wet wipes readily available.

- *PTSD:* hypervigilance or checking situations and people; carrying self-protective weapons; being with particular people or preferring to be alone.

Identifying Safety Behaviors and Signals

The first step is for clients and the therapist to work together to identify both subtle and obvious safety signals and behaviors. The therapist may observe clients during in-session exercises and activities and then ask clients whether they did anything in order to prevent catastrophic outcomes or make the situation less frightening. The therapist and client should compile a list of safety signals and behaviors and continually assess those domains, particularly as clients engage in exercises and activities in naturalistic contexts. It is not uncommon to find that clients utilize different safety signals and behaviors in different situations, or even several different safety signals and behaviors across similar situations (Taylor, 2000).

Review with clients examples of their own particular safety signals, and discuss concrete ways of going through FEEL exercises and goal-related activities without them. Also review the client's safety behaviors as they pertain to the FEEL exercises and chosen goal-related activities, and discuss ways of performing the task differently and without engaging in safety behavior.

Increasing Psychological Flexibility and Developing Repertoire-Expanding Solutions

From an ACT perspective, safety behaviors are really forms of experiential avoidance. They are used, sometimes consciously and sometimes automatically outside a person's awareness, to minimize or avoid the dreaded events associated with anxiety-related problems. As with other struggle and anxiety control strategies, safety-guided behavior tends to get in the way of living a full, rich, and meaningful life. For this reason, it is important for clients to experience that their safety signals and behaviors are ineffective as a solution for their problems. It is essential that therapists let clients experience the functional role safety signals and behaviors play in maintaining their problem, including how they have actually constricted their ability to live a full and valued life.

Conducting FEEL exercises and goal-related activities effectively means that clients face fear-provoking situations while weaning themselves off safety signals. It means facing the situations in a direct and open manner, without crutches. Many of the behaviors that have helped clients get through anxiety-provoking situations have ultimately not been helpful because they ended up trapping them and narrowing their options. By this point in therapy, many of these issues will be out on the table already. Yet clients will occasionally be reluctant to simply give up their tendency to use safety signals and behaviors and move the willingness thermostat up to its highest setting.

For this reason, it is important to let clients experience how such behaviors continuously get in the way of them living fully, richly, and without defense. This can be accomplished by doing mini in-session behavioral experiments that involve the client first engaging in an exposure FEEL exercise in the presence of a safety signal or while also engaging in a safety behavior, and then repeating the experiential exposure exercise without the safety signals or behaviors (Taylor, 2000). When safety signals and behaviors show up, therapists can ask the client "How well has this worked for you?" and "What does your experience tell you about doing XYZ? Are such actions taking you closer to or further away from where you want to be with your life?"

Therapists cannot promise what will happen to clients' anxiety as they engage in repeated exposure exercises. What therapists *can* promise clients is that those exercises will add flexibility and new choices in a way that clients will not have experienced for a long time. This is the most important aspect of exposure—or what we call FEEL exercises—from an ACT perspective. Recall that the problem for a socially anxious person is not that they get anxious or avoidant when asked to join a group meeting. The problem is that their repertoire has narrowed to avoidance only and it seems there is no other option available to them (Wilson & Murrell, 2004). The most important benefit of FEEL exercises is to broaden the client's repertoire and make it more flexible with respect to the avoided events. When combined with mindfulness and experiential openness, exposure creates a context where clients make full contact with many life events as they are, and without acting to change the experience because of what they think the experience is or means. While avoidance remains an option, FEEL makes other options available, such as joining the meeting without saying a word *and* feeling anxious. This client may subsequently attend the meeting again and say one or two sentences *and* feel anxious. The week after that, the client may attend the meeting and pose a question and say one or two sentences *and* feel anxious. The anxiety level may not have changed much, but the client has added two more response options that were not there before. Eventually anxiety levels may also go down due to extinction processes. This would simply be a welcome by-product of the more important behavioral repertoire expansion.

Problems with Values[*]

A number of different obstacles may arise that are related to values and the achievement of goals. Let us briefly deal with some of the more common issues clients come up with.

I Don't Have Any Values!

Some clients will say that they don't value anything. The reality, however, is that they do, in fact, have values. The problem is that they may feel too hopeless and afraid to express their values, or they may not have had the space to be in full contact with their values. Sometimes, caring hurts, especially if the value a client cares about has been a source of suffering. For instance, a client once told us, "I don't value being part of a loving family because I don't even know what a loving family is all about. Every time I try to reach out to a family member, they just push me away. My family is so

---

[*]   Some of the material in this chapter has been adapted from our ACT workbook for anorexia (Heffner & Eifert, 2004). It shows how many of the issues coming up in the ACT treatment of one clinical problem are similar to issues in other clinical problems—and how the solutions are similar in both cases, too.

dysfunctional that there is no point in me even thinking about family values." On the one hand, the client said that she does not value family. On the other hand, she mentioned that she reaches out to her family (and cares!). To help her out of this apparent dilemma, we asked her to reframe the way she identified her values. Instead of asking herself, "Can I *achieve* this?" we recommended she ask herself, "Do I *care about* this?"

Remember that values are different from goals, and they are not about achieving outcomes. The client was thinking in terms of goals and achievements. Values, in her view, were focused on outcomes: "If I care for my family, then they ought to reciprocate by showing caring for me." It was difficult for her to see that she could value and live her life as a caring individual even when others might not do the same toward her. She was correct that there was no point in setting the impossible goal of having the most loving family in town. However, she could certainly keep her value of caring about her family, and behave in ways that support that value, even knowing that her family's dysfunction might not yield the loving outcome she desired.

Second-Guessing Values and Goals

Some people complete the Valued Directions worksheet and easily identify what they care about. Their gut reaction is often, "Yes, I value parenting, friendship, communing with nature, and education." Then they begin to doubt and question their values. Do I have enough money? Do I have enough time? Am I too stupid to do this? What would my friends think if I chose this? With these worries, clients can literally second-guess themselves into behavioral paralysis, wondering if they truly hold their chosen values. We recommend using some of the defusion techniques described earlier to deal with these worries. Also remind clients that acceptance is about not judging their thoughts as "good" or "bad." Actually, there is no such thing as a good value or a bad value. Values are what they are and should be judged relative to their workability for clients in their social context. Values are not decisions—they are choices that need not be justified or defended. Encourage clients to go with their gut reaction and choose without judging. To explain the concept of choosing, we use an example described by Eugene Herrigel in his book *Zen in the Art of Archery* (1953). He described how animals and infants reach for objects without hesitation. On the other hand, adults tend to evaluate their choices, often hesitating before reaching for an object: "Do I really want to reach for that object?" All of us have much to learn from babies and animals in this regard. We and our clients can choose to act thoughtfully and without hesitation. Ask clients, "Will you step into this and stay committed to your valued direction and keep moving in that direction, no matter what your mind says?"

Is It Really the Client's Value?

At times, clients seem less than enthusiastic about their stated values. If that is the case, then examine whether the stated values and goals are really theirs and not the result of social pressure or wanting to please others. When people complete the Valued Directions worksheet, they sometimes choose values that sound socially appropriate or values that their loved ones expect of them. Be sure that the stated values are really *their* values, not values that society, friends, or family have imposed on them. Encourage clients to ask themselves: Why am I doing this? Am I doing this for me or for someone else? Remind them that the pursuit of values is about discovering or rediscovering their own life. It is time to put themselves first! If they are familiar with air travel, they know the standard safety instruction: "When the oxygen masks come down, *put your mask on first* before attending to others" (Heffner & Eifert, 2004).

We are not advocating that clients live their lives in a hedonistic, self-serving fashion with blinders that block how their chosen values affect people (including themselves). For instance, if a client values travel and seeing the world and is a parent with a spouse and children to care for, it would likely not be a good thing for this client to simply decide that from now on he is going to travel here and there whenever he can and for as long as he feels like it, without also considering the consequences of these actions on the family. In this situation, the client may feel a real tension between family values and other values, and these must be balanced. The same is true of most value-based decisions. Values do not occur in a vacuum. Values are not a one-at-a-time activity. They are situated in a stream of ongoing activity and multiple, competing value-based decisions that must be weighed. Clients can still be encouraged to put themselves first in the sense of living as a compassionate human being, which really is the crux of the matter. Values guided by good intention usually will not go wrong when the feet, hands, and mouth follow.

Valued Living Ain't Easy

Obviously, if valued living were easy, then we would all be living valued lives. Valued living is about ongoing commitment. It is a test of our integrity. Commitment means getting up after being knocked down. To face barriers as they come and as they are on the journey through life is true commitment. When clients report difficulty staying on course, remind them that they are the driver of their life bus. They really are in control of their destination. Their hands and feet, not the words of the unruly and loud passengers, steer that bus. Ultimately thoughts are just words and words are just sounds. The passengers' taunts are far less important compared with moving in a valued direction.

Also, your clients may bring up the issue of risk. It is undoubtedly risky to make changes. Things can and sometimes do go wrong. Yet, it is often the case that the biggest risk in life is not taking a risk at all. There are few outcomes in life that are certain. The future is, by definition, not knowable. Most choices involve risk for this very reason. Choosing to play it super safe is a surefire way to guarantee that nothing will change. Clients can count on that. And if nothing changes, they will definitely go where they were headed. Is that the place where their values are? Is that where they truly want to go?

Traveling with Your Fears

Clients need to travel with their anxieties, fears, and pain just as they do with their joys, hopes, dreams, and loves. This obviously is an enormous challenge for most anxious clients. When barriers come up, ask clients, "Are you 100 percent willing to go to the places that scare you so much that you do not live a valued life?" In the book *Hope for the Flowers* (1973), Trina Paulus writes, "How exactly does one become a butterfly? You must want to want so badly to fly that you are willing to give up being a caterpillar." Ask clients whether they are ready to change and want to fly so badly that they are willing to do things they may have avoided doing for years.

There is a Buddhist saying "If you don't decide where you are going, you will end up where you are headed." Values can prevent clients from heading toward a gloomy destination called "chronic and exhausting anxiety management." This is where clients have spent a good deal of their time already. After completing the values exercises and LIFE forms for some weeks, many clients have probably begun to recognize the cost of managing their anxiety and may wonder if they will ever become the person they want to be. They may realize that every minute they spend managing their anxiety is a minute that they are not devoting to their values and life goals. It is natural to feel impatient about the change process. Remind clients that valued living is a process comprised of a series of small commitments over time. It is recognized by actions, and often only upon reflection, when all of these small moments are considered in hindsight. Then, and usually only then, do we say, "Now there is a life lived well."

Therapists can occasionally remind clients that practicing FEEL exercises and life-goal activities with mindfulness is not about getting it right or attaining some ideal state. It is about helping them to stay present with themselves and continue on their path. For instance, when clients notice their response to anxiety-related thoughts getting in the way of what they wish to do, you may suggest coming back to the present moment using the "touch and let go" instruction. We touch thoughts by acknowledging them as thinking; we touch feelings by noticing them as feelings; we touch evaluations by noticing them as evaluations. We touch them lightly like we would touch a bubble with a feather so that we can let them go and continue with what we set out to do. In ACT, relaxation is not about relaxing muscles in your body. It is about relaxing our struggle and relaxing with ourselves. When clients notice intense feelings, the practice is to drop whatever story they are telling themselves and lean into the anxiety or fear and make space for it—just like in the finger trap exercise. This is what Chödrön (2001) calls "opening the fearful heart to the restlessness of our own energy" (p. 29). It is through this process that we learn to stay with and accept the experience of our emotional distress.

6. Dealing with Setbacks Through Mindful Acceptance and Compassion

No matter how often you remind clients to stay open to whatever arises, from time to time they are still going to use the techniques they have learned in this program as a way to suppress or escape from their emotions, thoughts, and painful memories. Reiterate some of the notions described in chapter 10 about how acceptance should not be abused as a clever way to fix anxiety. Remind clients that change is gradual and only occurs when they remember, day by day, and every month of every year, to move toward their emotional discomfort with compassion for themselves and without condemning their experience. There is no point in beating up on themselves for not being perfect at acceptance and keeping commitments. Trying to fix themselves is neither necessary nor helpful because it implies struggle and self-denigration. Although self-improvement can have temporary results, lasting change occurs only when we honor ourselves by approaching our imperfections with kindness, compassion, and patience. It is only when we begin to relax *with ourselves*, instead of relaxing our body, that acceptance becomes a transformative process (Chödrön, 2001). It is change if we stop running from ourselves, our imperfections, and our setbacks. Accepting ourselves is changing ourselves.

Tell clients that they cannot expect always to catch themselves spinning off into their old habitual patterns of evaluating and avoiding. When clients notice they are engaging in self-evaluative or catastrophic thinking, it is important they recognize such thinking without harshness and without putting themselves down for having such thoughts. As Chödrön (2001) puts it, staying with pain without loving-kindness for oneself is just warfare! That is why self-compassion and courage are vital. Ask clients to simply acknowledge thinking as thinking and return to the out breath during a mindfulness exercise, or at any other time, and continue with what they were doing. The label "thinking" becomes a code word for seeing "just what is." This activity is a move forward and an index of progress. "In essence, the practice is always the same: instead of falling prey to a chain reaction of self-hatred, we gradually learn to catch the emotional reaction and drop the story lines" (Chödrön, 2001, p. 33).

Chödrön (2001) also has an intriguing way of describing emotions as a combination of self-existing energy and thoughts, and she explains how we can use this energy in constructive ways. Emotions typically proliferate through our internal dialogue, that is, our evaluative thoughts. She reminds us that although we can label thoughts as "thinking" when we notice them, there is something that remains below the thoughts. There is a vital pulsating energy to our emotional experience, and there is nothing wrong, nothing harmful about that underlying energy. Just as we have repeatedly indicated in this book, there is nothing disordered about anxiety per se. The practice is to stay with it, experience it, leave it as it is, and when possible put it to good use. So when emotional distress arises uninvited, ask clients to let the story line, their thoughts, go and connect directly with the energy. What remains is a felt experience, not a verbal commentary on what is happening. Ask clients to feel the energy in their bodies. If they can stay with it, neither acting it out nor suppressing it, it can wake them up and provide them with energy to do things that move them forward toward their goals. This is somewhat similar to the amazingly large number of stage actors who never lose their "stage fright" and who typically use all the anticipatory anxiety and adrenaline as a source of energy for their subsequent acting. They do so because they will not sacrifice the acting they care about by quitting their career. So night after night they willingly go out on stage, do what they love to do, and take their anxiety with them.

7. Experiential Life Enhancement Exercises (Home)

- Practice the Acceptance of Anxiety exercise for at least 20 minutes daily and complete the practice sheet after each practice

- Practice FEEL exercises (interoceptive and/or imagery exercises) and/or Valued Life Goal Activities daily

- Keep track of FEEL practice and value-related activities by completing the Valued Life Goal Activities form each week and the Goal Achievement Record

- Continue monitoring anxiety and fear-related experiences using the LIFE form

- Complete the Daily ACT Ratings form

8. Preparing Clients for End of Treatment (Session 12)

Toward the end of treatment, it is essential to discuss relapse prevention and a plan for ongoing self-directed therapy using the strategies learned thus far. Monthly follow-up calls can be used to assess client progress and to minimize therapeutic setbacks, or what we think of as reverting to the old avoid and control agenda.

Provide Treatment Summary

In Session 12, therapists can help clients summarize the principles of this treatment program, what they have learned, and how it was learned. It is also important to revisit some of the most significant and frequent barriers that have come up and point out to clients that they will almost certainly continue to come up from time to time. Emphasize that clients have learned a great deal. They have made many changes. How clients are now approaching anxiety-related thoughts and feelings is different from their early tendency to run from them. Now, they are back in contact with their values and moving day by day on a path toward a valued life. A good way to illustrate a client's progress is to pull out some of the earlier LIFE forms and the Goal Achievement Record and ask them to compare where they were and where they are now. Do they see a difference? Have they allowed themselves to experience a difference?

There are numerous ways clients can maintain their process and learning. Here are two of them that you can discuss with your clients: *One way is to continue to practice mindfulness and acceptance exercises.* Encourage clients not to limit such exercises to anxiety-related situations. Mindfulness and acceptance are much bigger than anxiety. *The second strategy involves continuing to set short-term goals for each week in the post-treatment period.* Clients can make commitments to themselves to make progress in an area that is important to them and then monitor their progress in the same way they have done during treatment.

Prepare for Relapse and Setbacks

Therapists need to discuss the likelihood of experiencing a relapse. In an ACT program, relapse is a setback in a person's attempt to continue on their chosen path. Such setbacks are periodic failures to live up to or keep valued commitments. It is a return back to the old unworkable avoid and control agenda that landed clients in therapy in the first place. Informing clients to expect setbacks teaches them that recommitting to valued action after a setback is the key to getting back on track. These lapses or setbacks may be experienced as flare-ups of anxious symptoms that clients respond to with struggle, unwillingness and control efforts, or the reinstatement of safety signals or avoidance. How clients handle such setbacks is very important. Clients may quickly evaluate themselves as complete failures and use this evaluation to justify stopping all efforts at moving closer to their goals. In such cases, what is really happening is that clients are experiencing what it is like to be fully human. Our values do not ordinarily change because we fail to act consistently with them. Encourage clients to deal with self-deprecating thoughts with self-compassion and mindful acceptance, treating them as just another example of unruly passengers on their life bus. Their choice is to continue steering the bus in the direction that they truly want rather than where those passengers might tell them to go.

Identify High-Risk Situations

Relapse prevention is also about thinking ahead, during periods of success, to how clients might handle more difficult times. High-risk situations are events, thoughts, behaviors, and emotional reactions that increase the potential for lapsing into the old avoid and control agenda. Potential situations also include negative emotional states, interpersonal conflict, and social pressure, and life stress more generally. Continued practice of mindful acceptance can defuse such events from serving as relapse triggers, but they cannot and are not meant to prevent the actual experience of such events. The events can and will happen as clients expand their lives. What we want to do here is to ready clients to not give in to such events and to welcome them, always with an eye on living fully and moving in the direction of what they care about.

Therapists can assist clients with generating a list of high-risk situations and strategies to approach them. A good starting point is to revisit any previous setbacks a client has experienced during therapy and how they dealt with them. The aim of this exercise is to increase a client's awareness of the factors that contribute to setbacks and to prepare them for dealing with setbacks using what they learned so far.

A client may not recognize a relapse has taken place until they experience a full flare-up of anxiety or panic and find themselves in the middle of attempting to control or manage it. At that time, the client should engage in the mindful observing practices that they learned during FEEL exercises. In fact, typically such flare-ups are just another FEEL exercise waiting to be experienced. Therapists can emphasize that the client now has the skills to move through those events or situations. Ultimately, every situation is part of the totality of human experience and is time-limited. Therapy has given clients new strategies for living with such events and others that may come. The client's perception of their ability to handle situations is crucial to continued improvement beyond therapy. Remind clients of their prior accomplishments by referring back to the Goal Achievement Record. Reviewing the Goal Achievement Record is a useful strategy during good times to stay on track, and it is useful and important during setbacks to maintain perspective.

GOAL ACHIEVEMENT RECORD

Life Enhancement Exercise Record Form

First state the name of the goal (use a separate record form for each major goal). On the next line, record the date on which you have set your goal and committed to it. Use the following lines in the left column to record the activities (mini-goals) necessary to achieve the larger goal. In the middle column, always record the date you made a commitment to doing an activity. In the right column, always record the date you completed the activity. Once you have reached the larger goal stated at the top, you can also record the date you achieved it.

Name of Goal: _____

Date Committed to Goal: _____   **Date Goal Achieved:** _____

Activities	Date Committed	Date Completed
_____	_____	_____
_____	_____	_____
_____	_____	_____
_____	_____	_____
_____	_____	_____
_____	_____	_____
_____	_____	_____
_____	_____	_____
_____	_____	_____
_____	_____	_____
_____	_____	_____
_____	_____	_____
_____	_____	_____
_____	_____	_____
_____	_____	_____
_____	_____	_____
_____	_____	_____
_____	_____	_____
_____	_____	_____
_____	_____	_____

CHAPTER 12

Practical Challenges and Future Directions

Carefully watch your thoughts, for they become your words. Manage and watch your words, for they will become your actions. Consider and judge your actions, for they have become your habits. Acknowledge and watch your habits, for they shall become your values. Understand and embrace your values, for they become your destiny.

—Mahatma Gandhi

THE ROAD AHEAD

The psychotherapy scene is flooded with books promising new and "better" approaches to alleviate human suffering. We simply cannot promise you that an ACT approach applied to persons suffering from anxiety disorders will turn out to be better or more useful than other well-established approaches. It may. It may not. Only time will tell. What we can be relatively sure of is that ACT will change over time because of its coherent philosophical foundation, intriguing treatment technology, and rapidly evolving empirical base. Such changes, we hope, will move us closer to alleviating a wider range of human suffering.

This somewhat humble way to open the closing chapter of this book is meant to serve a function. Most of us genuinely wish to leave the world a better place than we found it. In a therapy context, this value usually translates into therapeutic actions that are designed to help our clients live better long after therapy has ended. This is the real legacy of our actions as therapists and what we usually mean when we talk about "good therapeutic outcomes." When a new treatment technology is disseminated in a practical form, as we have tried to do here, there is a risk that the approach and related technology may be held too tightly. This, we believe, would be a mistake. Throughout the book we have laid out the conceptual and practical foundation for using ACT with anxious clients. This book is not meant to be *the* way to do ACT with anxious persons. Rather, we hope you will use the material in a spirit of openness, creativity, flexibility, genuineness, curiosity, humility, sharing, respect, and investigative play. This is the spirit that guided us in writing this book and a posture that we believe is necessary when using ACT—or any psychotherapy approach—with other suffering human beings. We also recognize that there is more work to be done and that we still have a long way to go. There are no psychotherapies that are wholly curative. The same is true of ACT. Thus, it seems fitting and appropriate to explore some practical challenges that you may encounter when using ACT with your anxious clients, and where we see the third-generation behavior therapies headed in the years to come.

PRACTICAL CHALLENGES IN CONDUCTING ACT

We have said that ACT is a treatment approach, not merely a treatment technology. It flows naturally from a conceptualization of human suffering that underscores language traps and blind alleys, and unworkable self-regulation processes, and how these get in the way of living fully and meaningfully. It entails a therapeutic stance and a range of concepts that have been acknowledged and embraced by less behavioral schools of psychotherapy for some time. Some of you will find comfort in the ACT approach and technology because it fits your own training and experience. Others of you may find ACT hard to swallow. This is understandable given that many of us were trained in the tradition of "eliminating symptoms of disorders." Yet, we do not wish the ACT model to be a barrier for you or your clients.

The Approach Is Counterintuitive

The ACT approach is counterintuitive and goes against the grain of what most of us have learned needs to be done and ought to be done to alleviate human suffering, particularly in the West. Many (not all) of your anxious clients will also find the approach at odds with what they have come to expect from psychotherapy. That is, therapy is about alleviating suffering by focusing on the unwanted experiences. For anxious persons, suffering occurs because they typically focus on content (i.e., thoughts, feelings, physical sensations, and behavioral tendencies) that is undesired and the situations that may occasion such experiences. ACT, as we have seen, turns this view on its head by focusing on what people do about their pain, and how that doing creates suffering by getting in the way of living. Hence, the aim of ACT is not to fix people, because they are not broken, but to break them loose.

The counterintuitive nature of the treatment is, in part, what makes it effective. Yet, this feature can also be a real obstacle as you work to use ACT effectively with your clients. Remember that you are in the same soup as your clients. You have played the language game yourself when it comes to your own suffering. You have likely sought out solutions that resemble those tried by your anxious clients. Some of these probably include strategies to manage and control your own suffering. You also have likely received professional training and experiences that may have played into this very system. As a consequence, you may find yourself modeling nonacceptance by slipping back into control and symptom-focused kinds of talk, or by selectively suggesting that negatively evaluated experiences be reduced in the service of promoting more socially desirable experiences. You may even delve into the past history of your clients in an effort to achieve insight into the reasons for their problems, or find yourself wanting to offer solutions, explanations, and the like that would remove the discomfort your clients may be experiencing—and some of your own discomfort by extension. These and other actions are precisely what most anxious clients have been doing before coming into therapy. ACT is not about doing more of the same.

This is why it is so important to get your head and heart around the ACT model in your own life and in your professional role as a therapist. Acceptance is not something that can be instructed or faked. Nonacceptance may emerge in you and your clients in subtle forms during the course of therapy. When left unchecked, a lack of acceptance on your part can set up expectations about therapy that can be difficult to undo. As we have said, nonacceptance tends to play into the social-verbal system (i.e., rules, reasons, justifications, evaluations, avoidance, control) that an ACT approach is trying to help clients break loose from. This is why the counterintuitive nature of the treatment is so compelling. It functions to weaken verbal-cognitive forms of control, so as to make room for actions that are more flexible, less evaluative, and more experientially based. There is no magic to this. No smoke. No mirrors. It is what it is. As you struggle with the background material and its application in therapy, play with it and use it in your own life and in your clinical work. We think that you find ACT more experientially intuitive when you do so.

Handling Client Resistance

Resistance is ubiquitous in psychotherapy and everyday life. Virtually all psychotherapists have experienced client resistance in one form or another. All human beings have resisted some aspect of their experience. Though resistance can take several forms, it usually involves a fundamental dialectic between knowing what we should or should not do while at the same time not being able to do or not do it for reasons we often do not understand. Sometimes we cannot even see those reasons clearly. In ACT terms, resistance is fundamentally about verbal behavior getting in the way of effective action. It is a natural process of change and growth and a process that can keep people stuck. At the core, it is about taking charge of one's own life and living it!

Resistance to Action and Response-ability

Anxious persons tend to show up in therapy with quite a bit of resistance under their belts. At some level, they know what they should be doing with their lives, but cannot seem to get going and doing. They are on autopilot, listening and responding to what the mind says "is" or "ought" to be. The anxiety monster rules the roost. Anxiety News Radio is broadcasting 24/7, repeating again and again old habitual patterns of relating with oneself and the world. The old programming is in place, and behavioral tendencies follow automatically. There is little room for response-ability in this system, because the system runs the show. It is never challenged directly for what it is. Actions that run counter to this system, in turn, do not fit the programming. They are met with resistance. There is no room on Anxiety News Radio for doing something new. Nothing changes. Nothing needs to change.

The very act of coming into therapy challenges this system by providing an alternative to it. Yet, so long as the system remains in place, therapeutic efforts that challenge the system directly are met with more resistance, not less. This is why ACT goes after the system first, and hence the problem of resistance to change. All of the procedures contained in this book are about undermining subtle and at times obvious forms of client resistance (e.g., unwillingness, experiential avoidance, cognitive fusion) by fostering psychological flexibility, experiential openness, responsibility, and value-guided actions. Metaphors and experiential exercises weaken forms of resistance, in part, because they challenge the programming. We encourage clients to turn off Anxiety News Radio and tune in to Just So Radio instead. The anxiety monster need not be fed. Clients can be response-able and do what matters most to them. The bus can head north even while the mind is broadcasting, "Go south or else!" To get there, however, clients need to open up to the possibility that the programming is simply the programming. It will always be there. Clients can feed into the programming with more of the same, or choose not to buy into it by doing something different with their hands and feet. This is a moment of choice, personal response-ability, and courage, and quite often a turning point in therapy. It emerges once clients make contact with how they have lived up to this point and how they wish to live now and into the future.

Being with Noncompliance

One of the most common forms of resistance occurs when clients fail to complete a task they committed to doing. When that happens, therapists need to examine what got in the way of task completion and move through barriers to valued action using some of the strategies described in the previous chapter. In the process, therapists should attend to the possibility that the task was not clearly linked to client values or that the client fails to see the connection. It is important to note that noncompliance is not failure. Therapists should refrain from pressuring or threatening clients with statements such as, "If you don't keep your commitments, then things are not going to change much." Such statements are coercive and do not work. They model self-denigration. Instead of resorting to social pressure, confrontation, or interpretations of "resistance," this is a time for therapists to model acceptance and compassion:

> No matter how carefully the stage is set for the client to choose valued actions, it is a choice only the client can make. Choosing not to go forward with a plan is a legitimate choice, as long as it is actually a choice. The gentlest [and most compassionate] way to work with a client in such circumstances is to completely validate the client and the dilemma he or she is facing. The therapist might say, "If this were my life and I were seeing the consequences you are seeing, I could well imagine myself choosing not to go forward." (Hayes, Strosahl, & Wilson, 1999, p. 260)

As indicated earlier, the commitment is to do it and mean it 100 percent. The commitment is not that the client will never break it. What is important is that when clients do break a commitment, they recommit, mean it, and get back on their chosen path.

Resistance Is About Choice, Growth, and Change

Forms of resistance, including noncompliance, are neither good nor bad. They are what they are, and they reflect where the client may be with you as a person and with aspects of themselves. Resistance can be defused from, embraced, and experienced for its workability in the context of client goals and values. This is a critical point. When resistance emerges, evaluate whether you are operating from an equal stance with the client. Ask, who is setting the agenda here? Are you, as a therapist and another human being, operating in the role of bus driver? Are you setting the agenda for your client, or are they setting the agenda? Resistance cannot be overcome by therapeutic efforts to push the client harder, to set their goals, to make their choices. Pushing in this way typically will guarantee more resistance, not less. You can let them experience what hasn't worked and that there is a different radio station out there they can choose to tune into. Change is a choice only clients can make.

The same is true of resistance. For instance, most anxious clients are showing up for therapy in an effort to get help. The therapist, in turn, is there to help, and yet the client is resisting those helping efforts. In this sense, resistance seems to run counter to what therapists and clients are there for: to provide help and to receive help. Yet, this state of affairs is also a potential trap, for it places the therapist in the role of giver and the client in the role of receiver. Resistance emerges naturally from this relationship, particularly if one does not wish to take what is being offered.

Instead we suggest to keep the focus on how resistance is working for the client in the therapeutic moment. Is resistance just another barrier to valued living in disguise? Is resistance moving the client north or south? Be mindful that resistance is a process of change and growth, not an outcome. It is not about comfort or being comfortable. It is about confronting the familiar—the programming—and doing something different, perhaps even radically different. This view is nicely illustrated in the following Zen poem.

> *"Go to the edge," the voice said.*
> *"No!" they said. "We will fall."*
> *"Go to the edge," the voice said.*
> *"No!" they said. "We will be pushed over."*
> *"Go to the edge," the voice said.*
> *So they went*
> *and they were pushed*
> *and they flew.*

> —Anonymous

Jan Luckingham Fable (1998) described progress through resistance as an "Oops! I did it again," "Oops! I did it again," "Oops! I almost did it again" stage in a person's movement toward awareness and acceptance. The "Oops! I almost did it again" stage is the beginning of action and change, where resistance is transformed into willingness and movement north. This is the difficult part and why, even after we know and accept, we sometimes slip up and slip back. That is, acceptance and change may not occur in lockstep. Even with acceptance on board, there are times when we slip, fall, fail to keep commitments, and get caught up in self-doubt and don't do what we intend to do.

Dealing with Medication Management and Discontinuation

You will likely find that many anxious clients have used, or are currently taking, some form of anxiolytic or antidepressant medication. Indeed, clients often turn to medications as a first-line treatment for anxiety, guided by the view that reduction in symptoms will restore health and life functioning much like aspirin may alleviate a headache. Numerous medications (e.g., benzodiazapines, tricyclic antidepressants, SSRIs), in turn, are effective in reducing symptoms associated with anxiety disorders (Van Ameringen, Mancini, Oakman, & Farvolden, 2000). Yet, most clients do not wish to be on medications, largely because of their unpleasant side effects. Others, however, eventually make contact with the simple truth that life restoration does not necessarily follow from symptom reduction. They are right. There is no "life" pill that we know of. Your clients probably sense this too. Otherwise, they would not be in the room with you.

Medications Only Go So Far

We are learning from large-scale clinical trials that medications for anxiety typically result in faster symptom relief relative to psychotherapy. Yet, medications are not curative in the long term and are quite often associated with higher rates of relapse relative to psychotherapy. For instance, CBT for panic disorder by itself generally outperforms medications (i.e., imipramine) in the long term, but not in the short term (Barlow, Gorman, Shear, & Woods, 2000; see also Boyer, 1995; Clum, Clum, & Surls, 1993; Cox, Endler, Lee, & Swinson, 1992). Similar patterns have been observed with social phobia (Heimberg et al., 1994; Turner, Beidel, & Jacob, 1994); though with obsessive-compulsive disorder and generalized anxiety disorder, the tendency is for combined treatments to result in better long-term treatment gains relative to CBT or SSRIs alone (Cottraux et al., 1995; Kasvikis & Marks, 1988; Power, Simpson, Swanson, & Wallace, 1990). Data regarding the efficacy of combined treatments for PTSD are still too limited to draw any meaningful conclusions. Nonetheless, findings from such studies are converging on one simple conclusion, namely, that psychotherapy and life change alone result in the best long-term outcome for most anxiety disorders compared to medications alone or medications combined with psychotherapy.

Medications in the Context of ACT

There is nothing particularly problematic about medication use in the context of ACT for anxiety disorders. Past and present medication use would normally be addressed early on in the therapy process. For instance, in the context of fostering creative hopelessness, you will want to carefully evaluate why your client is taking anxiolytic medications. Is the client relying on medications so as to not experience anxiety? If so, this ought to be addressed experientially in the context of acceptance and mindfulness activities. One might anticipate, for example, that a client who routinely relies on benzodiazepines for anxiety or panic might be less inclined to do so as they become more willing to experience anxiety for what it is, not for what they say it is.

On the other hand, medication use may actually interfere with ACT-relevant treatment processes. Think about it this way: Most antianxiety medications diminish the frequency, intensity, and duration of problematic content associated with anxiety disorders. This is precisely the outcome that clients want ("*My control efforts are finally working!*"). This is problematic from an ACT perspective because it creates the illusion that we can successfully control our internal world if we only try hard enough. Most research studies, as we described in chapter 4, suggest the exact opposite to be the case. Remember that ACT is about making contact with problematic content, fully and without defense. As anxiolytic medications function to diminish full contact with problematic content, there is the real risk that clients may not derive maximum benefit from the treatment. They cannot fully make contact with the problematic content so long as medications change the properties of that content! FEEL exposure exercises that would normally evoke difficult content cannot possibly do so under such circumstances. This may, in turn, contribute to therapeutic setbacks or relapse following medication discontinuation. At present, we simply do not have any firm evidence to guide us here in recommending how best to address medication use in the context of ACT for anxiety disorders. Again, judging by the emerging data on the efficacy of combined treatments for anxiety disorders, our suggestion would be to help move clients in the direction of change that relies on their efforts in therapy, not temporary symptom relief that may be found by taking a pill.

Maintenance of Treatment Gains in a Nonaccepting World

This is perhaps the most important practical challenge you will face in using an ACT approach with your clients. They must live in a world where managing difficult psychological and experiential content is front and center stage. They must live in a world that largely devalues acceptance, mindfulness, openness, genuineness, experiential forms of knowing, and value-guided action. This context, in turn, runs counter to what you and your client have been trying to accomplish in therapy. The risk, therefore, for relapse or setbacks is quite real. Yet, that risk can be handled and addressed in a straightforward fashion prior to therapy termination.

Relapse and Value-Guided Action

Treatment gains are more likely to be maintained when clients set their eyes squarely on valued living and commit daily to living consistently with those chosen values. Obviously, this is easier said than done. Clients ought to expect a full range of psychological content to show up in their daily lives. The critical issue for clients is not to get caught up in the trap of letting that content get in the way of movements, however small, in the direction of their values. Relapse is not about a return of symptoms or difficult content. Rather it is about a return to old ways of responding to problematic content so as to not have it. In other words, relapse is about getting caught up in the experiential avoidance loop we discussed in chapter 4. The natural tendency, once in such a loop, is to fall into old habits and get stuck going round and round. Yet, this need not be the outcome.

Valued Living Is Not an All-or-None Affair

Valued living is not an all-or-none affair; it's not something that you either do or don't do (Hayes, Strosahl, & Wilson, 1999). It is not something that you gain or lose. Values may be hidden from view, but they are always there. Values also may change, but they do not go away simply because one fails to live consistently by them. North is north regardless of where you are. Values will be there long after therapy has ended.

Even the best parents in the world occasionally get tripped up and behave in ways that do not reflect the value of good parenting. In such cases, persons who value parenting do what is necessary to get back on track because being a good parent matters. Remember, values are directions with no clear end point. They may change over time. This is fine. What is not okay is when relapse gives the appearance that values have changed when they have not. Typically, what has changed is confidence in one's ability to live out those values, not the actual values. In such cases, therapists can simply return to the Life Compass described in chapter 9. By recalling the Life Compass and bus driver exercise, ask clients to consider the following:

> Imagine driving your life bus headed north toward your Value Mountain [pick a client value here]. Along the way, you realize that you must have taken a wrong turn and now find yourself about one hour out of your way, headed south. What do you do? What does your mind tell you that you should do? You are, in a sense, lost, but not directionless. Is there anything that would prevent you from turning the bus around and heading north toward the mountain? If getting to the mountain is important to you, then what you need to do is stay in the driver's seat of the bus and keep on driving north toward the mountain. Now, let's suppose that I throw in some of those anxious thoughts and feelings that your mind and body will kindly dish out once in a while. Remember, they are the passengers that are in the bus with you. As you get on the road to Value Mountain, they creep in and scream, "Pay attention to us, turn around, go back, you can't drive to Value Mountain with us ... We are more important ... Spend time with us ... Don't go there! ... Take that detour ... It is safer, easier ... It will make you feel better." What will you do? Stopping won't get you to the mountain, and neither will the detour. Only you and you alone can take yourself there—and you have no choice but to take all of you with you.

The point of going back to the bus driver metaphor is to illustrate that relapse is fundamentally about choice and action. It represents the reality that, every once in a while, each of us fails to live consistently with our values. Yet, every day requires a renewed commitment to take actions that move us in life directions that we care about.

Relapse is not about a return of anxiety, fear, or any of a number of possible human sensations that are part of living. Relapse is about not committing to small actions that make life worthwhile and meaningful. It is about not living! This is why we have emphasized values repeatedly throughout this book.

Use Booster Sessions to Foster Client Autonomy and Growth

A sensible way to evaluate therapeutic progress is to gradually taper the number of client visits over time. Hayes, Strosahl, and Wilson (1999) refer to these as "field experiments" in that they allow you to evaluate how well your client is doing without regular therapy as a support. They are also helpful in determining whether the termination point in therapy was adequate. A good rule of thumb here is to move from weekly to monthly to quarterly booster visits. Although we have written this book as a twelve-session weekly program, the total number of sessions and how you space the final sessions should be kept flexible. The content of the booster sessions will vary depending on the unique circumstances of your client. Normally, you will want to review the client's efforts in moving in the direction of chosen values and address weak points where experiential avoidance tends to show up and how it may continue to get your client off track. More generally, you should reinforce some of the concepts discussed over the course of therapy. Remember that we are looking to foster the growth and development of fully functioning human beings. This is a process that will take a lifetime, considerable effort, and commitment. It does not end when therapy ends. Therapy can only help clients take the first steps in this process that must continue after therapy has ended.

What About Anxiety Reduction?

As indicated throughout the book, anxiety is likely to go down as clients start engaging in FEEL exercises and goal-related activities. For mere anxiety-reduction purposes, it does not matter whether a man with agoraphobic avoidance drives in his car for one hour in the context of a naturalistic exposure exercise to extinguish fear and to correct catastrophic thoughts about driving, or whether he drives one hour to a job center to get information on a training program in the context of pursuing a chosen value-guided goal. The principle of extinction will work regardless of the reasons why clients engage in previously avoided activities. Interestingly, in the context of valued activities, extinction may work on more than just the conditioned fear response. Previous avoidance behavior may have been set off by a rule ("To get a job, I must first get my anxiety under control") or evaluation ("I can't drive because I have too much anxiety"). If the client's current behavior proves that rule and evaluation to be ineffective with respect to a chosen value, the relation between the ineffective rule or evaluation and the avoidance behavior that used to follow it is weakened. Moreover, an interesting study by Bach and Hayes (2002) with psychotic individuals has shown that the believability of unwanted cognitions (hallucinations and delusions) went down drastically with ACT compared to treatment as usual (TAU). Interestingly, the frequency of unwanted cognitions also went down with ACT but less than in the TAU group. However, ACT patients were 50 percent less likely to be rehospitalized compared to TAU patients.

We have deemphasized anxiety reduction as a treatment goal because it puts the old control agenda right back on the table. When therapists hold out anxiety reduction as a promise in even subtle ways, they may reinforce old experiential avoidance tendencies and undermine the ACT process. Nonetheless, therapists need to be sensitive to the goals of clients, which may still include anxiety relief (see also our discussion in chapter 6, Session 1). It may no longer be the only goal for clients, and perhaps no longer the most important one, but some clients will hold on to it at least to some degree. As therapists, we need to respect and accept that. There are no dogmas in ACT. It is not necessary for clients to buy into ACT 100 percent. If clients give up the old avoidance agenda and embark and stay on their path to valued goals, they are on the right track, regardless of whether they occasionally still dream of and wish for an anxiety-free life. So instead of categorically declaring that anxiety control and reduction is not a treatment goal, we recommend that therapists consistently frame therapy as an opportunity for clients to learn new ways of moving with anxiety on their way to doing what matters to them rather than allowing anxiety or the goal of anxiety reduction to be an obstacle. FEEL exercises and other goal-related activities are opportunities for clients to learn and practice new and more flexible ways of responding when they experience anxiety. We prefer simply to leave the question of anxiety reduction open; the client's experience will eventually provide the answer.

PRACTICAL INTEGRATION OF ACT WITHIN TRADITIONAL FORMS OF CBT

ACT is very much part of the behavior therapy tradition. It is not a movement to undermine that tradition. ACT brings into the behavior therapy movement a radically different model of psychological health and human suffering. In so doing, it places the therapeutic prize clearly in focus: namely, promotion of human value, growth, and dignity. It normalizes human suffering and redirects clinical attention on feeling well because of living well, not feeling well so as to live well.

How Far Are We Going to Go?

The treatment agenda we have outlined is radically different from the typical mainstream cognitive behavioral therapies for anxiety disorders. We have tried to make it ACT consistent as much as possible. Yet, we also recognize that we are treading on new territory and that ACT is still very much under development. Still, we do think that we are on to something that is worthwhile and important. A rapidly growing group of behavior therapists seems to think so too (Hayes, Follette, et al., 2004).

ACT and other third-wave behavior therapies are challenging the symptom- and syndrome-focused change agenda that has come to characterize behavior therapy as much as it has psychiatry. This shift in focus emphasizes broadband functional outcomes and process-oriented changes that are clinically meaningful and life altering. Acceptance is one such process. Contextualizing therapy in the service of value-guided actions is another development that is quite different from the tendency to focus on altering thoughts and feelings as a means to a life and at times as an end unto itself. Though this movement is making its way into several domains of empirical practice, it still remains unclear just how far researchers and clinicians are willing to go with it. Some researchers and clinicians will no doubt see the revival of interest in nontraditional concepts like acceptance, mindfulness, values, choice, spirituality, commitment, meaning, and purpose as passing fads. This is a real possibility. Yet, we believe it is unlikely for several reasons.

ACT Is Moving Forward on Several Fronts

First, ACT has a solid empirical base focused on the very nature of human language and cognition. It is built upon solid behavioral principles that flow from, and are in some sense guided by, a coherent philosophical and theoretical foundation (i.e., functional contextualism and relational frame theory; Hayes et al., 2001, 1994). This bottom-up approach was precisely the recipe that paved the way for many of the early and continuing successes of first-wave behavior therapy. In fact, treatments that followed this formula, such as exposure therapies for anxiety problems, have been enormously successful and have showed staying power (Barlow, 2002).

Second, the philosophical, theoretical, and empirical strands of ACT are highly integrated, and have yielded an applied technology that flows naturally from them. Applied process and outcome research on ACT is moving forward at a rapid clip, and therapeutic developments are closely tied with advances in the basic and conceptual branch of acceptance research (Hayes, 2004a). This again is highly unusual, but advantageous for the empirical base of ACT. It protects from the kind of faddish trends in psychotherapy that often attract many followers, but yield few lasting good outcomes.

Third, it is becoming increasingly clear that the worldwide ACT research and applied community are a generally kind and sharing bunch. There is a high level of communication among its growing members, and a real sense of common vision and purpose. All share a commitment to advancing an understanding of why humans suffer and the promotion of psychological health. This model of health, as should now be clear, stands in stark contrast to most Western views of health, happiness, and syndrome-based criteria used to judge psychological suffering and therapeutic success. The group as a whole is vital, energetic, and eschews dogma. There are many researchers and clinicians who are working to push ACT to its limits. They are willing to be wrong, just as we are, and do not hold to any particular hidden agenda. This level of communication truly stands to help advance the integration of science and practice in a manner that is relatively uncommon and much needed.

Finally, ACT is behavior therapy. Although ACT has borrowed and integrates techniques from a variety of Western and Eastern schools of psychotherapy, ACT is firmly rooted in psychological science at both the conceptual and practical levels. At a conceptual level, ACT heavily draws on and is derived from new developments in the behavior analysis of verbal and other behavior (for a detailed account, see Hayes et al., 2001). At a practical level, ACT focuses on experiential learning and value-related behavioral change and activation—the hallmarks of good behavior therapy practice. ACT has been developed with the same dedication to rigor and empirical evaluation that has been characteristic of behavior therapy at large and continues to be one of the main reasons for behavior therapy's remarkable success, growth, and impact. We are optimistic that these roots and strengths, along with a growing empirical support base, provide a unique and solid foundation for the advancement and further growth of ACT at a rapid pace.

THE FUTURE

The future of third-generation behavior therapies, such as ACT, will depend on their practical utility. ACT is not an easy treatment to learn, let alone apply. The evidentiary base of ACT is growing, but still sparse compared with well-established CBT for anxiety disorders. We recognize that this presents a challenge and an opportunity.

The Empirical Base Is Growing

The staying power of ACT will depend on whether it yields outcomes that therapists and clients consider worthwhile. A comprehensive review of clinical outcome studies (Hayes, Masuda, et al., 2004) and a number of studies published in a special issue of the journal *Behavior Therapy* (2004, Vol. 35, Issue 4) show that ACT is an effective intervention for an unusually broad range of clinical problems ranging from depression, substance abuse, chronic pain, and eating disorders, to work-related stress and other problems, some of which are quite severe (e.g., schizophrenia; see Bach & Hayes, 2002). ACT has also proven effective for anxiety-related problems such as OCD (Twohig et al., in press) and trichotillomania (Twohig & Woods, 2004). One of the core findings of most outcome studies to date is that ACT produces rapid and significant decreases in the believability of negative or unwanted thoughts. Interestingly, in many cases, the frequency of such thoughts and other unwanted "symptoms" goes down as well, although such reductions were not targeted outcomes.

Several of the studies examining core processes of ACT, such as acceptance, defusion, and willingness (e.g., Eifert & Heffner, 2003; Karekla et al., 2004; Levitt et al., 2004; Twohig et al., in press), have been done in the anxiety area. So far, all of the published tests of ACT components have been positive. All of this work is consistent with the view that ACT is not merely another narrowband, disorder-specific treatment package. It is much bigger than that. As Hayes pointed out in his foreword to this book, it is a model, an approach, and a set of associated technologies, with data spanning the range from basic process, to experimental psychopathology, to inductive studies of treatment components, to studies of processes of change, to outcome research. It is designed to get at the heart of human suffering by addressing processes that rest at the core of suffering. This is why ACT works well across a broad spectrum of psychological problems.

Though the treatment program we have outlined has not been tested empirically as a whole package, almost every element of this protocol has empirical support. In some cases this support comes from experimental psychopathology studies or clinical outcome research—in other cases it comes from both sources. So there is a growing base of support for this technology and the treatment approach we describe in this book. Researchers in several places around the world are busy testing ACT in experimental settings and randomized clinical trials doing component analyses and testing processes of change. Much of the data are preliminary but strongly supportive. It is time to put this approach before the psychological community.

The fact that not all of these data come from anxiety-related studies is not particularly relevant because the processes accounting for pathology (e.g., experiential avoidance and control) as well as the processes of change (greater acceptance, willingness, cognitive defusion, and valued living) apply to anxiety as much as they do to substance abuse, depression, or chronic pain. Though forms of human suffering may differ from one person to the next, the underlying issues tend to revolve around these basic processes. To further advance this work in the area of anxiety disorders requires bundling the approach into a technology that is suitable for use by clinicians and researchers alike. The next step calls for systematic empirical evaluation. For instance, we are currently conducting a randomized clinical trial comparing our program with traditional CBT at UCLA, and a related trial will soon start in Albany, New York. We sincerely hope that some of you will also contribute to this empirical effort by reporting on your work with this treatment via single case reports or other studies. To enable you to do so is one of the main purposes of this book.

Challenges

There are other challenges that the ACT community faces that may work against its staying power. For instance, we are still far from having psychometrically sound assessment devices to evaluate core processes that are believed to underlie this treatment and related interventions. For instance, assessment of experiential avoidance and acceptance is limited to a self-report device (i.e., the AAQ; Hayes, Strosahl et al., 2004), and several researchers (e.g., Frank Bond) are working to evaluate a revised and expanded version of the AAQ. Yet, it is unclear whether acceptance is a construct that is best assessed via self-report devices. In our view, acceptance and nonacceptance denote actions—what people do, not what they say or think about what they do. We therefore need behavioral methods of assessing acceptance. Similar problems exist in the assessment of mindfulness and values, and, less so, with defusion. Efforts to develop more adequate and versatile measures to assess these key constructs and processes are underway. We are not there yet though.

There is also some concern about whether ACT can or ought to be manualized. Those who see ACT as an approach would say no. Those who see it as a technology guided by the approach, including us, would say "why not?" We have obviously gone to great lengths to manualize the present treatment. We struggled intensely with this activity. We tried to get it right. We hope we have provided a useful tool, because there is a need to make ACT and other related technologies accessible to therapists who wish to use them. It is simply not workable to rely on seminars and workshops to accomplish such goals. Though we encourage you to catch an ACT workshop or two to reinforce points and stay abreast of the latest developments in this area, we ultimately believe that workshops alone are neither the most cost-effective nor most efficient way to disseminate ACT. Therapists should not have to rely on such venues in order to learn how to apply new psychotherapies.

Treatment manuals are necessary now more than ever. As Barlow et al. (2004) suggested, manuals need to be more simple and user-friendly by focusing on a single set of therapeutic principles for all anxiety disorders rather than creating diverse protocols for each anxiety disorder. This is precisely the unified approach we have taken with our protocol. Manuals are also required as part of federally funded clinical trials testing new psychotherapies. They are required for treatments to be considered as empirically supported. And, they help with dissemination efforts and are useful for training purposes. When used in a flexible fashion and when guided by a clear rationale and conceptualization, as we have stressed in this book, manuals can be quite useful to you and your clients and tend to improve therapy outcome (Schulte & Eifert, 2002). At the same time, do not feel compelled to follow the outline we have provided "exactly by the book." Instead, spend time with the material and then use it as a guide or framework in your work with clients. Stay clinically present and let the approach and technology we have outlined flow from that, not the other way around. This book is not about setting a treatment agenda for your clients. This would be ACT inconsistent and not good clinical practice anyway.

OUTLOOK

Making a difference is what psychotherapy is all about. This book was conceived in the spirit of making ACT accessible to therapists who face human suffering—their own and that of their clients. It was created in the spirit of helping you make a difference in the lives of clients who suffer about anxiety and fear. The differences we hope that you and your clients will achieve are quite broad and sweeping. Imagine, if you will, changes that have a broad impact on the lives of your clients. This may be in their families, their work, their ability to derive joy and pleasure from the world in which they live, freedom of movement, expanded choices and opportunities, new friendships, and deeper interpersonal relationships. It is in these and other areas where our clients' lives are lived, where joys can be found, and where suffering has its greatest impact. How our clients function in such domains is what matters most. Lives continue long after therapy has ended. Actions do not occur in a vacuum. How we live affects others. The consequences of dropping a small pebble into a still pond is a ring of widening ripples that remain present, ever expanding, long after the pebble has disappeared below the surface. Therapy is like the pebble in this respect. We expect that changes in psychotherapy will have a broad impact on the lives of our clients long after therapy has ended. This is our legacy as therapists and the kind of legacy we hope to achieve with the treatment program outlined in this book. The ACT approach we outline for anxious clients is a pebble. Our hope is that clients will drop the rope so that they can take the pebble.

Acceptance and Action Questionnaire (AAQ-Rev-19)

Below you will find a list of statements. Please rate how true each statement is for you by circling a number next to it. Use the scale below to make your choice.

1	2	3	4	5	6	7
never true	very seldom true	seldom true	sometimes true	frequently true	almost always true	always true

1. I am able to take action on a problem even if I am uncertain what is the right thing to do.   1 2 3 4 5 6 7

2. When I feel depressed or anxious, I am unable to take care of my responsibilities.   1 2 3 4 5 6 7

3. I try to suppress thoughts and feelings that I don't like by just not thinking about them.   1 2 3 4 5 6 7

4. It's okay to feel depressed or anxious.   1 2 3 4 5 6 7

5. I rarely worry about getting my anxieties, worries, and feelings under control.   1 2 3 4 5 6 7

6. In order for me to do something important, I have to have all my doubts worked out.   1 2 3 4 5 6 7

7. I'm not afraid of my feelings.   1 2 3 4 5 6 7

8. I try hard to avoid feeling depressed or anxious.   1 2 3 4 5 6 7

9. Anxiety is bad.   1 2 3 4 5 6 7

10. Despite doubts, I feel as though I can set a course in my life and then stick to it.   1 2 3 4 5 6 7

11. If I could magically remove all the painful experiences I've had in my life, I would do so.   1 2 3 4 5 6 7

12. I am in control of my life.   1 2 3 4 5 6 7

13. If I get bored with a task, I can still complete it.   1 2 3 4 5 6 7

14. Worries can get in the way of my success.   1 2 3 4 5 6 7

15. I should act according to my feelings at the time.   1 2 3 4 5 6 7

16. If I promised to do something, I'll do it, even if I later don't feel like it.   1 2 3 4 5 6 7

17. I often catch myself daydreaming about things I've done and what I would do differently next time.   1 2 3 4 5 6 7

18. When I evaluate something negatively, I usually recognize that this is just a reaction, not an objective fact.   1 2 3 4 5 6 7

19. When I compare myself to other people, it seems that most of them are handling their lives better than I do.   1 2 3 4 5 6 7

White Bear Suppression Inventory

Please indicate the degree to which you agree with each of the following items using the scale below. Simply circle your response to each item.

1	2	3	4	5
strongly disagree	disagree somewhat	neither agree nor disagree	agree somewhat	strongly agree

1.	There are things I prefer not to think about.	1 2 3 4 5
2.	Sometimes I wonder why I have the thoughts I do.	1 2 3 4 5
3.	I have thoughts that I cannot stop.	1 2 3 4 5
4.	There are images that come to mind that I cannot erase.	1 2 3 4 5
5.	My thoughts frequently return to one idea.	1 2 3 4 5
6.	I wish I could stop thinking of certain things.	1 2 3 4 5
7.	Sometimes my mind races so fast I wish I could stop it.	1 2 3 4 5
8.	I always try to put problems out of mind.	1 2 3 4 5
9.	There are thoughts that keep jumping into my head.	1 2 3 4 5
10.	Sometimes I stay busy just to keep thoughts from intruding on my mind.	1 2 3 4 5
11.	There are things that I try not to think about.	1 2 3 4 5
12.	Sometimes I really wish I could stop thinking.	1 2 3 4 5
13.	I often do things to distract myself from my thoughts.	1 2 3 4 5
14.	I often have thoughts that I try to avoid.	1 2 3 4 5
15.	There are many thoughts that I have that I don't tell anyone.	1 2 3 4 5

Mindfulness Attention Awareness Scale (MAAS)

Please indicate the degree to which you agree with each of the following items using the scale below. Simply circle your response to each item.

1	2	3	4	5	6
almost always	very frequently	somewhat frequently	somewhat infrequently	very infrequently	almost never

1. I could be experiencing some emotion and not be conscious of it until some time later. 1 2 3 4 5 6

2. I break or spill things because of carelessness, not paying attention, or thinking of something else. 1 2 3 4 5 6

3. I find it difficult to stay focused on what's happening in the present. 1 2 3 4 5 6

4. I tend to walk quickly to get where I'm going without paying attention to what I experience along the way. 1 2 3 4 5 6

5. I tend not to notice feelings of physical tension or discomfort until they really grab my attention. 1 2 3 4 5 6

6. I forget a person's name almost as soon as I've been told it for the first time. 1 2 3 4 5 6

7. It seems I am "running on automatic" without much awareness of what I'm doing. 1 2 3 4 5 6

8. I rush through activities without being really attentive to them. 1 2 3 4 5 6

9. I get so focused on the goal I want to achieve that I lose touch with what I am doing right now to get there. 1 2 3 4 5 6

10. I do jobs or tasks automatically, without being aware of what I'm doing. 1 2 3 4 5 6

11. I find myself listening to someone with one ear, doing something else at the same time. 1 2 3 4 5 6

12. I drive places on "automatic pilot" and then wonder why I went there. 1 2 3 4 5 6

13. I find myself preoccupied with the future or the past. 1 2 3 4 5 6

14. I find myself doing things without paying attention. 1 2 3 4 5 6

15. I snack without being aware that I'm eating. 1 2 3 4 5 6

Web Sites and Other Resources

ACT *for Anxiety Disorders*—Our Book

http://www.ACT-for-Anxiety-Disorders.com

This is a Web site for this book, with information on workshops, contact information for the authors, and additional information about the book and the ACT approach in general. Our intent is to make this Web site useful to you. Thus, we plan to include a section where you will be able to find audio and video training materials and additional clinical resources to help you improve the treatment of your anxious clients. We will also share some feedback and suggestions from readers that we think might be of interest and useful for other therapists. Most of the materials are available for everyone visiting the site. To access some of the advanced electronic training materials and clinical resources will require that you type in the following universal case-sensitive access code: ACTonAnxiety. A must see!

ACT-Related Books and Materials

http://www.acceptanceandmindfulness.com

This Web site contains information on other New Harbinger books in which acceptance and mindfulness approaches are applied to a variety of clinical problems.

Acceptance and Commitment Therapy

http://www.acceptanceandcommitmenttherapy.com

This Web site has many useful resources for those interested in learning more about ACT as well as those actively engaged in ACT research and application. There is also an extensive collection of research support (e.g., you can find updated lists of empirical studies on ACT, and many of them can be downloaded directly from the Web site).

Center for Mindfulness in Medicine

http://www.umassmed.edu/cfm/

This is the Web site for the Center for Mindfulness in Medicine, Health Care, and Society at the University of Massachusetts Medical School. This site is dedicated to furthering the practice and integration of mindfulness in the lives of individuals, institutions, and society through a wide range of clinical, research, education, and outreach initiatives. One of these initiatives is the Stress Reduction Program, the oldest and largest academic medical center–based mindfulness program in the country.

Relational Frame Theory

http://www.relationalframetheory.com/

This Internet site describes relational frame theory (RFT) and relevant related research and theory. RFT is the core theoretical conceptual foundation of ACT. This Web site includes numerous articles and resources describing RFT work (many may be downloaded for free). You will also find a nice online tutorial on the basics of RFT.

References

American Psychiatric Association (2000). *Diagnostic and statistical manual of mental disorders* (4th ed.). Washington, DC: Author.

Antony, M. M., & Barlow, D. H. (2002). Specific phobias. In D. H. Barlow (Ed.), *Anxiety and its disorders: The nature and treatment of anxiety and panic* (2nd ed.) (pp. 380-417). New York: Guilford Press.

Antony, M. M., Orsillo, S. M., & Roemer, L. (2001). *Practitioner's guide to empirically based measures of anxiety*. New York: Kluwer Academic/Plenum.

Ascher, L. M. (1989). Paradoxical intention and recursive anxiety. In L. M. Ascher (Ed.), *Therapeutic paradox* (pp. 93-136). New York: Guilford.

Bach, P., & Hayes, S. C. (2002). The use of Acceptance and Commitment Therapy to prevent the rehospitalization of psychotic patients: A randomized controlled trial. *Journal of Consulting and Clinical Psychology, 70* (5), 1129-1139.

Barlow, D. H. (1988). *Anxiety and its disorders: The nature and treatment of anxiety and panic*. New York: Guilford Press.

Barlow, D. H. (2001). *Clinical handbook of psychological disorders: A step-by-step treatment manual* (3rd ed.). New York: Guilford.

Barlow, D. H. (2002). *Anxiety and its disorders: The nature and treatment of anxiety and panic* (2nd ed.). New York: Guilford Press.

Barlow, D. H., Allen, L. B., & Choate, M. L. (2004). Toward a unified treatment for emotional disorders. *Behavior Therapy, 35*, 205-230.

Barlow, D. H., & Durand, V. M. (2004). *Essentials of abnormal psychology* (4th ed.). New York: Wadsworth.

Barlow, D. H., Gorman, J. M., Shear, M. K., & Woods, S. W. (2000). Cognitive-behavioral therapy, imipramine, or their combination for panic disorder: A randomized controlled trial. *Journal of the American Medical Association, 283*, 2529-2536.

Beck, A. T., & Emery, G. (1985). *Anxiety disorders and phobias: A cognitive perspective*. New York: Basic Books.

Becker, C. B., & Zayfert, C. (2001). Integrating DBT-based techniques and concepts to facilitate treatment for PTSD. *Cognitive and Behavioral Practice, 8*, 107-122.

Biglan, A., & Hayes, S. C. (1996). Should the behavioral sciences become more pragmatic? The case for functional contextualism in research on human behavior. *Applied and Preventive Psychology: Current Scientific Perspectives, 5,* 47-57.

Bishop, S. R., Lau, M., Shapiro, S., Carlson, L., Anderson, N., Carmody, J., et al. (2004). Mindfulness: A proposed operationalized definition. *Clinical Psychology: Science and Practice, 11,* 230-241.

Blackledge, J. T., & Hayes, S. C. (2001). Emotion regulation in Acceptance and Commitment Therapy. *JCLP/In Session: Psychotherapy in Practice, 57,* 243-255.

Bond, F. W. & Bunce, D. (2000). Mediators of change in emotion-focused and problem-focused worksite stress management interventions. *Journal of Occupational Health Psychology, 5,* 156-163.

Bond, F. W., & Bunce, D. (2003). The role of acceptance and job control in mental health, job satisfaction, and work performance. *Journal of Applied Psychology, 88,* 1057-1067.

Borkovec, T. D., Alcaine, O., & Behar, E. (2004). Avoidance theory of worry and generalized anxiety disorder. In R. G. Heimberg, C. L. Turk & D. S. Mennin (Eds.), *Generalized anxiety disorder: Advances in research and practice* (pp. 77-108). New York: Guilford Press.

Borkovec, T. D., & Newman, M. G. (1998). Worry and generalized anxiety disorder. In A. S. Bellack & M. Hersen (Series Eds.), *Comprehensive Clinical Psychology* (Vol. 6, pp. 439-459). New York: Elsevier.

Bouton, M. E., Mineka, S., & Barlow, D. H. (2001). A modern learning theory perspective on the etiology of panic disorder. *Psychological Review, 108,* 4-32.

Boyer, W. (1995). Serotonin uptake inhibitors are superior to imipramine and alprazolam in alleviating panic attacks: A meta-analysis. *International Journal of Clinical Psychopharmacology, 10,* 45-49.

Brown, K. W., & Ryan, R. M. (2003). The benefits of being mindful: Mindfulness and its role in psychological well-being. *Journal of Personality and Social Psychology, 84,* 822-848.

Brown, T. A., & Barlow, D. H. (2002). Classification of anxiety and mood disorders. In D. H. Barlow (Ed.), *Anxiety and its disorders: The nature and treatment of anxiety and panic* (2nd ed.) (pp. 292-327). New York: Guilford Press.

Brown, T. A., DiNardo, P. A., & Barlow, D. H. (1994). *Anxiety Disorders Interview Schedule for DSM-IV.* Boulder, CO: Graywind.

Centers for Disease Control and Prevention (2002). *Web-based Injury Statistics Query and Reporting System (WISQARS) [Online].* National Center for Injury Prevention and Control, Centers for Disease Control and Prevention. Available from: URL: www.cdc.gov/ ncipc/wisqars.

Chambless, D. L., & Gracely, E. J. (1989). Fear of fear and the anxiety disorders. *Cognitive Therapy and Research, 13,* 9-20.

Chödrön, P. (2001). *The places that scare you.* Boston: Shambhala.

Chorpita, B. F., & Barlow, D. H. (1998). The development of anxiety: The role of control in the early environment. *Psychological Bulletin, 124,* 3-21.

Cioffi, D., & Holloway, J. (1993). Delayed costs of suppressed pain. *Journal of Personality and Social Psychology, 64,* 274-282.

Clark, D. M., Ball, S., & Pape, D. (1991). An experimental investigation of thought suppression. *Behaviour Research and Therapy, 29,* 253-257.

Clum, G. A., Clum, G. A., & Surls, R. (1993). A meta-analysis of treatments for panic disorder. *Journal of Consulting and Clinical Psychology, 61*, 317-326.

Cottraux, J., Note, I., Cungi, C., Legeron, P., Heim, F., Chneiweiss, L., et al. (1995). A controlled study of cognitive behaviour therapy with buspirone or placebo in panic disorder with agoraphobia. *British Journal of Psychiatry, 167*, 635-641.

Cox, B. J., Endler, N.S., Lee, P.S., & Swinson, R.P. (1992). A meta-analysis of treatments for panic disorder with agoraphobia: Imipramine, alprazolam, and in vivo exposure. *Journal of Behaviour Therapy and Experimental Psychiatry, 23*, 175-182.

Cox, B. J., Swinson, R. P., Norton, G. R., & Kuch, K. (1991). Anticipatory anxiety and avoidance in panic disorder with agoraphobia. *Behaviour Research and Therapy, 29*, 363-365.

Craske, M. G. (1991). Phobic fear and panic attacks: The same emotional states triggered by different cues? *Clinical Psychology Review, 11*, 599-620.

Craske, M. G. (1999). *Anxiety disorders: Psychological approaches to theory and treatment.* Boulder, CO: Westview Press.

Craske, M. G. (2003). *Origins of phobias and anxiety disorders: Why women more than men?* Amsterdam: Elsevier.

Craske, M. G. (2005). *Cognitive-behavioral treatment of anxiety disorders.* Unpublished treatment manual. Available from the author at Department of Psychology, University of California at Los Angeles.

Craske, M. G., Antony, M. M., & Barlow, D. H. (1997). *Mastery of your specific phobia.* Boulder, CO: Graywind.

Craske, M. G., & Barlow, D. H. (2000). *Mastery of your anxiety and panic, 3rd ed. (MAP III).* Boulder, CO: Graywind.

Craske, M. G., Miller, P. P., Rotunda, R., & Barlow, D. H. (1990). A descriptive report of features of initial unexpected panic attacks in minimal and extensive avoiders. *Behaviour Research and Therapy, 28*, 395-400.

Craske, M. G., Rowe, M., Lewin, M., & Noriega-Dimitri, R. (1997). Interoceptive exposure versus breathing retraining within cognitive-behavioural therapy for panic disorder with agoraphobia. *British Journal of Clinical Psychology, 36*, 85-99.

Craske, M. G., Street, L., & Barlow, D. H. (1989). Instructions to focus upon or distract from internal cues during exposure treatment of agoraphobic avoidance. *Behaviour Research and Therapy, 27*, 663-672.

Dahl, J. (in press). *Living beyond your pain.* Oakland, CA: New Harbinger Publications.

Dahl, J., Wilson, K. G., & Nilsson, A. (2004). Acceptance and commitment therapy and the treatment of persons at risk for long-term disability resulting from stress and pain symptoms: A preliminary randomized trial. *Behavior Therapy, 35*, 785-802.

Davis, M. D., Eshelman, E. R., & McKay, M. (2000). *The relaxation and stress reduction workbook* (5th ed.). Oakland, CA: New Harbinger Publications.

Denollet, J., Sys, S. U., Stoobant, N., Rombouts, H., Gillebert, T. C., & Brutsaert, D. L. (1996). Personality as an independent predictor of long-term mortality in patients with coronary heart disease. *The Lancet, 347*, 417-421.

Dollard, J., & Miller, N. E. (1950). *Personality and psychotherapy: An analysis in terms of learning, thinking, and culture.* New York: McGraw-Hill.

Eaton, W. W., Dryman, A., & Weissman, M. M. (1991) Panic and phobia. In L. N. Robins, & D. A. Regier (Eds.), *Psychiatric disorders in America: The epidemiologic catchment area study* (pp. 155-179). New York: The Free Press.

Eifert, G. H., & Heffner, M. (2003). The effects of acceptance versus control contexts on avoidance of panic-related symptoms. *Journal of Behavior Therapy and Experimental Psychiatry, 34,* 293-312.

Eifert, G. H., & Wilson, P. H. (1991). The triple response approach to assessment: A conceptual and methodological appraisal. *Behaviour Research and Therapy, 29,* 283-292.

Eifert, G. H., & Zvolensky, M. J. (2004). Somatoform disorders and psychological factors in physical health and illness. In J. E. Maddux & B. A. Winstead (Eds.), *Psychopathology: Contemporary issues, theory, and research* (p. 281-300). Hillsdale, NJ: Erlbaum.

Eifert, G. H., Zvolensky, M. J., & Lejuez, C. W. (2000). Heart-focused anxiety and chest pain: A conceptual and clinical review. *Clinical Psychology: Science and Practice, 7,* 403-417.

Ellis, A. (2004). *The road to tolerance: The philosophy of rational emotive behavior therapy.* Amherst, NY: Prometheus.

Ellis, A., & Robb, H. (1994). Acceptance in rational-emotive therapy. In S. C. Hayes, N. S. Jacobson, V. M. Follette, & M. J. Dougher (Eds.), *Acceptance and change: Content and context in psychotherapy* (pp. 91-102). Reno, NV: Context Press.

Eysenck, H. J. (1987). Behavior therapy. In H. J. Eysenck & I. Martin (Eds.), *Theoretical foundations of behavior therapy* (pp. 3-34). New York: Plenum.

Feldner, M. T., Zvolensky, M. J., Eifert, G. H., & Spira, A. P. (2003). Emotional avoidance: An experimental test of individual differences and response suppression during biological challenge. *Behaviour Research and Therapy, 41,* 403-411.

First, M. B., Spitzer, R. L., Gibbon, M., & Williams, J. B. W. (1996). *Structured Clinical Interview for DSM-IV Axis I Disorders, Clinician Version* (SCID-CV). Washington, DC: American Psychiatric Press.

Foa, E. B., & Emmelkamp, P. M. G. (1983). *Failures in behavior therapy.* New York: Wiley.

Foa, E. B., & Kozak, M. J. (1997a). Beyond the efficacy ceiling? Cognitive behavior therapy in search of a theory. *Behavior Therapy, 28,* 601-611.

Foa, E. B., & Kozak, M. J. (1997b). *Mastery of obsessive-compulsive disorder (OCD): A cognitive-behavioral approach.* Boulder, CO: Graywind.

Folke F., & Parling, T. (2004). *Acceptance and Commitment Therapy in group format for individuals who are unemployed and on sick leave suffering from depression: A randomized controlled trial.* Thesis, University of Uppsala, Uppsala, Sweden.

Forsyth, J. P. (2000). A process-oriented behavioral approach to the etiology, maintainance, and treatment of anxiety-related disorders. In M. J. Dougher (Ed.), *Clinical behavior analysis* (pp. 153-180). Reno, NV: Context Press.

Forsyth, J. P., Daleiden, E., & Chorpita, B. F. (2000). Response primacy in fear conditioning: Disentangling the contributions of the UCS vs. the UCR. *The Psychological Record, 50,* 17-33.

Forsyth, J. P., & Eifert, G. H. (1996). The language of feeling and the feeling of anxiety: Contributions of the behaviorisms toward understanding the function-altering effects of language. *The Psychological Record, 46,* 607-649.

Forsyth, J. P., & Eifert, G. H. (1998a). Phobic anxiety and panic: An integrative behavioral account of their origin and treatment. In J. J. Plaud & G. H. Eifert (Eds.), *From Behavior Theory to Behavior Therapy* (pp. 38-67). Needham, MA: Allyn & Bacon.

Forsyth, J. P., & Eifert, G. H. (1998b). Response intensity of systemic alarms in content-specific fear conditioning: Comparing 20% versus 13% CO_2-enriched air as a UCS. *Journal of Abnormal Psychology, 107,* 291-304.

Forsyth, J. P., Eifert, G. H., & Barrios, V. (in press). Fear conditioning research as a clinical analogue. In M. G. Craske, D. Hermans, & D. Vansteenwegen (Eds.), *Fear and learning: Basic science to clinical application*. Washington, DC: American Psychological Association.

Forsyth, J. P., Eifert, G. H., & Thompson, R. N. (1996). Systemic alarms in fear conditioning— II: An experimental methodology using 20% CO_2 inhalation as a UCS. *Behavior Therapy, 27*, 391-415.

Forsyth, J. P., Parker, J. D., & Finlay, C. G. (2003). Anxiety sensitivity, controllability, and experiential avoidance and their relation to drug of choice and addiction severity in a residential sample of substance-abusing veterans. *Addictive Behaviors, 28*, 851-870.

Freud, S. (1920). *Introductory lectures on psychoanalysis*. New York: Norton.

Friman, P. C., Hayes, S. C., & Wilson, K. G. (1998). Why behavior analysts should study emotion: The example of anxiety. *Journal of Applied Behavior Analysis, 31*, 137-156.

Gaudiano, B. A., & Herbert, J. D. (in press). Acute treatment of inpatients with psychotic symptoms using Acceptance and Commitment Therapy. *Behaviour Research and Therapy*.

Gifford, E. V., Kohlenberg, B. S., Hayes, S. C., Antonuccio, D. O., Piasecki, M. M., Rasmussen-Hall, M. L., & et al. (2004). Applying a functional acceptance based model to smoking cessation: An initial trial of Acceptance and Commitment Therapy. *Behavior Therapy, 35*, 689-705.

Gold, D. B., & Wegner, D. M. (1995). Origins of ruminative thought: Trauma, incompleteness, nondisclosure, and suppression. *Journal of Applied Social Psychology, 25*, 1245-1261.

Greco, L. A., & Eifert, G. H. (2004). Treating parent-adolescent conflict: Is acceptance the missing link for an integrative family therapy? *Cognitive and Behavioral Practice, 11*, 305-314.

Greenberg, L. (1994). Acceptance in experiential therapy. In S. C. Hayes, N. S. Jacobson, V. M. Follette, & M. J. Dougher (Eds.), *Acceptance and change: Content and context in psychotherapy* (pp. 53-67). Reno, NV: Context Press.

Gregg, J. (2004). *Development of an acceptance-based treatment for the self-management of diabetes*. Unpublished doctoral dissertation, University of Nevada, Reno.

Gross, J. J. (1998). Antecedent and response-focused emotion regulation. *Journal of Personality and Social Psychology, 74*, 224-237.

Gross, J. J. (2002). Emotion regulation: Affective, cognitive, and social consequences. *Psychophysiology, 39*, 281-291.

Gross, J. J., & Levenson, R. W. (1997). Hiding feelings: The acute effects of inhibiting negative and positive emotion. *Journal of Abnormal Psychology, 106*, 95-103.

Gutiérrez, O., Luciano, C., Rodríguez, M., & Fink, B. C. (2004). Comparison between an acceptance-based and a cognitive-control-based protocol for coping with pain. *Behavior Therapy, 35*, 767-784.

Hand-Boniakowski, J. (1997). Hope. *Metaphoria*, Vol. 4, No. 7, Issue 43. Retrieved on January 13, 2005, from http://www.metaphoria.org/ac4t9703.html

Hayes, S. C. (1993). Analytic goals and the varieties of scientific contextualism. In S. C. Hayes, L. J. Hayes, H. W. Reese, & T. R. Sarbin (Eds.), *Varieties of scientific contextualism* (pp. 11-27). Reno, NV: Context Press.

Hayes, S. C. (1994). Content, context, and the types of psychological acceptance. In S. C. Hayes, N. S. Jacobson, V. M. Follette, & M. J. Dougher (Eds.), *Acceptance and change: Content and context in psychotherapy* (pp. 13-32). Reno, NV: Context Press.

Hayes, S. C. (2002). Acceptance, mindfulness, and science. *Clinical Psychology: Science and Practice, 9*, 101-106.

Hayes, S. C. (2004a). Acceptance and Commitment Therapy and the new behavior therapies: Mindfulness, acceptance, and relationship. In S. C. Hayes, V. M., Follette, & M. Linehan (Eds.), *Mindfulness and acceptance: Expanding the cognitive-behavioral tradition* (pp. 1-29). New York: Guilford Press.

Hayes, S. C. (2004b). Acceptance and Commitment Therapy, Relational Frame Theory, and the third wave of behavior therapy. *Behavior Therapy, 35*, 639-665.

Hayes, S. C., Barnes-Holmes, D., & Roche, B. (2001). Relational frame theory: A post-Skinnerian account of human language and cognition. New York: Kluwer-Plenum.

Hayes, S. C., Bissett, R., Korn, Z., Zettle, R. D., Rosenfarb, I., Cooper, L., et al. (1999). The impact of acceptance versus control rationales on pain tolerance. *The Psychological Record, 49*, 33-47.

Hayes, S. C., Bissett, R., Roget, N., Padilla, M., Kohlenberg, B. S., Fisher, G., Masuda, A., Pistorello, J., Rye, A. K., Berry, K., & Niccolls, R. (2004). The impact of acceptance and commitment training and multicultural training on the stigmatizing attitudes and professional burnout of substance abuse counselors. *Behavior Therapy, 35*, 821-835.

Hayes, S. C., Follette, V. M., & Linehan, M. M. (Eds.). (2004). *Mindfulness and acceptance: Expanding the cognitive behavioral tradition*. New York: Guilford Press.

Hayes, S. C., Hayes, L. J., Reese, H. W., & Sarbin, T. R. (Eds.). (1993). *Varieties of scientific contextualism*. Reno, NV: Context Press.

Hayes, S. C., Jacobson, N. S., Follette, V. M., & Dougher, M. J. (Eds.). (1994). *Acceptance and change: Content and context in psychotherapy*. Reno, NV: Context Press.

Hayes, S. C., Luoma, J., Bond, F., & Masuda, A. (in press). Acceptance and Commitment Therapy: Model, processes, and outcomes. *Behaviour Research and Therapy*.

Hayes, S. C., Masuda, A., Bissett, R., Luoma, J., & Guerrero, L. F. (2004). DBT, FAP, and ACT: How empirically oriented are the new behavior therapy technologies? *Behavior Therapy, 35*, 35-54.

Hayes, S. C., & Pankey, J. (2003). Psychological acceptance. In W. T. O'Donohue, J. E. Fisher, & S. C. Hayes (Eds.), *Cognitive behavior therapy: Applying empirically supported techniques in your practice* (pp. 4-9). New York: Wiley.

Hayes, S. C., & Shenk, C. (2004). Operationalizing mindfulness without unnecessary attachments. *Clinical Psychology: Science and Practice, 11*, 249-254.

Hayes, S. C., & Strosahl, K. D. (Eds.).(2004). *A Practical Guide to Acceptance and Commitment Therapy*. New York: Springer-Verlag.

Hayes, S. C., Strosahl, K. D., & Wilson, K. G. (1999). *Acceptance and Commitment Therapy: An experiential approach to behavior change*. New York: Guilford Press.

Hayes, S. C., Strosahl, K., Wilson, K. G., Bissett, R. T., Pistorello, J., Toarmino, D., et al. (2004). The Acceptance and Action Questionnaire (AAQ) as a measure of experiential avoidance. *The Psychological Record, 54*, 553-578.

Hayes, S. C., & Wilson, K. G. (1994). Acceptance and commitment therapy: Altering the verbal support for experiential avoidance. *The Behavior Analyst, 17*, 289-303.

Hayes, S. C., & Wilson, K. G. (2003). Mindfulness: Method and process. *Clinical Psychology: Science and Practice, 10*, 161-165.

Hayes, S. C., Wilson, K., Afari, N., & McCurry, S. (1990, November). *The use of Acceptance and Commitment Therapy in the treatment of agoraphobia.* Paper presented at the meeting of the Association for Advancement of Behavior Therapy, San Francisco.

Hayes, S. C., Wilson, K. G., Gifford, E. V., Bissett, R., Piasecki, M., Batten, S. V., et al. (2004). A randomized controlled trial of twelve-step facilitation and acceptance and commitment therapy with polysubstance abusing methadone maintained opiate addicts. *Behavior Therapy, 35*, 667-688.

Hayes, S. C., Wilson, K. G., Gifford, E. V., Follette, V. M., & Strosahl, K. (1996). Experiential avoidance and behavioral disorders: A functional dimensional approach to diagnosis and treatment. *Journal of Consulting and Clinical Psychology, 64*, 1152-1168.

Heffner, M., & Eifert, G. H. (2004). *The anorexia workbook: How to accept yourself, heal suffering, and reclaim your life.* Oakland, CA: New Harbinger Publications.

Heffner, M., Eifert, G. H., Parker, B. T., Hernandez, D. H., & Sperry, J. A. (2003). Valued directions: Acceptance and Commitment Therapy in the treatment of alcohol dependence. *Cognitive and Behavioral Practice, 10*, 379-384.

Heffner, M., Greco, L. A., & Eifert, G. H. (2003). Pretend you are a turtle: Children's responses to metaphorical and literal relaxation instructions. *Child Family and Behavior Therapy, 25*, 19-33.

Heffner, M., Sperry, J., Eifert, G. H., & Detweiler, M. (2002). Acceptance and Commitment Therapy in the treatment of an adolescent female with anorexia nervosa: A case study. *Cognitive and Behavioral Practice, 9*, 232-236.

Heide, F. J., & Borkovec, T. D. (1983). Relaxation-induced anxiety: Paradoxical anxiety enhancement due to relaxation training. *Journal of Consulting and Clinical Psychology, 51*, 171-182.

Heimberg, R. G., Juster, H. R., Brown, E. J., Holle, C., Schneier, F. R., & Gitow, A. (1994, November). *Cognitive-behavioral versus pharmacological treatment of social phobia: Posttreatment and follow-up effects.* Paper presented at the Annual Meeting of the Association for Advancement of Behaviour Therapy, San Diego, CA.

Hennessey, T. M., Rucker, W. B., & McDiarmid, C. G. (1979). Classical conditioning in paramecia. *Animal Learning and Behavior, 7*, 417-423.

Herrigel, E. (1953). *Zen in the art of archery.* New York: Random House.

Hollon, S. D., & Kendall, P. C. (1980). Cognitive self-statements in depression: Development of an Automatic Thoughts Questionnaire. *Cognitive Therapy and Research, 4*, 383-395.

Hofmann, S. G., & Barlow, D. H. (2002). Social phobia. In D. H. Barlow (Ed.), *Anxiety and its disorders: The nature and treatment of anxiety and panic* (2nd ed.) (pp. 454-476). New York: Guilford Press.

Hopko, D. R., Hopko, S. D., & Lejuez, C. W. (2004). Behavioral activation as an intervention for co-existent depressive and anxiety symptoms. *Clinical Case Studies, 3*, 37-48.

Hopko, D. R., Lejuez, C. W., Ruggiero, K. J., & Eifert, G. H. (2003). Behavioral activation as a treatment for depression: Procedures, principles, and progress. *Clinical Psychology Review, 23*, 699-717.

Jacobson, N. S., Christensen, A., Prince, S. E., Cordova, J., & Eldridge, K. (2000). Integrative behavioral couple therapy: An acceptance-based, promising new treatment for couple discord. *Journal of Consulting and Clinical Psychology, 68*, 351-355.

Jaycox, L. H., & Foa, E. B. (1998). Post-traumatic stress disorder. In A. S. Bellack & M. Hersen (Series Eds.), *Comprehensive Clinical Psychology* (Vol. 6, pp. 499-517). New York: Elsevier.

Juster, H. R., & Heimberg, R. G. (1998). Social phobia. In A. S. Bellack & M. Hersen (Series Eds.), *Comprehensive Clinical Psychology* (Vol. 6, pp. 475-498). New York: Elsevier.

Kabat-Zinn, J. (1990). *Full catastrophe living: Using the wisdom of your body and mind to face stress, pain, and illness.* New York: Delacorte.

Kabat-Zinn, J. (2005). *Coming to our senses: Healing ourselves and the world through mindfulness.* New York: Hyperion.

Karekla, M. (2004). *A comparison between acceptance-enhanced panic control and panic control treatment for panic disorder.* University of Albany, SUNY, Albany, New York. Unpublished Doctoral Dissertation.

Karekla, M., & Forsyth, J. P. (2004, November). A comparison between acceptance-enhanced cognitive behavioral and Panic Control Treatment for panic disorder. In S. M. Orsillo (Chair), *Acceptance-based behavioral therapies: New directions in the treatment development across the diagnostic spectrum.* Paper presented at the 38th annual meeting of the Association for Advancement of Behavior Therapy, New Orleans, LA.

Karekla, M., Forsyth, J. P., & Kelly, M. M. (2004). Emotional avoidance and panicogenic responding to a biological challenge procedure. *Behavior Therapy, 35,* 725-746.

Kasvikis, Y., & Marks, I. (1988). Clomipramine, self-exposure, and therapist-accompanied exposure in obsessive-compulsive ritualizers: Two-year follow-up. *Journal of Anxiety Disorders, 2,* 291-298.

Kessler, R. C., McGonagle, K. A., Zhao, S., Nelson, C. B., Hughes, M., Eshleman, S., et al. (1994). Lifetime and 12-month prevalence of DSM-III-R psychiatric disorders in the United States: Results from the National Comorbidity Study. *Archives of General Psychiatry, 51,* 8-19.

Khan, A., Leventhal, R. M., Khan, S., & Brown, W. A. (2002). Suicide risk in patients with anxiety disorders: A meta-analysis of the FDA database. *Journal of Affective Disorders, 68,* 183-190.

Kohlenberg, R. J., & Tsai, M. (1991). *Functional analytic psychotherapy: Creating intense and curative relationships.* New York: Plenum.

Koster, E. H., Rassin, E. G., Crombez, G., & Näring, G. W. (2003). The paradoxical effects of suppressing anxious thoughts during imminent threat. *Behaviour Research and Therapy, 41,* 1113-1120

Lang, P. J. (1993). The network model of emotion: Motivational connections. In R. S. Wyer & T. K. Srull (Eds.), *Perspectives on anger and emotion: Advances in social cognition* (Vol. 6, pp. 109-133). Hillsdale, NJ: Erlbaum.

Lavy, E. H., & van den Hout, M. A. (1990). Thought suppression induces intrusions. *Behavioural Psychotherapy, 18,* 251-258.

Leary, M. R. (1986). Affective and behavioral consequences of shyness: Implications for theory, measurement, and research. In W. H. Jones, J. M. Cheek, & S. R. Briggs (Eds.), *Shyness: Perspectives on research and treatment* (pp. 27-38). New York: Plenum.

LeDoux, J. E. (1996) *The Emotional Brain.* New York: Simon and Schuster.

LeDoux, J. E. (2000) Emotion circuits in the brain. *Annual Review of Neuroscience, 23,* 155-184.

Lejuez, C. W., Eifert, G. H., Zvolensky, M. J., & Richards, J. B. (2000). Preference between predictable and unpredictable administrations of 20% carbon dioxide–enriched air: Implications for understanding the etiology of panic disorder. *Journal of Experimental Psychology: Applied, 6,* 349-358.

Lejuez, C. W., Hopko, D. R., & Hopko, S. D. (2001). A brief behavioral activation treatment for depression: Treatment manual. *Behavior Modification, 25,* 255-286.

Lejuez, C. W., Hopko, D. R., & Hopko, S. D. (2002). *The brief behavioral activation treatment for depression (BATD): A comprehensive patient guide.* Boston: Pearson Custom Publishing.

Levitt, J. T., Brown, T. A., Orsillo, S. M., & Barlow, D. H. (2004). The effects of acceptance versus suppression of emotion on subjective and psychophysiological response to carbon dioxide challenge in patients with panic disorder. *Behavior Therapy, 35,* 747-766.

Linehan, M. M. (1993). *Skills training manual for treating borderline personality disorder.* New York: Guilford Press.

Linehan, M. M. (1994). Acceptance and change: The central dialectic in psychotherapy. In S. C. Hayes, N. S. Jacobson, V. M. Follette, & M. J. Dougher (Eds.), *Acceptance and change: Content and context in psychotherapy* (pp. 73-86). Reno, NV: Context Press.

Luckingham Fable, J. (1998). *Some thoughts about resistance.* Fairfield, CT: Center for Transformational Psychotherapy. Available at http:/www. Forhealing.org/resistance. html

Marks, I. M. (1979). Conditioning models for clinical syndromes are out of date. *The Behavioral and Brain Sciences, 2,* 175-177.

Masuda, A., Hayes, S. C., Sackett, C. F., & Twohig, M. P. (2004). Cognitive defusion and self-relevant negative thoughts: Examining the impact of a ninety year old technique. *Behaviour Research and Therapy, 42,* 477-485.

McCracken, L. M, Vowles, K. E., & Eccleston, C. (in press). Acceptance-based treatment for persons with complex, long-standing chronic pain: A preliminary analysis of treatment outcome in comparison to a waiting phase. *Behaviour Research and Therapy.*

McDowell, J. J. (1982). The importance of Hernstein's mathematical statement of the law of effect for behavior therapy. *American Psychologist, 37,* 771-779.

Mennin, D. S., Heimberg, R. G., Turk, C. L., & Fresco, D. M. (2002). Applying an emotion regulation framework to integrative approaches to generalized anxiety disorder. *Clinical Psychology: Science and Practice, 9,* 85-90.

Menzies, R. G., & Clarke, J. C. (1995). The etiology of phobias: A nonassociative account. *Clinical Psychology Review, 15,* 23-48.

Mower, O. H. (1939). A stimulus-response analysis of anxiety and its role as a reinforcing agent. *Psychological Review, 46,* 553-565.

Mower, O. H. (1960). *Learning theory and behavior.* New York: Wiley.

Nardone, G., & Watzlawick, P. (1993). Clinical practice, processes, and procedures. In G. Nardone & P. Watzlawick (Eds.), *The art of change* (pp. 45-72). San Francisco: Jossey-Bass.

Orsillo, S. M., Roemer, L., Lerner, J. B., & Tull, M. T. (2004). Acceptance, mindfulness, and cognitive-behavioral therapy: Comparisons, contrasts, and application to anxiety. In S. C. Hayes, V. M. Follette, & M. M. Linehan (Eds.), *Mindfulness and acceptance: Expanding the cognitive-behavioral tradition* (pp. 66-95). New York: Guilford Press.

Otto, M. W., & Deckersbach, T. (1998). Cognitive-behavioral therapy for panic disorder: Theory, strategies, and outcome. In J. F. Rosenbaum & M. H. Pollack (Eds.), *Panic disorder and its treatment* (pp. 181-204). New York: Marcel Dekker.

Paulus, T. (1973). *Hope for the flowers*. Mahwah, NJ: Paulist Press.

Pennebaker, J. W., & Beall, S. K. (1986). Confronting a traumatic event: Toward an understanding of inhibition and disease. *Journal of Abnormal Psychology, 95*, 274-281.

Perls, F. P. (1973). *The Gestalt approach and eye-witness to therapy*. Palo Alto, CA: Science and Behavior Books.

Peterson, R. A., & Reiss, S. (1992). *Anxiety Sensitivity Index Manual* (2nd ed.). Worthington, OH: International Diagnostic Systems.

Power, K. G., Simpson, R. J., Swanson, V., & Wallace, L. A. (1990). A controlled comparison of cognitive-behaviour therapy, diazepam, and placebo, alone and in combination, for the treatment of generalized anxiety disorder. *Journal of Anxiety Disorders, 4*, 267-292.

Purdon, C. (1999). Thought suppression and psychopathology. *Behaviour Research and Therapy, 37*, 1029-1054.

Rachman, S. (1976). The passing of the two-stage theory of fear and avoidance: Fresh possibilities. *Behaviour Research and Therapy, 14*, 125-131.

Rachman, S. (1977). The conditioning theory of fear acquisition: A critical examination. *Behaviour Research and Therapy, 15*, 375–387.

Rachman, S. (1991). Neo-conditioning and the classical theory of fear acquisition. *Clinical Psychology Review, 11*, 155-173.

Rapee, R. M. (Ed.) (1996). *Current controversies in the anxiety disorders*. New York: Guilford Press.

Reiss, S., Peterson, R. A., Gursky, D. M., & McNally, R. J. (1986). Anxiety sensitivity, anxiety frequency and the predictions of fearfulness. *Behaviour Research and Therapy, 24*, 1-8.

Robins, C. J. (2002). Zen principles and mindfulness practice in Dialectical Behavior Therapy. *Cognitive and Behavioral Practice, 9*, 50-57.

Roemer, E., & Orsillo, S.M. (2002). Expanding our conceptualization of and treatment for generalized anxiety disorder: Integrating mindfulness/acceptance-based approaches with existing cognitive-behavioral models. *Clinical Psychology: Science and Practice, 9*, 54-68.

Rogers, C. R. (1961). *On becoming a person: A therapist's view of psychotherapy*. Boston: Houghton Mifflin.

Salkovskis, P. (1998). Panic disorder. In A. S. Bellack & M. Hersen (Series Eds.), *Comprehensive Clinical Psychology* (Vol. 6, pp. 400-437). New York: Elsevier.

Samoilov, A., & Goldfried, M. R. (2000). Role of emotion in cognitive-behavior therapy. *Clinical Psychology: Science and Practice, 7*, 373-385.

Schmidt, N. B., Woolaway-Bicke, K., Trakowski, J., Santiago, H., Storey, J., Koselka, M., et al. (2000). Dismantling cognitive-behavioral treatment for panic disorder: Questioning the utility of breathing retraining. *Journal of Consulting and Clinical Psychology, 68*, 417-424.

Schulte, D., & Eifert, G. H. (2002). What to do when manuals fail: The dual model of psychotherapy. *Clinical Psychology: Science and Practice, 9*, 312-328.

Segal, Z. V., Williams, J. M. G., & Teasdale, J. D. (2002). *Mindfulness-based cognitive therapy for depression: A new approach to preventing relapse.* New York: Guilford.

Selden, N. R. W., Everitt, B. J., Jarrard, L. E., Robbins, T. W. (1991) Complementary roles for the amygdala and hippocampus in aversive conditioning to explicit and contextual cues. *Neuroscience, 42,* 335-50.

Seligman, M. E. P. (1971). Phobias and preparedness. *Behavior Therapy, 2,* 307-320.

Shafran, R., Thordarson, D. S., & Rachman, S. (1996). Thought-action fusion in obsessive compulsive disorder. *Journal of Anxiety Disorders, 10,* 379-391.

Sloan, D. M. (2004). Emotion regulation in action: Emotional reactivity in experiential avoidance. *Behaviour Research and Therapy, 42,* 1257-1270.

Smari, J. (2001). Fifteen years of suppression of white bears and other thoughts: What are the lessons for obsessive-compulsive disorder research and treatment? *Scandinavian Journal of Behaviour Therapy, 30,* 147-160.

Solomon, R. L., & Wynne, L. C. (1954). Traumatic avoidance learning: The principles of anxiety conservation and partial irreversibility. *Psychological Review, 61,* 353-385.

Spira, A. P., Zvolensky, M. J., Eifert, G. H., & Feldner, M. T. (2004). Avoidance-oriented coping as a predictor of anxiety-based physical stress: A test using biological challenge. *Journal of Anxiety Disorders, 18,* 309-323.

Staats, A. W., & Eifert, G. H. (1990). The paradigmatic behaviorism theory of emotions: Basis for unification. *Clinical Psychology Review, 10,* 539-566.

Steketee, G. S., & Barlow, D. H. (2002). Specific phobias. In D. H. Barlow (Ed.), *Anxiety and its disorders: The nature and treatment of anxiety and panic* (2nd ed.) (pp. 516-550). New York: Guilford Press.

Steketee, G. S., & Frost, R. O. (1998). Obsessive-compulsive disorder. In A. S. Bellack & M. Hersen (Series Eds.), *Comprehensive Clinical Psychology* (Vol. 6, pp. 367-398). New York: Elsevier.

Strosahl, K. D., Hayes, S. C., Wilson, K. G., & Gifford, E. V. (2004). An ACT primer: Core therapy processes, intervention strategies, and therapist competencies. In S. C. Hayes & K. D. Strosahl (Eds.), *Acceptance and Commitment Therapy: A practical clinical guide* (pp. 31-58). New York: Springer Science.

Taylor, S. (2000). *Understanding and treating panic disorder.* Chichester, UK: Wiley.

Turner, S. M., Beidel, D. C., & Jacob, R. G. (1994). Social phobia: A comparison of behaviour therapy and atenolol. *Journal of Clinical and Consulting Psychology, 62,* 350-358.

Twohig, M. P., Hayes, S. C., & Masuda, A. (in press). Increasing willingness to experience obsessions: Acceptance and Commitment Therapy as a treatment for obsessive compulsive disorder. *Behavior Therapy.*

Twohig, M. P., & Woods, D. W. (2004). A preliminary investigation of Acceptance and Commitment Therapy and habit reversal as a treatment for trichotillomania. *Behavior Therapy, 35,* 803-820.

Van Ameringen, M., Mancini, C., Oakman, J. M., & Farvolden, P. (2000). In K. J. Palmer (Ed.), *Pharmacotherapy of anxiety disorders* (pp. 17-30). Hong Kong: Adis International.

Watson, J. B., & Rayner, R. (1920). Conditioned emotional reactions. *Journal of Experimental Psychology, 3,* 1-14.

Wegner, D. M. (1994). Ironic processes of mental control. *Psychological Review, 101,* 34-52.

Wegner, D. M., Schneider, D. J., Carter, S. R., & White, T. L. (1987). Paradoxical effects of thought suppression. *Journal of Personality and Social Psychology, 53*, 5-13.

Wegner, D. M., Schneider, D. J., Knutson, B., & McMahon, S. R. (1991). Polluting the stream of consciousness: The effect of thought suppression on the mind's environment. *Cognitive Therapy and Research, 15*, 141-152.

Wegner, D. M., & Zanakos, S. (1994). Chronic thought suppression. *Journal of Personality, 62*, 615-640.

Williams, S. L. (2004). Anxiety. In J. E. Maddux & B. A. Winstead (Eds.), *Psychopathology: Contemporary issues, theory, and research* (pp. 127-154). Hillsdale, NJ: Erlbaum.

Wilson, K. G., & Groom, J. (2002). *The Valued Living Questionnaire.* Available from the first author at the Department of Psychology, University of Mississippi, Oxford, MS.

Wilson, K. G., & Murrell, A. R. (2004). Values-centered interventions: Setting a course for behavioral treatment. In S. C. Hayes, V. M. Follette, & M. M. Linehan (Eds.), *Mindfulness and acceptance: Expanding the cognitive-behavioral tradition* (pp. 120-151). New York: Guilford Press.

Wilson, K. G., & Roberts, M. (2002). Core principles in acceptance and commitment therapy: An application to anorexia nervosa. *Cognitive and Behavioral Practice, 9*, 237-243.

Wolpe, J. (1958). *Psychotherapy by reciprocal inhibition.* Stanford, CA: Stanford University Press.

Wolpe, J., & Rowan, V. C. (1988). Panic disorder: A product of classical conditioning. *Behaviour Research and Therapy, 26*, 441-450.

Yerkes, R. M., & Dodson, J. D. (1908). The relation of strength of stimulus to rapidity of habit formation. *Journal of Comparative Neurology and Psychology, 18*, 459-482.

Zettle, R. D. (2003). Acceptance and commitment therapy (ACT) versus systematic desensitization in treatment of mathematics anxiety. *The Psychological Record, 53*, 197-215.

Zettle, R. D., & Hayes, S. C. (1986). Dysfunctional control by client verbal behavior: The context of reason giving. *The Analysis of Verbal Behavior, 4*, 30-38.

Zettle, R. D., & Raines, J. C. (1989). Group cognitive and contextual therapies in treatment of depression. *Journal of Clinical Psychology, 45*, 438-445.

Zinbarg, R. E., Craske, M. G., & Barlow, D. H. (1993). *Mastery of your anxiety and worry.* Boulder, CO: Graywind.

Zuercher-White, E. (1997). *Treating panic disorder and agoraphobia: A step-by-step guide.* Oakland, CA: New Harbinger Publications.

Zvolensky, M. J., Lejuez, C. W., & Eifert, G. H. (1998). The role of control in anxious responding: An experimental test using repeated administrations of 20% CO_2-enriched air. *Behavior Therapy, 29*, 193-209.

Zvolensky, M. J., Lejuez, C. W., & Eifert, G. H. (2000). Prediction and control: Operational definitions for the experimental analysis of anxiety. *Behaviour Research and Therapy, 38*, 653-663.

Index

Georg H. Eifert, Ph.D., is professor and chair of the department of psychology at Chapman University in Orange, CA. He was ranked in the top thirty of Researchers in Behavior Analysis and Therapy in the 1990s and has authored over 100 publications on psychological causes and treatments of anxiety and other emotional disorders. He is a clinical fellow of the Behavior Therapy and Research Society, a member of numerous national and international psychological associations, and serves on several editorial boards of leading clinical psychology journals. He also is a licensed clinical psychologist. He is the author of *The Anorexia Workbook* and *From Behavior Theory to Behavior Therapy*.

John P. Forsyth, Ph.D., is associate professor and director of the Anxiety Disorders Research Program in the Department of Psychology at the University at Albany, State University of New York. He has written widely on acceptance and experiential avoidance, and the role of emotion regulatory processes in anxiety disorders. He has been doing basic and applied work related to Acceptance and Commitment Therapy (ACT) for well over 10 years. He is a licensed clinical psychologist in New York State, serves on the editorial boards of several leading clinical psychology journals, and is associate editor of the *Journal of Behavior Therapy and Experimental Psychiatry*.

Eifert and Forsyth are also authors of a forthcoming book—*ACT on Life, Not on Anger*—describing the application of ACT for persons struggling with problem anger. They routinely give talks and workshops on acceptance and commitment therapy and cognitive behavior therapy for anxiety and related disorders.

Foreword writer **Steven C. Hayes, Ph.D.,** is University of Nevada Foundation Professor of Psychology at the University of Nevada in Reno, NV. He is the author of *Acceptance and Commitment Therapy* and *Relational Frame Theory*, among many other books and articles, and he is one of the founders of acceptance and commitment therapy.